Rangers and pioneers of Texas

Sowell, Andrew Jackson, 1848- [from old catalog]

RANGERS

AND

Pioneers of Texas.

WITH A

CONCISE ACCOUNT

OF THE

EARLY SETTLEMENTS, HARDSHIPS, MASSACRES, BATTLES, AND WARS,

BY WHICH

TEXAS WAS RESCUED FROM THE RULE OF THE SAVAGE AND CONSECRATED TO THE EMPIRE OF CIVILIZATION.

BY

A. J. SOWELL,

SEGUIN, TEXAS.

SAN ANTONIO, TEXAS:
SHEPARD BROS. & CO., PRINTERS AND PUBLISHERS.
1884

D.M.
8 M'oo.

F 38.
.13

RANGERS

AND

PIONEERS OF TEXAS.

EMBRACING

A Concise Account of the Settlement of the Greater Part of the State.

Personal Adventures Incident to the Settlement of a New Country.

An Account of Nearly One Hundred of the Mexican and Indian Battles of Burleson, Hays, Ford, Caldwell, the Mc-Cullochs, Moore, Bowie, Van Dorn, Mustang Grey, Big Foot Wallace, and Other Noted Texas Rangers.

With Incidents in the Battles of San Jacinto, Goliad, Salado, Dawson's Massacre, Plum Creek, Mill Creek, Storming of the Alamo, Etc., Etc., Giving the Names of 500 Rangers and Pioneers.

Campaign of the Texas Rangers to the Wichita Mountains in 1871: Burning of a Government Wagon Train by Indians: Capture of "Big Tree," Sittanke, Satante, and "Kicking Bird," Noted Kiowa and Comanche Chiefs.

Slaughter of United States Troops and Rangers in the "Lost Valley" Fight.

Fight Between Rangers and Indians on "Paradise Prairie:" Terrible Fight at Ball's Ranch, in which "Red Cap," War Chief of the Comanches, was Killed.

Perilous Journey of the Lost Scouts, Etc., Etc.

•

By A. J. SOWELL.

[The Writer was connected with the Wichita Campaign, and writes from his own personal knowledge.]

SAN ANTONIO, TEXAS:
SHEPARD BROS. & CO., PRINTERS AND BINDERS.
1884.

PREFACE.

In the following pages the Author has attempted to recite a part of what is as yet the unwritten history of the country. Many brave and heroic men have lived and died, and did their country glorious service upon the frontiers of Texas, whose names have as yet found no place in history. They were the men who cut the brush and blazed the way for immigration, and drove the wild beast and the red man from the path of civilization. They bore the heat and burden of the day, and their deeds should live, like monuments, in the hearts of their countrymen. Where commerce now holds its prosperous marts was then the camping ground and rendezvous of these rangers and pioneers. The incidents of history herein contained have been gathered from sources most reliable, and he that peruses this volume may feel assured that he is not reading fiction, but facts which form part of the history of Texas. If this volume serves the purpose for which it is written, *i. e.*, that the names and deeds of these good and brave men may not be forgotten, and the writer occupy one fresh green spot in the folds of their memory, he will not think his labor has been in vain.

AUTHOR.

CHAPTER I.

"I HEAR the tread of pioneers,
Of nations yet to be;
The first low wash of waves, where soon
Shall roll a human sea."
—WHITTIER.

INTRODUCTION—INDIAN RAIDS IN NACOGDOCHES COUNTY —HUTCHINSON FAMILY—DEATH OF CAPT. DENTON— CHASED BY INDIANS—DEATH OF CALAHAN—SETTLING FANNIN COUNTY—A SAD MISTAKE—TREACHERY OF A MEXICAN.

WHEN the white settlers of Texas, composing Austin's and De Witt's colonies, first began to erect their cabin in this wild and beautiful country, all the Indian tribes were friendly. The Comanches were the most numerous, numbering several thousand warriors. Hostilities commenced by thieving parties of Indians stealing horses from the whites; and, when caught by the exasperated settlers, were roughly handled: in fact, there was not much law in the country in those days regulating the punishment for such offenses, and the unfortunate red man caught under such circumstances was generally shot on the spot. White horse thieves were served the same way, or strung up to the limb of a tree.

The consequence of these severe measures was that all the tribes (then numbering twenty or more) sooner or later became hostile, with the exception, perhaps, of

the Tankaways, who always lived on good terms with
the whites, and were very useful in scouting and trailing
hostile bands when they made incursions into the settlements, and some of them went with Taylor's army to
Mexico.

From the time the Indians became hostile, almost up
to the present time (1883), every settler who pitched
his cabin in the West, from the coast to the Staked
Plains, had to contend with hostile Indians, and if all
the incidents were related, connected with these settlements, of Indian battles. adventures of the settlers, mas-
sacres, etc. which occurred while these settlements
gradually extended out towards the Rio Grande (Big
River), which was the boundary line between Texas
and Mexico in the West, it would fill a volume ten times
the size of the one I contemplate writing. My object is
to give as many of such incidents as the size of this work
will admit, and try to convey a correct idea of what the
brave men and women of that period had to contend
with in settling this fair land of Texas and paving the
way for capital, railroads and more immigrants. Being
myself raised in Texas, and spending some time on the
frontier, I have, from time to time, collected such incidents as I thought worth relating and which would be
interesting to the reading public, as Indian battles, mas-
sacres, and scalp dances are now a thing of the past in
Texas.

In commencing this little work, I will relate a few incidents which occurred as the settlers gradually pushed
out into the unsettled wilds of the West; then, under
the head of Incidents in the Life of an Old Texan, I
will bring in other scraps of unwritten history which
I wish to relate in memory of those veterans, who
have now nearly all passed away. and who did deeds,

worthy the pen of our best historians. I will close with an account of the campaign of the Texas rangers to the Wichita mountains in 1871. In that I will give some account of the settling of that part of the state; that is, the Indian troubles mostly. One thing which greatly bothers me in collecting these incidents, is being deficient in dates, which is very necessary, but which sometimes have to be omitted; but I will try to give the facts as near as I can, as they were related to me by the old pioneers. For instance, one will be relating some incident, with which he was connected or was acquainted, and you will ask, "When did that occur?" "Well," he will say, "I do not recollect exactly, but I think it was in the fall or winter or spring of so and so;" and, of course, there are likely to be some errors of this kind.

I will commence this part of the work by relating an incident which occurred in Nacogdoches County, which I learned from an old Texan, named Baily, who was well acquainted with the parties concerned in this horrible deed of savage cruelty. In the early settlement of this county, in the eastern part of the State, a family, named Hutchinson, settled between the Neches and Trinity rivers, near Fort Houston. The family consisted of the old man, his wife, and daughter, Anna. They lived in peace and quiet for some time, with plenty around them to live on comfortably, but in 1838 the Indians, then being hostile, began committing depredations between the two rivers, and armed bands of men began scouring the country in order to run them out. Late one evening nine armed settlers came to the house of old man Hutchinson stating that they were out after Indians and would like to spend the night with him, and go on up the country next morning, where they were to meet another party who were also scouting. The old man cordially invited them to dismount and come in; their horses were attended to. and the old lady and her daughter prepared supper.

When supper was announced, the men went back into the shed room, on the north side of the cabin, where the meal was spread, and took their seats at the table leavin· their guns standing in the corner near an open door which fronted to the south.   The meal was

(Settlers driving the Indians from Nacogdoches County.)

not more than half over, when, hearing a slight noise in the direction of the south door, they looked and saw three hideously painted Indians between them and their guns. Not knowing how many more there were close at hand, they all sprang from the table and escaped through an east door in the shed room. the old man Hutchinson among the balance. thinking, of course, I suppose, that the women would follow, but such was not the case.

The brave old lady seized a heavy iron shovel, and dashing into the house, commenced a most furious attack upon the Indians, and succeeded in beating one of them to the floor before she was tomahawked. Anna also procured a weapon of some kind, and came to the assistance of her mother, but she was also struck on the head and fell to the floor, apparently lifeless. The savages not satisfied with this, then cut out her left breast, and left her lying on the floor in this horrible condition. They then brought some lard out of the kitchen, and emptying it in one corner of the house, set fire to it and then left, carrying some of the guns with them. Before the fire spread much, Anna returned to consciousness, and barely made her escape from the burning building. Her mother's body was consumed.

The girl wandered about in a dazed sort of way until morning, and succeeded in getting about two miles from the house, and being overcome with fatigue and pain, could go no further, and sank almost fainting to the ground. In this condition she was found by three rangers and carried to the nearest house, and by close and careful attention, finally recovered. It is likely the men, had they known there were but three Indians to deal with, would have rushed in and overpowered them; but be this as it may, the women were the bravest, for they remained and fought them. The Indians succeeded in eluding the search, which was made for them, and escaped out of the country.

In 1840–42 the Indians were very troublesome along the Trinity and Brazos rivers. Captain Denton raised a company of forty men, and set out in pursuit of a large band, which had been depredating and were going back. They struck the trail on the Sulphur Fork of the Brazos, and followed it for several days, and finally came up with them in a bend of the Trinity river, about sixty miles below where Fort Worth now stands. Here the Indians had a village with growing corn, pumpkins and water melons. The settlers furiously charged in among them, and a short, but bloody fight ensued. The Indians soon gave way and fled through the bottoms, leaving fourteen of their number dead on the ground. But the settlers did not come out unscathed; the brave and fearless Denton was killed at the first onset, and Lieutenant Stout was wounded. The village was set on fire, the dead Captain buried, and the pioneers returned to their homes, having broken up one of the strongholds of the hostiles.

John D. Pickens, a resident of Guadalupe County, was in this fight, and furnished me the items in regard to it. He was then but fourteen years old. He saw Captain Denton when he fell from his horse.

About this time the Indians were committing depredations among the settlers of Gonzales County. Horses were stolen, cattle killed, and children carried into captivity.

In July, 1841, Hardin Turner, ——— Callahan, and another man, whose name I cannot learn, went out horse hunting near Peach Creek, about twelve miles east of Gonzales. They camped out, and were up early next morning hunting for their horses, while it was cool, and ascended a ridge for the purpose of looking over into the valley to see if they could discover any horses, but instead saw a band of about fifteen Indians. The odds were too much against them to think of making a stand, unless compelled to, and they instantly turned their horses and fled, closely pursued by the Indians, who were on good horses. Turner and Callahan made for a dense thicket, some distance off, keeping close together in this race for life. The other man. being mounted on a splendid horse, left his companions, and was soon out of sight, carrying off a double-barreled shot gun belonging to Callahan, who had handed it to him a few minutes before to shoot a turkey.

The Indians, being well mounted. gained on them at every jump, at the same time uttering loud and exultant yells, as they felt confident of their victims; and when the two white men neared the thicket, were close upon their heels. Turner shouted to Callahan to leave his horse and run into the thicket, when he saw him about to pass around it, at the same time leaping from his horse and plunging in himself. The Indians were so near one of them threw his lance at Turner, striking him between the shoulders, near the left shoulder blade, but he still continued to tear his way through the brush, dragging the lance after him, until it pulled out. Being weak from loss of blood and exertion, he lay down at the base of a large pecan tree, with his rifle beside him, ready to shoot the first Indian who found him.

Callahan was overtaken and killed near the thicket, having failed to heed the warning cry of Turner. After stripping and mutilating his body, and taking off his scalp, they hung him up in a tree, and danced and sang around it, one of them every now and then saying: "Yankee Doodle," "Yankee Doodle." Turner could see most of this performance from where he lay, thinking it would be his time next, but determined to sell his life dearly as possible. and get one Indian at least. After getting through with their pow-wow around the dead body of his companion, the Indians prowled around the thicket, in search of Turner. but were afraid to enter, as they knew the white man carried his rifle with him, and it would be certain death to the foremost Indian, and none were willing to sacrifice himself. Once a lot of them charged through on their horses, almost running over him, but went in such a hurry they did not look much.

The Indians finally all left but one, a hideous, old, crooked-mouth fellow, who still continued the search for some time longer. Turner was sorely tempted to shoot this old demon, but fearing the report of his gun would bring the others back, he refrained from doing so until the old Indian should discover him, and then he calculated to kill him. The Indian would stoop down and peer into the thicket, and sometimes Turner was almost certain the Indian saw him, and once started to raise his gun to fire, but the Indian saved his handsome face from being spoiled by a bullet, by turning off and looking somewhere else.

Turner's shirt was stained with green fodder, which he had been pulling, and so nearly resembled the green foliage beneath which he lay was one reason, I suppose, why the Indians failed to see him.

The old Indian finally gave up the search and left, to overtake his companions. Turner lay where he was until late in the evening and then crawled out from his hiding-place and looked around. His horse, of course, was gone. The body of Callahan was still dangling in the tree, and presented a horrible sight as it swayed to and fro in the breeze. Faint and weary, he then made his way to a small pool of water near by, and pulling off one of his shoes, washed the blood out of it, which had run down from his wound, and drank out of it. He was so weak from loss of blood he was afraid to lie down and drink from the pool, fearing he would not be able to rise again. He drank several times before attempting to leave the place, but after his burning thirst was quenched, he felt stronger, and set out for the nearest house, which was three miles nearer than his own, and arrived there before midnight. The family were still up, for they had heard the news from the man who escaped. He said that Turner and Callahan were both killed, and when Turner stepped in with his white haggard face and bloody garments, the lady of the house fell fainting to the floor. A runner was then sent to inform his parents that he was there, for he was an unmarried man and lived with them. They soon came, and he was carried home, but it was sometime before he recovered from that terrible lance thrust. The body of Callahan was brought in the next morning after he was killed.

At this time the settlements had extended a considerable distance up the Colorado, Brazos, Guadalupe, San Marcos and other streams, the more adventurous pioneers still pushing further west, trailing and fighting Indians as they went, and being killed and scalped by them in return. Hundreds of miles of beautiful country still lay ahead of them, and only inhabited by the buffalo, deer, antelope, etc., and the red man.

After the annexation of Texas to the United States, in 1845, counties were rapidly laid off and organized: several counties, however, were organized and named prior to that period, for judicial and other purposes. Among the number was Fannin, named in honor of the brave Col. Fannin, who was, with his command, brutally murdered by the Mexicans after he had surrendered, at Goliad, in 1836.

The county was organized in 1838, but owing to the hostilities of the Indians, few settlers came into it until about 1842. As I am not attempting to write a history of Texas, but the battles and adventures of pioneers, I will have to make extracts from other works to make it complete, as I was unable to obtain all the information I wanted otherwise. Therefore, I take the following sketches from the American Sketch Book, published at Austin, in 1880, by Mrs. Bella French Swisher.

"Among those who emigrated in 1842, was Phillip Smith and family, a brother-in-law to Judge Inglish, first settled at the place where Fort Inglish was afterwards built. Smith did not fear the danger incident to settling, and living on the frontier: but came fixed up with all the regalia of high life, fine wagons and carriages, and ten or twelve extra fine horses. He did not look at the possibility of his fine stock being taken from him in a few months of time: he did not know that an Indian would risk his life, lose his reputation and character as an honest man for the value of a horse. In 1841 Smith had his confidence shaken by the loss of nearly all his horses. Indians captured them during the night. His loss was discovered early in the morning, and eight or ten men started in pursuit. The watchword was, quick step and sharp lookout for Indians. The Indians must be captured and horses retaken at all hazards.

"The south boundary line of the county, not having as yet been run, Col. Montague, the county surveyor, had sent his deputy surveyor, John B. Black, with a guard of eight or ten men, regular soldiers, to do the work.

"Those in pursuit discovered, a short distance ahead, on Pilot Knob, a smoke arising from camp fires on the Indian trail. Now, the Indians must be killed and scalped and horses rescued in quick time for fear of being discovered. The company dismounted, tied their horses and the priming of guns examined. Every man being his own commander, it was not necessary to give orders. All, from the color of the face, would pass for white men: no stiff joints, but trembling with eagerness for battle or something else. The pursuers arose, and fired: with a shout and a yell, the camp was charged upon. Three Indians were seen to fall at the first fire, and the others ran for life. When the camp was reached, there lay two dead white men and three badly wounded, they being the men sent out with John B. Black to guard when running the county line, who unfortunately had camped a few hours before upon the trail of the pursued

Indians. The dead were buried as best they could: the wounded brought back and cared for, and the search for the culprits abandoned."

In 1838 the land system was organized in the Republic of Texas. Land certificates were issued to citizens, also immigrants under the donation laws. When individuals having obtained certificates. went to locating their claims. litigation resulted. which was settled by a justice of the peace and twelve jurymen. A case of this kind came up in what was then called Washita Bend, but now Preston, between Col. Holland Coffee and Capt. John Hart, both parties contending for preference of location. A jury was summoned from the Bois d'Arc neighborhood, where Bonham now stands. who went to the Bend to try the case at issue. As they were returning home, they met a Mexican. whose name was Andrew Penaro. He said he had been trading with the wild Indians. He was riding on an extra fine Mexican mule, with superior Mexican saddle, equipped fantastically, a fine brace of holster pistols attached to the saddle, a fine double-barreled shot gun in his hand. He was dressed like a prince, from head to foot; a fine gold watch and plenty of cash in his pockets. Suspecting he had been guilty of a foul deed, he was questioned closely. He stated, that ten days before, he had met with a Mexican officer with the Indians, making presents and inducing them to war with the whites. and that he decoyed him from camp and killed him. Suspecting this statement to be false, he was questioned closely, and promises made if he would tell the truth he should go unpunished, whereupon he confessed that he had engaged as pilot to a Mexican Colonel and decoyed him in a wrong direction and shot him in the back, when he had dismounted to arrange his saddle girths. He then led them to the spot where the deed had been done. There lay the body of the Mexican Colonel, dead, bereft of clothing, robbed by his Mexican brother. In hunting around, Mr. Simpson found his hat with a bullet hole through the band. It had three rows of gold braid around it. He carried the hat home; his wife mended it, and he had the honor of wearing the officer's hat. Had not promises been sacred things with them, Andrew Penaro would have pulled hemp to pay for his treachery.

CHAPTER II.

VOLUNTEERS — THE FALSE ALARM — CAPTAIN HART SCALPING INDIANS—JOHN F. HUNTER, THE OLD TEXAS RANGER—MISS HUNTER CARRIED INTO CAPTIVITY—FIGHT WITH INDIANS NEAR RED RIVER—LOCATION OF FANNIN COUNTY.

IN 1838 the first volunteer companies for the defense of Fannin County were raised and organized by Captain Robert Sloan and N. L. Journey. These two companies consisted of forty men each. The first night at camp the captain's charger and two other horses were stolen. The next night the two companies met and camped ready for an early start for the Indian village on the west fork of the Trinity river. Guards were stationed around the encampment for the night, and each mess went to spinning yarns. In the midst of this amusement one of the guards fired his gun. In an instant the pickets fled for camp; men ran for their guns. Some guns were misplaced; shot pouches and ammunition missing. All was hurry and confusion. The captain dispatched to learn the cause of alarm—no guard at his post. One of the guards dashed into camp, saying he had seen and shot an Indian trying to steal horses. His heart beat so hard he declared it was the sound of Indians' feet flying from the fire of his gun.

The officer returned and made his report, and stated that he had found no dead or wounded Indian, but supposed he had found an Indian's blanket, but upon examination it proved to be the paunch of the beef

2

slaughtered that day for rations. No more yarns that night. Next morning march was taken for the Indian village. They marched three days and camped for the last night until the Indian village should be desolated by the heroes of Fannin County. Next morning a council of war was held. Scouts were sent out to reconnoiter the village. Scouts returned, reporting the village close at hand. Now, their bravery must be tried, or they must run.

Three hundred Indian warriors, fortified in their huts to defend themselves, squaws and children, and only ninety-nine to attack and enter into deadly conflict with them. Many a pale face was to be seen in the ranks.

But, lo! when they got to the scene of action only a small camp of Indians were there. The Indians were soon dispatched, and their scalps taken by Captain John Hart. One white man was wounded, and one horse killed. After the battle, one wounded Indian lay concealed in the grass, with his tomahawk in hand. A man by the name of Pangborn, usually called "Brandy," from his long and intimate acquaintance with that beverage, was in search of the Indian, and came upon him so closely that he could not shoot. The Indian arose, with tomahawk in hand, striking at Pangborn's head. The latter wheeled and ran, shouting for help at every jump. One gun was fired from our ranks; the Indian fell, and Captain Hart was on him in an instant, taking his scalp. This fight took place at Bird's Fort, in Tarrant County. Thus ended the scouting till a more formidable force was raised, which was done that winter, under the command of General John H. Dyer, of Red River County.

Mr. John F. Hunter, of Rosston, Cook County, says that he settled in Fannin County in 1838; that he has been ranging in northwest Texas for forty-one years.

In 1843 the Indians made a raid in Fannin County, murdered his mother, captured his sister, killed his cousin, seven years old, a negro woman, and robbed the house of its contents. The prisoner, Lovicia, was carried to the Keechi mountains, in western Texas, and kept forty-six days. She was purchased by Delaware Frank, who paid the ransom sum of $750. He brought her safely to the settlements.

Mr. Hunter then, clad in leather pants and hunting shirt, buckled on his moccasins, shouldered his old flint-lock rifle, and took the war path, which he tramped for thirteen years. He formed one of the seventy-two, under Tarrant's command, that drove the thousand warriors from their village on Village creek. Mr. Hunter had many a hard chase after Indians. He passed through where Pilot Point is now situated in 1841, and says that the summit of the great hill, which then loomed up and stood out in bold relief against the western horizon, piloting the pioneer fathers in their exploits against the red men, was covered with buffalo trails. Now it is graced with the beautiful little city of Pilot Point, and he is here to-day to behold the change of thirty-eight years.

In the winter and spring of 1839-40 the citizens of Fort Inglish, Warren and Preston moved home from the forts, with the determination to defend themselves and property against the ravages of the Indians, the efforts of the government having proved ineffectual in giving protection to its subjects on account of a lack of men and resources adequate for the purpose. The president was opposed to a war policy, thus favoring pacific and treaty measures instructed the officers and requested the citizens to use their influence in collecting the detached tribes of Indians then over the republic, in order that treaties might be made with them, and reservations of land granted them for settlements.

Dr. D. Rowlett, congressman for this district, had collected a small tribe of Coushattas at his place on Red river, and had the care of them, until they could be provided for by the government. The depredations of this tribe became frequent in the neighborhood, and resulted in the terrible conflict with the Duggan family, (the particulars of which the writer has not been able to get). After this battle, the Indians left Dr. Rowlett's and fled to the Indian Territory, north of Red river. The Texans (pronounced Texian), being greatly incensed at the course practiced by them while living in Texas, determined they should not remain so near them. Captain Joseph Sowell, with ten or twelve men, crossed the river at night, ascertained where they were camped, stole upon them, and fired into their wigwams, killing ten or twelve of their number. This matter was kept secret for some time, the act being a violation of the international law with the United States Government.

The Indians retaliated by charging on Captain Sowell's posse shortly after. The District Court of Fannin County was to commence in 1841, at Warren, then the county seat, on a Monday morning. Owing to the sparse and scattered settlements of the citizens, and the long distances those summoned to witness and jurymen had to travel, many went on Sunday evening to be in readiness Monday morning.

Their stopping place was at the tavern kept by Captain Sowell and J. S. Scott. During the night, when the men were busily engaged in spinning yarns, and drinking whisky, the Coushattas made their raid upon the stable of the tavern, wherein were placed the horses of the guests, and a fine charger, owned by Captain Sowell. They secured the stallion, one of them saddled and mounted him, preparatory to driving the other horses from the stable, while others laid down in the corner of the fence or secreted themselves near the bars. The neighing of the horses alarmed the men, who rushed from the house in the wildest excitement, most of them without their guns or pistols. Sowell and Scott ran to the gap, laid down by the Indians. Sowell, being in front, discharged his pistol without effect, when they retorted with a volley of arrows. One passed through his stomach, another through his back. He fell at the Indians' feet, called to Scott to shoot the Indian, and expired without a groan. Scott killed one Indian; the rest fled precipitately in every direction. They collected again, and arranged a trap for those whites who should pursue them, but no other encounter took place.

After the murder of Captain Sowell, the citizens were greatly excited on account of the attack. District Court met at Warren, and was organized for business, and had not proceeded far with the cases on docket, when a scout came dashing into town with the intelligence that a large trail of Indians was discovered, going in the direction of Fort Inglish. The judge immediately adjourned the court, and all started for their homes except two or three, Mr. Simpson and Major Bird, after whom the fort was named, among the number, who waited until night fall, this being the safest mode of travel to avoid Indians. They traveled in the most profound silence for some time, till Major Bird, who was under the influence of liquor, lost his hat. While stopping to look for it, the Major, very much trammeled by his befuddled condition, a squad of Indians ran upon them, and came within fifteen or twenty paces of them, when Mr. Simpson fired his shot gun at them and at the same time shouted "charge, charge!" This gave the impression that a large company was under his command, and the effect was magical among the Indians; they scattered in every direction.

At this time depredations became so numerous that houses were attacked in daylight, and many murders committed. Captain John Youree and Daniel Davis were attacked, the latter killed.

The County of Fannin is located in the north central portion of the State, the Red river, forming its northern boundary, being the dividing line between the Indian Territory and the State of Texas.

CHAPTER III.

INDIAN TROUBLES IN FAYETTE COUNTY—WACO BROWN—
CHILDREN CARRIED INTO CAPTIVITY—INDIAN FIGHT
ON ROSS CREEK—SETTLEMENT ON THE BRAZOS—DEN-
TON COUNTY—INDIAN RAIDS—FORT PARKER TAKEN BY
INDIANS—CAPTIVITY OF MRS. PLUMMER.

THE County of Fayette was organized in 1837, but settlements were commenced some time before.

In 1821, the Buckners, A. C. and Oliver, settled on the creek that bears their name. In 1823, the Castlemans settled on the western bank of the river (Colorado), and Stephen F. Austin for a time made Fayette County his home. Among other settlers of the county, were Col. John Moore, Jesse Burnham, Andrew Rabb, J. J. Ross, James Tombleson, John Cryer, S. A. Anderson, C. Cummings, James Lester, Redden Andrews, and John Rabb.

In 1833-34 came John E. Lewis, Breedings, Joel Robinson, J. G. Robinson, Walter Robinson, John W. Dancy, Ed Manton, Henry Manton, M. Hill and I. H. Hill. The Indians, as usual, commenced depredating on the whites as soon as they began to form a settlement. John Duff, or Waco Brown, was captured by the Waco Indians in August, 1825, and by them kept for fifteen months, in their favorite region, of which the present town-site of Waco was one of the chief villages. He, by his stay among the Indians, acquired a vast amount of information about the Waco and other tribes which proved to be of great value to General Austin and the early settlers. It was thought by his wife and Captain Henry S. Brown (his brother) that he had been killed by the Indians. But in 1826 he made his escape from a war party of seventeen Wacos on Cummings' creek, in this county, the party having come down to kill and rob the settlers. They brought him with them, as he had promised to assist them in stealing horses. He made his escape at night, while they were all asleep, and hastened to San Felipe, on the Brazos, where he found his brother, H. S. Brown, who had just returned from Mexico, having a well-armed party with him.

With these and some volunteer citizens, Captain Brown hastened in search of the Indians, completely surprised them at daylight on the following morning, and killed all but one. J. D. Brown was afterwards known as Waco Brown.

In February, 1837, as J. G. Robinson and his brother Walter were on their way to see a gentleman on business, they were both killed by Indians, on Cummings' creek. The same day Mr. and Mrs. Gocher were killed by Indians, on Rabb's creek, and three of their children carried into captivity, one girl and two boys. They were afterwards redeemed by Mr. Spalding, who married the young lady.

During the "Runaway" in 1836, the Indians captured a young German girl. At this time the Indians kept their captives for trade; they could be purchased by relatives or friends. A German purchased this young lady, and made her his wife.

In 1828 or '29, says Mr. James. T. Ross, a party of Indians were camped on Ross's creek. They made their camp in the bed of the creek, that they might be protected by the cliffs from the chilling winds. It was thought by the old settlers that they were there on a stealing expedition until they killed a Mexican and scalped him. Mr. James J. Ross, J. Tombleson, John Cryer, S. A. Anderson and several others, whose names are forgotton, got together and attacked their camp. When they reached the camp some were lying down and others were dancing around with their scalps, and some were parching corn. The number of Indians were sixteen; eight of them were killed, and an attempt was made to burn them, but only the skin was burned off, and the bones were left to bleach in the bed of the creek. Seven were wounded, but succeeded in making their escape, and were never heard from afterwards. It was thought they died ere they reached their tribe. Mr. Pennington was allowed to trade with this tribe of Indians. and while there on one of his trading expeditions, one of these Indians returned to the tribe, and it was always supposed that he was the only one left to tell the story.

In 1833 the Indians were very bad about killing and stealing. About this time Tom Alley was out hunting horses, and unexpectedly came on a camp of these Indians. As soon as he was discovered by them, they immediately commenced shooting at him, and he was badly wounded. He put spurs to his horse and made his escape, and was fortunate enough to reach home.

The next day several of his friends trailed them towards the head of Cummings' creek, and there the Indians burned the grass, and the pursuers lost the trail.

Those of my readers who have never seen a new country can hardly conceive of its wild beauty and grandeur as it appeared to the first settlers of this country.

The following is an extract from a sketch of Fort

Bend County, which is as near as pen can describe it:

"Texas, and its native loveliness, we have been told, had impressed other discoverers and pioneers long ere Austin visited the country. Yet their footprints in the vast wilderness were effaced as fast as made, and the legendary relations we have heard, and the slight visible remains made impressions on the early settlers, as dim traditions, like the poetry of the Scottish Border, which relates incidents verified by latter chronicles.

"The first settlers found this portion of Texas a new country, rich in primeval beauty, and so many of the old Texans speak of the emotion of wonder aroused on their first view of this strange wild beauty of the land; how the undulating formation impressed them; how the exuberance of verdure, and the wide flower-germed prairies, and clear running streams, fringed with trees to the water's edge, excited their love of the beautiful, and this portion of Texas was thought by them to be a land of plenty and a paradise of beauty."

In 1821, (says J. J. Sullivan), William Little with others of the "old three hundred," had reached the city of New Orleans on their way to Texas as colonists. At this point William Little received orders from Stephen F. Austin to take with him as many families as would be sufficient to establish a small settlement, and sail with them to the mouth of the Brazos river; from there to proceed up that stream, until he should find a desirable situation, and then land there and make a settlement. In obedience to this order, Little and his party ascended the river until they had reached the spot where Richmond now stands. From the tide to this point, on each side of the river nothing but low banks, dense forests, cane-brakes and the richest body of land, perhaps in the world, was to be seen. But here the eyes and the hearts of the whole party were gladdened by finding the banks much higher than anywhere below, whilst on the west the prairie came full up to the river, spreading out as far as the eye could reach, westward, one vast and unbroken sea of rich waving grass, interspersed with an endless variety of most beautiful and fragrant flowers.

With what alacrity and gladness did this little party of pioneers go ashore, just at the foot of the large bend in the river, which circles for some ten or twelve miles around, just above the present town of Richmond.

Soon the work of preparation of their future homes commenced. Among the first and most important things to be done, was the building of a small fort for the protection of the pioneers against the savage tribes of Indians then numerous on the Brazos. This was soon accomplished, and before long this great bend in the river came to be called "Fort Bend," and hence the county of Fort Bend came by its name.

The first settlements in what is now known as Denton County, was on Hickory and Prairie creeks, in 1842, up to 1845, by the Wagners, Prices, Clarys, Kings, and others. In June, 1845, there were in all seventeen families. In the latter part of 1845 came Murphy, the Harmosons, Halfords, Weldors, Frenches and others, and in the early part of '46 the Carters, S. A. Venters and the Yochonis settled on Clear creek and the Stricklins on Isle De Bois.

Denton County was organized in July, 1846. The Indians were numerous and hostile, and often bloody encounters took place between them and the pioneers. In 1868 a party of Indians, supposed to be about twenty strong, made a raid into Wise and Denton Counties. Crossing Denton creek near the overland road and meeting no opposition, the red skin marauders at twelve o'clock, one night, dashed into the town of Denton, unperceived, and drove out about thirty horses. The next morning horses were missed from lots and pastures.

Indian trails were discovered in the fields and every circumstance attested that their very doors had been visited by the savages. Scouts were sent out in several directions, when it was discoverd that the Indians had gone out by the Gainesville road to the crossing on Clear creek, gathering all the horses on the route.

No attempt had been made by them to kill, scalp, or capture any of the citizens whose houses they had passed. When crossing Clear creek, they attempted to capture two of Mr. Rol's little boys who happened to be some distance from the house. Their main object seemed to be to get as many horses as possible. They gathered all the horses on the way, until the drove amounted to some fifty or sixty, then left the settlements beyond Clear creek, and started out in the direction of Cook County. Captain R. H. Hopkins, Stephenson Curley, and three other men, whose ranches on Clear creek were swept of a good deal of valuable stock, mounted fleet horses and went out in pursuit. Another force of ten men also joined in the chase farther in the rear, not being able to keep pace with the Indians, all of whom were now mounted upon fresh horses. The chase continued for many miles over the prairie, the party keeping in sight of the Indians all the time until Hopkins' squad made a flank movement, for the purpose of getting re-enforcements from some ranches on the right. This move so confused the Indians, who thought this was some stratagem, that they turned into the brakes and briers on Clear creek, where they were charged upon by Hopkins and his men, and nearly all the stolen horses recaptured. The Indians escaped with the horses they were riding and went off in the direction of Montague County.

.Soon after this raid a runner hastened to town and

reported Indians in force, between the residence of Thomas Eagan and that of George McCormick, five miles from the town of Denton, gathering horses. Some twenty-five of the citizens immediately armed themselves as best they could, mounted horses and started out in pursuit. About ten miles from town the scouts observed a couple of Indians on Hickory creek, driving some fifteen horses to the main herd, when they raised the yell and charged, recapturing the horses. Mr. Tarleton Bull was in the lead and fired first at close range, the ball taking effect near the spine, when the Indian turned and fired upon Mr. Bull but missed his aim. He then raised his bow, but was pierced with three more balls before he could use it. Mr. Bull secured his pony, and Mr. E. Allen returned with his gun, bow and quiver. The other Indian escaped. The scouts then pushed on closely after the main body of the savages up North Hickory, but did not come up with them until they halted at Chism ranch. Here at the sound of their bugle the Indians formed in line of battle. A dog, belonging to one of the scouting party, hearing the sound of the bugle, ran over to the Indians, and was instantly killed. The force of the scouting party by this time had increased to forty-three men; the number of savages was estimated at one hundred and fifty.

Firing commenced on both sides, when the Indians, seeing the comparative smallness of the squad, raised the war whoop, and charged. The men retreated in disorder and formed on the bank of a little prairie creek. In the retreat Mr. Severe Fortenberry was killed, scalped, stripped of his clothes, and disfigured in too barbarous a manner to relate. Mr William Eaves received a slight wound, and Mr. George McCormick's horse was shot and killed under him, but he succeeded in making his escape across the creek. The Indians were successful in the fight, and succeeded in getting away with two or three hundred head of horses.

Early in the fall of 1835, a small colony of whites, known as Austin Colony (now Grimes County), arrived and settled at a point about two and a half miles north of the present county seat. The following persons composed the colony: Silas M. Parker, John Parker, James Parker, L. T. M. Plummer, Benjamin Parker, Elisha Anglin and his son, Abraham, Samuel Frost and family, Seth H. Bates and son. Geo. E. Dwight, J. Nickson and the heroic Mrs. Plummer. The early outlook for this little band of brave and industrious people were first of the most pleasing and encouraging nature, indeed they were all happy upon the realization of long anticipated hopes for they were seeking, what apparently laid at their feet, rich and productive soil, broad and flourishing pasturage, good timber, excellent water, and abundant game : but, alas! these pleasing realizations were soon to be overclouded by the dark and frustrating clouds of adversity, warfare and death.

The sad sequel of this little band has been verbally related to the author of this sketch (Maggie Abercrombie) by one of the old settlers, above mentioned, who is still alive, but too decrepid and and old to write. From his conversation is gathered the following data : The first evidence of trouble that appeared to the people was caused by a small party of settlers from Colorado, who, not being content to pursue their avocations peaceably and honestly, attempted to infringe upon the rights of a tribe of Tehaucano Indians, who had a small village upon the hills of the same name (Tehaucano), situated in the northern part of the county. These Colorado settlers repeatedly molested and annoyed the Indians by attempting to steal their horses. The Indians had manifested a civil disposition until these annoyances provoked their resentment and revenge, and in the instances alluded to, they repulsed the white Colorado settlers, killing Williams, the leader, and wounding Huldaman, a small boy. From this unfortunate event, the Indians exhibited no little degree of malice and revenge, and would frequently glide into the white settlements at midnight and steal their stock and cattle. They appeared perfectly defiant in their village, which stands on one of the highest hills in central Texas, and overlooks the broad green prairies for miles and miles around. They seemed to believe these hills, like Cæsar, did the hills of Rome, a formidable fortification against any and all intrusion, and would often in daytime commit fearful crimes, and immediately repair to their quarters on the hills.

No sooner had the settlers begun to take the preliminary steps for shelter and comfort, than did the alarming indications of molestation become more manifest, and the propriety of defense manifest itself. They therefor soon erected that rude fortification known to the darker pages of Texas history as "Fort Parker," and which shall ever live in the hearts of the countrymen, as does the recollections of San Jacinto and the Alamo. Of these trials, scenes and dangers one of the old survivors has written as follows:

"After our log fort had been erected, we pursued our avocations with better satisfaction than before, and not until May, the succeeding year, did we suffer any very great depredations from the Indians. During this month the fearful and cowardly massacre of Fort Parker was enacted. It was no day for the awful deeds committed, for nature had ushered into light a May-day as gentle and as serene as the soft light of the dawning sun that stole carelessly over our sleeping farms. At an early hour, and while a few of our more delicate ones were still engaged in slumber, we noticed upon an eminent point on the the prairie, not exceeding four hundred yards from the fort, a body of restless Indians.

" This unexpected spectacle created the usual result among the women and children, and while the men were naturally surprised they knew that discipline, composure and fortitude, were their imperative duty and safeguard. A white flag was conspiciously hoisted by the Indians as an indication of peace. Very soon afrerwards, a warrior from their camp approached the fort and in a civil manner offered to make a treaty. To this, Captain Benjamin Parker, commander of the fort, responded. After a short interview he returned and notified the inmates that he believed the Indians intended to fight. He, however, returned to the hostile camp, which was no sooner reached, than he was a mangled corpse, literally chopped into pieces by the bloodthirsty demons. They immediately began their hideous war-whoop, and with wild, infuriated yells, charged upon the fort. Fortunately, several of the inmates had left the stockade by this time, while others were endeavoring to escape. Mrs. Nixon, a brave little woman, heroically made her way through an exposed field, where she notified her father, husband and brother, of the imminent danger that threatened them.

" Mr. John Parker and wife, with Mrs. Kellogg, had gotten a mile or more away when they were overtaken, the old man killed and scalped, his wife speared and left for dead, and Mrs Kellogg made captive. Samuel M. Frost and his son were brutally killed, also Silas M. Parker. Mrs. Plummer in trying to escape by flight, was knocked down by a huge Indian, and with her child, seventeen months old, made prisoners. Cynthia Ann and John, two children of Silas Parker, were also captured. The survivors met a few days afterwards, when it was discovered that only eighteen of the original number of their party were present.

"The alarm spread through the settlements like wild fire, and a small body of men soon repaired to the fort, but seeing no line of defense against the great number of Indians which approximated near eight hundred, they, after close concealment in ambush, retreated to their respective homes, and in a short time all moved away to Fort Houston, about three miles distant from the present city of Palestine.

"The wounded wife of John Parker, covered with blood and scarcely able to walk, was found after night by a party of three or four, by whom she was conveyed to the Fort Houston settlement. She did not survive a great while. Soon afterwards a party repaired to Fort Parker and buried the remains of the dead. Mrs. Kellogg was, a few months afterwards, purchased by General Sam Houston from some friendly Delaware Indians, who held her at one hundred and fifty dollars ransom. Mrs. Plummer was also purchased from her captors by Colonel Donnahue, and after weeks of suffering and trial, reached Santa Fe. She was a captive over two years, and had many thrilling adventures."

Mr. R. F. Mattison writes of Mrs. Plummer's adventures and of "old Fort Parker," as follows.

"Mrs. Plummer, whose captivity and sufferings among the Comanche Indians we are now about to relate, was the daughter of Rev. James W. Parker, the captain of a small company of rangers, and the commander of Fort Parker. When the fort fell into the hands of the Indians, by means of a ruse to which they resorted, she attempted to escape, carrying in her arms her little son, James Pratt, only eighteen months old. Nothing could give us a more exalted estimation of female courage and fortitude, than the act of this frail, delicate little woman, who was willing to risk her life that she might save her infant child; while with the heartrending screams of friends were mingled with the terrible yells of the brutal and savage foe, she ventured out alone, risking all to save her dear one; with no shield, no protection, save the burning eye of God and the feeble prayers that were ascending to Him. With the infant pressed close to her bosom, she rushes across the field in the direction of adjoining timber. She strains every nerve and speeds onward, urged only by fear and affection.

"It was not, however, in the providence of God, that Mrs. Plummer and her child should meet death heroically or escape. A huge, savage warrior, painted and begrimmed with dust and blood, discovers and pursues her with a savage yell of triumph. Though fear lent swiftness to her feet, she is not fleet enough to leave him behind. He overtakes her, clutches a hoe left in the field, fells her to the ground and seizing her by the hair of

3

the head, drags her, still clinging to her boy, though stunned and unconcious, past the fort and into presence of the main body of Indians. She awakes to consciousness only to see her child torn from her bosom and hear the groans and cries of her wounded and dying friends.

Her anxiety was increased and her suspense rendered almost intolerable by seeing the dead and mutilated body of her uncle, Benjamin Parker, the reeking scalp of the aged grandfather, Rev. John Parker, and many other signs of the butchery now going on in and near the fort, where all was hushed in the silence of death, except the fiendish yells of triumph from the treacherous Indians. It was not till then she was made aware of her captivity. Mrs. Plummer was not allowed to speak to her relations, not even to her own little boy, Pratt. She and the rest were beaten with clubs by the Indian braves and lashed with rawhide thongs by the squaws.

"After leaving the fort the two tribes, Comanches and Kiowas, remained and traveled together until midnight. They halted on an open prairie, staked out their horses, placed their pickets, and pitched their camp. Bringing all their prisoners together for the first time, they tied their hands behind them with rawhide thongs so tightly as to cut the flesh, tied their feet close together, and threw them upon their faces. Then the braves gathered around with their yet bloody dripping scalps, commenced their usual war dance. They danced, screamed, yelled, stamping upon their prisoners, beating them with bows until their own blood came near strangling them.

"The remainder of the night these frail women suffered and had to listen to the cries and groans of three tender children. Add to this heart-sickening scene, one more heartless and cruel still. The infant of Mrs. Plummer, born during her captivity, and while only six weeks old, was torn madly from her bosom by six giant Indians, one of them clutched the little prattling innocent by the throat, and like a hungry beast with defenseless prey, he held it out in his iron grasp until all evidence of life seemed extinct. Mrs. Plummer's feeble efforts to save her child were utterly fruitless. They tossed it high in the air and repeatedly let it fall on rocks and frozen earth. Supposing the child dead they returned it to its mother but discovering traces of lingering life they again, by force, tore it angrily from her, tied plaited ropes around its neck, and threw its unprotected body into hedges of prickly pear. They would repeatedly pull it through these lacerating rushes with demoniac yells. Finally, they tied the rope attached to its neck to the pommel of a saddle and rode triumphantly around a circuit until it was not only dead but literally torn to shreds. All that remained of that once beautiful babe was then tossed into the lap of its poor distracted mother. This truly-drawn picture portrays some of the dark deeds of woe and strife that befel this little band."

Mrs. Plummer also said that in one of her rambles, after she had been with the Indians some time, she discovered a cave in the mountains and, in company with an old squaw that guarded her, she explored it and found a large diamond, but when she was ransomed the Indians stole it from her and she was compelled to leave it. She said also here in these mountains she saw a bush which had thorns on it resembling fish hooks which the Indians used to catch fish with, and she herself has often caught trout with them in the little mountain streams.

In the year 1838 another colony arrived near Fort Parker, with a view of locating, etc., but in this purpose they were disappointed, for the Indians had lost none of their troublesome and treacherous spirit, and in the year 1839 they were again compelled to flee the Indian annoyances, not, however, without having improved considerable land, built several log houses, and selected their town site, which was donated to them in a five hundred acre tract of land, by Mr. Herrin, who lived near Nacogdoches.

Limestone County was organized permanently two years afterwards, 1846: that is two years after the return of some of the families, in 1844.

CHAPTER IV.

INDIAN RAIDS IN COLORADO COUNTY—LAY AND ALLEY KILLED — INDIAN RAIDS IN PARKER COUNTY — MRS. SHERMAN KILLED — TERRIBLE FIGHT BETWEEN RANGERS AND INDIANS AT THE HEAD OF THE TRINITY RIVER COW-BOYS FIGHT WITH INDIANS—BESIEGING THE CAVE.

SETTLEMENTS were commenced in Colorado County in 1822. The first was at the Atasca Sitta crossing of the Colorado, a little below the present town of Columbus. Among the early settlers were Leander Beeson, W. W. Dewees, Ross Alley, William Alley, Peter and John Tumbleson, Jesse Burnham, J. W. C. Wallace, Thomas Buens. In 1831-'33 came F. Peters, Levi Bostick, William Hunt, John Matthews, Major Montgomery, David Cole, the Cooper's, and others. The tribe of Indians which gave the most trouble to the early settlers were the Carankaways, a fierce and warlike tribe. They are spoken of as being strongly built, and of tall stature, and over six feet in height.

It is said that each warrior carried a bow exactly his own length, so powerful that few Americans could bend them, and with these they could shoot their arrows with unerring accuracy. From what can be learned it is highly probable that this tribe were cannibals, indeed, they were always spoken of and regarded as such by the early settlers, and the facts certainly seem strongly to indicate that such was the case.

Colonel Dewees says:

"In 1823, three of our young men had been down the Colorado

river in a canoe to obtain corn.   (This corn had been raised on
the river.   The manner in which the ground was prepared seems
a little strange to the people of the present day.   They first
burned off the cane brakes, and then made holes in the ground
with a hand-spike, where they planted the corn.   The land being
very rich, a large crop was raised in this manner.)

"The Carankaway Indians had encamped at the mouth of
Skull creek, in Colorado County.   They saw the young men as
they returned with their canoe-load of corn and lay in ambush
for them.   When they were sufficiently near, the Indians fired
upon them and killed two, a Mr. Loy and Mr. Alley.   Mr. Clark,
the only one now remaining, leaped into the river and endeavored
to save himself by swimming, but ere he reached the opposite
bank he received some seven wounds from the arrows.   He succeeded in escaping by crawling into a very heavy cane-brake.
Here he lay all night, being unable to crawl, from the loss of blood.

A young man by the name of Brotherton had left the settlement that same evening to go down the river to the mouth of
Skull creek, on horseback.   Not apprehending any danger from
the Indians, he rode up the creek quite late in the evening, when
he was surrounded by the savages.   Thinking them to be friendly
Indians living in the neighborhood he still feared not.   He dismounted from his horse, when an Indian stepped up to him and
took hold of his gun as though wishing to look at it.   Just then
he discovered them to be a tribe with whom he was not acquainted.
He endeavored to retain possession of his gun, but the Indian
succeeded in wresting it from him.   The Indian attempted to
shoot but the gun being double-triggered, he was unable to fire.
He threw down the gun, and catching up his bow, shot Brotherton.
The arrow entered his back, doing no material injury.   Brotherton made his escape into the timber, and in a few hours succeeded
in reaching the settlements.   Fourteen men started in pursuit of
the Indians, and at midnight arrived at the place where Brotherton had been wounded.   Five of the number went to search out
the encampment of the Indians.

" After finding out the situation of their camp, says one of their
number, we returned to our comrades.   Here we remained until
about half an hour before day, then proceeded to the Indian encampment as silently as possible.   We crawled into a thicket
about ten steps behind the camp, placing ourselves about four or

five steps apart in a sort of half-circle, and completely cutting off their retreat from the swamp. The Indians were up and busily engaged apparently in getting breakfast. When the light was sufficient for us to see clearly we could not see anything of the Indians. We now commenced talking in order to draw them from their wigwams. In this we succeeded. They rushed out as if greatly alarmed. We fired upon them and killed nine. The rest attempted to escape but had no way to run except into the open prairie. We rushed upon them and killed all but two who had made their escape, though wounded, after the first fire. The number killed was nineteen.

"The Indians were so greatly alarmed that they did not even attempt to fire on us. After the fatigue of the night and the toils of the morning, being quite hungry, we entered the wigwams, where we found plenty of provision. We made a hearty breakfast, then loaded our horses with such things as we found in the wigwams, and returned to the settlements."

Parker County was created in 1855. Among those who settled Parker County who were here in 1856 and still reside in the county, are Thomas Allen, William Allen, Charles Baker, Joseph Baker, Samuel R. Barbee, W. C. Brashear, George W. Brock, Thomas Caldwell, Dr. H. G. Cantwell, Calvin Carr, William Carr, Joseph Carroll, Loving Clifton, Jeremiah Cockburn, J. P. Cole, Wilson Copeland, Isam Cranfield, William Cuthbert, Solomon Deroche, William Dixon, Thomas Derrett, Rev. Reuben A. Eddleman, J. C. Edwards, Jesse Ellison, M. S. Emberlin, and Mrs. Ensy.

In December, 1859, two families named Brown and Sherman, lived respectively eleven and sixteen miles from the county seat at Weatherford. They were farmers, highly respected and industrious. John Brown was about half a mile from his dwelling attending to his horses when five of the national assassins surrounded, killed and scalped him, and took eighteen horses from his farm. They then rode to Mr. Thompson's farm, two miles distant, and stole seven horses from him, and thence to Mrs. Sherman's residence, near the Palo Pinto line. The family, comprising six persons, were at dinner. The demons numbered nearly fifty. Six of them galloped into the yard, alighted from their horses, entered the house, and cordially took each member by the hand as if all had been on terms of intimacy. Without much ceremony the Indians told them to "vamose, vamose, no hurt, vamose." They did so, Mrs. Sherman, her husband and the four children, without the slightest resistance, as they had been assured that no danger should befall them. It was a very cold and rainy day and the exiles paced along the highway rapidly. They reached a point half a mile from the premises, joyful over their escape from a horrible death, when the brutes overtook them and captured Mrs. Sherman. The family begged for life. The monsters said they wanted "squaw," and suiting the action to the word, tore the frantic woman from those she loved best—the mother from the husband and children—carried her back to the house, where she was maltreated in a manner most outrageous and inhuman. Her screams and shrieks seemed to afford enjoyment to the merciless wretches. They deliberately applied all sorts of tortures, scalped her, stripped all the clothing from her person, shot several arrows into her body, and compelled her to pass through an ordeal that few could endure. They left her for dead, but soon after their departure she managed to crawl into the house, where the husband managed to find her several hours afterwards. Mr. Sherman, as soon as he had placed the children out of danger, with others started in pursuit of those who had so fiendishly robbed him of his wife, and destroyed the happy family of a few hours previous. When discovered she was suffering from almost every conceivable indignity, and was beyond the slightest hope of recovery. At sight of Mr. Sherman the poor woman rallied sufficiently to relate all she had so bitterly experienced at the hands of the miscreants. Strange to say, she lived four days after the perpetration of the outrage. The children were brought back to the house the following day, and it is said the meeting with the dying woman was one of the most touching and heartrending ever witnessed in this or any other country.

In June, of 1860, General John R. Baylor, who now resides in San Antonio, with his brother George W. Baylor, his two sons, Walker K. and John W. Baylor, and Wat. Reynolds, visited the Clear Fork of the Brazos, where the General formerly lived. While there hunting cattle these gentlemen were informed of the killing of Joseph Browning and the serious wounding of Frank Browning, by a large body of Comanches. They immediately went to the Browning ranch on the Clear Fork, near the mouth of Hubbard's creek, where they met other gentlemen who had been attracted to the spot by the murderous acts of the Indians.

General Baylor, George W. Baylor, Elias Hale, Minn Wright, and John Dawson, started in pursuit of the demons, and on the fifth day, June 28th, overtook them on Paint creek, where a fierce contest ensued, during which Baylor and his friends killed thirteen of the Indians. On their return to Weatherford they brought the scalps of nine of them, a white woman the Indians had killed, several bows and arrows, darts, quivers, shields, tomahawks, and other paraphernalia of savage warfare.

General Baylor took his scalps and other spoils of the victors to various cities and towns and soon after the people of the southwestern portion of the State sent flour, meal and all other kinds of provisions, clothing, boots and shoes, blankets, pistols, guns, etc., to Weatherford, for the support and protection of the people of the frontier. There was a universal cry; it seemed to be the heartfelt desire of every person: "Exterminate the Indians," was the watchword, and it is not to be wondered that such was the case when we fully realize the destruction of property and human life. Up to the close of 1875, it is estimated that the Indians captured and destroyed property within a circle of one hundred miles of Parker county, worth at least $6,000,000, and killed and took into captivity nearly 400 persons.

In 1837, the Indians were very numerous and hostile in Travis and adjoining counties, the Texas congress therefore authorized several persons to raise companies of rangers, to scour the country, and drive them out. Among the most noted rangers and Indian fighters of Texas, were Jack Hays, Henry and Ben McCulloch, Colonel Edward Burleson, Mathew Caldwell, James and Resin Bowie, Kit Ackland, Tom Green, Ad Gillespie, Mike Chevalier, W. W. Wallace, (Bigfoot), Jim Hudson, Sam Walker, Robert Neighbors, Colonel John S. Ford, Major Van Dorn, John H. Moore, and a great many other gallant men, too numerous to mention. The following account of an expedition of the Texas rangers against the Indians. I get from " Morphis: "

" On the 7th of October, 1837, Captain L. Lynch and William Eastland, with sixty-eight men, started from Fort Prairie, five miles below where Austin now stands, on the look-out for Indians. On arriving at the sources of Pecan Bayou and the Clear Fork of the Brazos, a jealousy sprang up between the officers as to right of command, when they partly divided, and Lieutenants Van Benthuyson and Miles, with sixteen men, continued their Indian hunt, while Captain Lynch and Eastland, with the remainder returned to the fort. Van Benthuysen, Miles, and company, soon fell in with a party of Keechis, attacked and defeated them, killing two of their warriors.

" Emboldened by success the little party pushed on to the
headwaters of the Trinity, near the " Knobs," called by the Indians " the stone houses." On the 10th of November they were
surrounded and attacked by about 180 or 200 savage warriors.
The little band of eighteen men took position at the head of
a ravine near a forest of trees, but where the grass was abundant,
and their horses could eat while the fight lasted. The battle was
desperate, and for hours the Texans kept off the Indians, killing
their chief, among others, when they retired from the contest,
elected another chief, and renewed the struggle. During the
fight the rangers would pull off their hats, place them on the end
of their ramrods, raise them above the walls of the ravine, and
the Indians, mistaking the empty hats for hats with heads in
them, would fire at them, sometimes putting as many as half
a dozen balls through one hat, when immediately the rangers
would rise, take aim, and fire at the Indians.

At last the wily savages resorted to the expedient of setting the
prairie on fire, and almost in an instant vast volumes of flames
and smoke forced the little band to leave their advantageous
position and seek safety in the woodland near by, to arrive at
which point they must necessarily charge through the Indians
as well as the flames. Having lost three men already, the remaining fifteen left their horses, baggage, provision and dead, and at
the word of command, bounded off on their run for life.

" In the charge through the Indians and run to the timber, a
distance of about eighty yards, seven of the rangers were killed,
including Lieutenant Miles, and three wounded. In the engagement ten of eighteen were killed and three of the survivors
wounded, while the Indians, as they reported at a trading house,
lost sixty-three killed and wounded. Night coming on soon after,
the rangers gained the woods, under the friendly protection of its
dark mantle they retreated before the victorious savages, and after
much suffering and many hardships, going for two or three days
without any thing to eat, they finally struck the settlements, and
found rest for their weary limbs, nourishing food for their empty
stomachs, no doubt esteeming themselves fortunate in the possession of their scalps, fully appreciating the language of the poet,

> For he who fights and runs away
> May live to fight another day,
> But he who is in battle slain
> Can never rise and fight again."

One of these eight rangers, J. O. Rice, verified the truth of this poetry, for in 1842, only five years afterwards, he joined the ill-fated expedition under General Somerville, and was wounded and captured. The Somerville campaign wound up with the unfortunate expedition to Mier, under Cameron, who, with a part of Somerville's force, after it was dissolved, crossed the Rio Grande and captured the town of Mier, and fortified himself in some of the buildings. Cameron was soon besieged by a large force of Mexicans, and after several days of hard fighting, it was left to a vote whether they should surrender or not, and it resulted in a majority of the men favoring a surrender. The barricades were removed from the doors, and the men marched out and gave up their guns in the street. Captain Cameron was opposed to a surrender, and when they came out, grasped his rifle by the muzzle, and raising it aloft, dashed it to pieces against the stone sidewalk. After the Mexicans had fully disarmed the Texans, they sentenced every fifteenth man to be shot. The lots were cast by the men drawing beans. To every fourteen white ones was placed one black one until they corresponded to the number of prisoners. The beans were then put in a hat and covered up, and the drawing commenced. Those drawing the black beans were placed off to one side by themselves and that evening led a short distance from the town and shot. The following are the names of those who drew the black beans: L. L. Cash, Pennsylvania; J. D. Cocke, Virginia; Robert Durham, Tennessee; William N. Eastland, Tennessee; Edward Este, New Jersey; Robert Harris, Mississippi; T. L. Jones, Kentucky; Patrick Mahan, Ireland; James Ogden, Virginia; Charles Roberts, Tennessee; William Rowan, Georgia; J. L. Shepherd, Alabama; J. M. N. Thompson, Tennessee; James

N. Torry, Connecticut; James Turnbull, Scotland; Henry Whaling, Indiana; M. C. Wing, New York. Although Captain Cameron drew a white bean he was afterwards shot by his treacherous captors. When the unfortunate men were formed in line to be shot the Mexicans marched up with loaded carbines and halted, each one opposite his man, and almost instantly fired. Every man fell dead except J. L. Shepherd, of Alabama. He was only wounded in the shoulder, but fell and feigned death. The Mexicans, after the discharge, wheeled and marched back to town. Shepherd lay with his dead comrades until after night set in, and then crept away, but becoming bewildered in the mountains, he wandered about until nearly starved, and was finally recaptured, carried back to Mier, and placed in the public square, where he served as a target for the Mexican soldiers to shoot at until he was literally riddled with bullets although his old wound was festering and badly swollen.

The Texas cow-boys had quite a remarkable chase once after Indians in northwest Texas, the particulars of which I learned from a frontiersman, who was familiar with the circumstance. and is as follows:

"It was in 1868 or 1869, near the brakes of the Brazos river, twenty-five of the boys were out hunting cattle, when they suddenly came upon twenty Comanche Indians, all afoot. The cow-boys had no guns, but each one had a revolver, and raising a yell, charged, and commenced firing. The Indians returned the fire with a volley of arrows and fled, closely pursued by the boys. The Indians being on foot, ran through the roughest places, while the boys being mounted, had to pick their way, but kept so close after them, and the Indians being so nearly run down, finally entered a cave. Nineteen were counted as they ran in, one being killed in the chase.

"The boys soon arrived at the mouth of the cave and dismounted, examined the place closely, and held a council as to what was best to do. It was throwing their lives away to enter the cave after them, as the Indians would have all the advantage, and it was agreed to starve them out, and accordingly sent one of their party back to bring up a wagon load of provision for themselves during the siege. In the meantime they built a wall of rock around the mouth of the cave, about four feet high, and guards were kept around it day and night, for they knew the Indians were bound to make a break sooner or later. The provision arrived with some more men with it, who were anxious to see the fun, and there, for five days and nights they eat, drank, sang and wondered when the Indians would come out, and finally, they came, on the sixth morning, just before day, screaming and yelling, and making the arrows fly, but they were literally riddled with bullets, and none got outside the rock enclosure. Some of the whites were wounded, but none killed. That was one band of Comanche warriors who left their tribe on a horse stealing expedition, and was never heard of any more by them."

CHAPTER V.

IN 1832, occurred one of the most remarkable Indian battles on record in Texas history. Considering the number engaged it, it has no equal. It occurred on the San Saba river, and was fought by James Bowie and his brother Rezin P. Bowie, David Buchanan, Mr. Hamm, Mathew Doyle, Thomas McCaslin, Robert Armstrong, James Corriell, and three others. They were out prospecting for gold in the San Saba mountains, and were in camp, when they were suddenly confronted by a large body of Indians. The following account of the affair is from the pen of Rezin P. Bowie:

" Their number," says he " being so far greater than ours, 164 to eleven, it was agreed that Rezin P. Bowie should be sent out to talk with them, and endeavor to compromise rather than attempt to fight. He accordingly started, with David Buchanan in company, and walked up to within forty yards of where they had halted, and requested them in their own tongue to send forward their chief, as they wanted to talk with him, as they wanted to talk with him. Their answer was ' How do you do! how do you do! ' in English, and a discharge of twelve shots at us, one of which broke Buchanan's leg. Bowie returned their salutation with the contents of a double-barreled gun, and a pistol. He then took Buchanan on his shoulder, and started back to the encampment. They then opened a heavy fire upon us, which wounded Buchanan in two more places slightly, and piercing Bowie's hunting shirt in several places without doing him any injury. When they found their shot failed to bring down Bowie, eight Indians, on foot, took after him, with toma-

'hawks, and when close upon him were discovered by his party, who rushed out with their rifles, and brought down four of them: the other four retreating back to the main body. We then returned to our position, and all was still for about five minutes.

"We then discovered a hill to the northwest, at the distance of sixty yards, red with Indians, who opened a heavy fire upon us, with loud yells, their chief on horseback, urging them, in a loud audible voice, to the charge, walking his horse, perfectly composed. When we first discovered him, our guns were all empty, with the exception of Mr. Hamm's. James Bowie cried out, 'Who is loaded?' Mr. Hamm answered, 'I am.' He was then told to shoot that Indian on horseback. He did so, and broke his leg and killed his horse. We now discovered him hopping around his horse on one leg with his shield on his arm to keep off the balls. By this time, four of our party being reloaded, fired at the same instant, and all the balls took effect through the shield. He fell and was immediately surrounded by six or eight of his tribe, who picked him up and bore him off. Several of these were shot by our party. The whole body then retreated back of the hill out of sight, with the exception of a few Indians, who were running about from tree to tree out of gun shot. They now covered the hill the second time, bringing up their bowmen, who had not been in action before, and commenced a heavy fire with balls and arrows, which we returned with a well directed aim with our rifles. At this instant another chief appeared on horseback, near the spot where the last one fell. The same question of 'Who is loaded?' was asked. The answer was 'nobody,' when little Charles, the mulatto servant, came running up with Buchanan's rifle, which had not been discharged since he was wounded, and handed it to James Bowie, who instantly fired and brought him down from his horse. He was surrounded by six or eight of his tribe, as was the last, and was borne off under our fire.

"During the time we were defending ourselves from the Indians on the hill, some fifteen or twenty of the Caddo tribe had succeeded in getting under the bank of the creek, in our rear, at about forty yards distant, and opened a heavy fire upon us, which wounded Mathew Doyle, the ball entering the left breast and coming out at the back. As soon as he cried out that he was wounded, Thomas McCaslin hastened to the spot, when he fell, and observed 'Where is the Indian that shot Doyle?' He was told by a more experienced hand not to venture there, as from the reports of their guns, they must be riflemen. At that instant he discovered an Indian, and, while in the act of raising his piece, was shot through the center of the body and expired. Robert Armstrong exclaimed, 'D——n the Indian that shot McCaslin; where is he?' He was told not to venture there as they must be riflemen, but, on discovering an Indian, and, while bringing his gun up, was fired at, and part of the stock of his gun cut off, the ball lodging against the barrel. During this time our enemies had formed a complete circle around us, occupying the points of rocks, scattering trees and bushes. The firing then became general from all quarters. Finding our situation too much exposed among the trees, we were obliged to leave them, and take to the thickets.. The first thing necessary was to dislodge the riflemen from under the bank of the creek, who were within point-blank shot. This we soon succeeded in doing, by shooting the most of them in the head, as soon as we had the advantage of seeing them, when they could not see us. The road we had cut around the thicket the night previous, gave us now an advantageous situation over that of our enemy, as we had a fair view of them in the prairie, while we were completely hid. We baffled their shots by moving six or eight feet the moment we had fired, as their only mark was the smoke of our guns. They would put twenty balls within the size of a pocket handkerchief when they had seen the smoke. In this manner we fought them two hours, and had one man wounded, James Corriell, who was shot through the arm, the ball lodging in the side, first cutting away a small bush which prevented it from penetrating deeper than then size of it. They now discovered that we were not to be dislodged from the thicket, and the uncertainty of killing us at random, they suffering very much from the fire of our rifles, which brought half a dozen down at every round, they determined to resort to strategem, by putting fire to the dry grass in the prairie, for the double purpose of routing us from our position, and, under cover of the smoke, to carry away their dead and wounded, which lay near us. The wind was now blowing from the west, and they placed the fire in that quarter, where it burned down all the grass to the creek, and then bore off to the right and left, leaving around our position a space of about five acres untouched by the fire. Under cover of their smoke they succeeded in carrying off a portion of their dead and wounded. In the meantime our party was engaged in scraping away the dry grass and leaves from our wounded men and baggage, to prevent the fire from passing over them; and likewise in piling up rocks and bushes to answer the place of breastwork. They now discovered that they had failed in routing us, as they had anticipated. They then re-occupied the points of rocks and trees in the prairie, and commenced another attack. The firing continued for some time, when the wind suddenly shifted to the north and blew very hard. We now discovered our dangerous situation, should the Indians succeed in putting fire to the small spot which we occupied, and kept a strict watch all around. The two servant boys were employed in scraping away dry grass and leaves from around the wounded men. The point from which the wind now blew being favorable to fire our position, one of the Indians succeeded in crawling down the creek, and putting fire to the grass that had not been burnt, but, before he could retreat back to his party, was killed by Robert Armstrong.

"At this time we saw no hope of escape, as the fire was coming down rapidly before the wind, flaming ten feet high, and directly for the spot we occupied. What must be done? We must either be burnt up alive, or be driven into the prairie among the savages. This encouraged the Indians; and, to make it more awful, their shouts and yells rent the air—they, at the same time, firing about twenty shots a minute. As soon as the smoke hid us from their view we collected together and held a consultation as what was best to be done. Our first impression was, that they might charge on us under cover of the smoke, as we could make but one effectual fire. The sparks were flying about so thickly that no man could open his powder horn without running the risk of being blown up. However, we finally came to a determination; had they charged us, to give them fire, place our backs together, draw our knives, and fight them as long as any of us were alive. The next question was, should they not charge on us and we retain our position, we must be burnt up. It was then decided that each man should take care of himself as well as he could until the fire arrived at the ring around our baggage and wounded men, and there it should be smothered with buffalo robes, bear skins, deer skins, and blankets; which, after a great deal of exertion, we succeeded in doing. Our thicket being so

4

much burnt and scorched that it afforded little or no shelter, we all got into the ring, that was made around our wounded men and baggage, and commenced building our breastwork higher, with the loose rocks from the inside, and dirt dug up with our knives and sticks. During the last fire the Indians had succeeded in removing all their killed and wounded which lay near us. It was now sundown, and we had been warmly engaged with the Indians since sunrise, and they, seeing us still alive and ready for fight, drew off at a distance of a hundred yards and encamped for the night."

No other attack was made upon the little party which remained upon the field of battle eight days, when the Indians, who were Caddos, and Tehuacanas, having retired, they saddled up and returned to the settlements, with the loss of one man killed, and three wounded. Five horses were killed, and three wounded. While the Indians loss, as reported by the Comanches, were eighty-two killed and wounded.

I will here state that Rezin P. Bowie was supposed by some to have been killed at the storming of Monterey, Mexico, as he was seen during the hottest of the fire, when men were falling on every side, and the streets and sidewalks were being literally torn to pieces by grape and canister shot; but after this, one writer says, Lieutenant Bowie was seen no more.

In 1839, the Texans began to have trouble with the Cherokee tribe of Indians, who had, prior to this time, been peaceable. Morphis says: "Although the Cherokees, under their chief, Bolles, had settled on the Neches, a few miles north of Nacogdoches, in 1822, with the permission of the Mexicans and a promise of uninterrupted possession, which had been guaranteed to them by the *consultation* and the treaty made by Houston and Forbes in 1836, yet they were intruders and should be removed. Depredations and murders were frequent on the frontier, and when accused of doing them, the Cherokees laid the blame upon '*the wild Indians.*'"

In order to guard the frontier as well as watch the Cherokees, Major Walters, with two companies of troops, was ordered to occupy the *Neches Saline*, which the Cherokees claimed as belonging to them. The chief, Bolles, notified Major Walters that the Cherokees would resist this occupation *by force and arms*. Major Walters reported the fact to the Secretary of War in November, 1839, but did not enter the territory of the Cherokees.

Now, before this time, Manuel Flores, an agent of the Mexican government, with some twenty-five men, passed between Seguin and San Antonio, where they murdered and robbed the defenseless, but were afterwards pursued, and overtaken, and entirely defeated by Lieutenant James O. Rice, on the San Gabriel fork of Little river, about fifteen miles from Austin. Rice captured 300 pounds of powder, a like quantity of shot, balls and bar lead, and more than a hundred mules and horses. Flores was killed, and on his person were found papers and letters showing the grand strategy of the Mexican policy of arousing and inciting all the border Indians to aid them with their war in Texas. Flores had messages from General Canalizo, the successor of Filisola, at Matamoras, to the chief of the Caddoes, Seminoles, Biloxies, Cherokees, Kickapoos, Brazas, Tehuacanas, and perhaps others, promising the lands on which they had settled, and assuring them that they need expect nothing from those greedy adventurers for land, who wish even to deprive the Indians of the sun that warms and vivifies them, and who would not cease to injure them while the grass grows and the water runs. By concert of action at the same time that the Mexican army marched into San Antonio, the Indians were to light up

the whole frontier with the flames of Texan dwellings
and cause the very air to resound with the cries of their
women and children.

Whatever title the Cherokees had to their lands, and
without doubt it was a good one, they forfeited it by entering into the war with Mexico against Texas.   So upon
receiving notification of Bolles, through Major Walters,
the Secretary of War, General A. S. Johnson, ordered
General Ed Burleson, with 400 men, from Colorado,
Colonel Landrum's regiment from eastern Texas, and
the Nacadoches regiment, under General Rusk, to march
into the Cherokee nation, and the entire force to act
under the command of General K. H. Douglas.

Commissioners proceeded the troops and met the Indians in council, whom they promised to pay for their
improvements, but required to surrender their gun-locks
and retire to the Cherokee nation of their brethren north
of the Red river, which the Indians refused to do, whereupon General Douglas and troops attacked the Indians,
and after two engagements, on the 15th and 16th of July,
1839, wherein the Indians were defeated with the loss of
about 100 warriors, including their chief, Bolles, (or
Bowles — like Texan, Texian, use justifies either), while
the whites lost eight killed and thirty wounded, drove
them out of the country, burned their villages, etc.''

This expulsion of the Indians from Texas was contrary to the advice and wishes of General Houston.

CHAPTER VI.

FLACCO, THE LIPAN CHIEF—COMANCHES ATTACK THE
SETTLEMENTS AROUND AUSTIN—DEATH OF MRS. COLE-
MAN AND HER SON—GENERAL BURLESON DEFEATS THE
INDIANS ON BRUSHY CREEK — JACK HAYS — COLONEL
FORD—DEATH OF IRON JACKET.

IN 1839, the Comanches were very hostile, and committed many depredations all along the frontier. Rangers
were ordered out. The settlers would often band together,
and with the aid of the friendly Indians, who were good
trailers and understood the Indian character, they would
penetrate into the wilds of the west and attack them in
their camps. Flacco and Castro were two noted chiefs
of the friendly Lipan. Flacco delighted to go with Jack
Hays' celebrated ranging company, hated the Comanche
tribe, and was always glad of an opportunity to fight
them. Although the Lipans were a branch of the
Comanche tribe, a quarrel had arisen in time between
two chiefs of this tribe, which terminated in Lipan, one
of the rival chiefs, leaving his tribe, and, with a number
who adhered to his cause, going into another part of the
country and forming a new tribe, calling themselves
Lipans, after their chief. The fate of Flacco is uncertain.
Some say he perished, while trapping, with nearly all of
his band, on the Staked Plains, for want of water. When
but few of them were left, they scattered, each one going
his own way and according to his own judgment. The
last seen of the gallant Flacco, he was standing by his
horse on this waterless waste of prairie. He had bled his

horse and was drinking the blood. This is the report that some of his tribe brought to Gonzales after this ill-fated trapping expedition.

The following incident of Indian warfare I get from Morphis: "On the 22nd of February, 1839, Colonel John H. Moore, W. P. Hardeman, Flacco, Castro, and others, aggregating sixty-five whites and forty-one Lipans, mostly from La Grange and Bastrop, attacked the Comanches in their camp on Wallace creek, seven miles from San Saba, and completely surprised them, but failing to push their advantage, they lost their horses, and marched home on foot, with the loss of one man accidently killed and seven wounded."

The early history of Texas and a life on the frontier may be exemplified by the following incidents, the truth of which many living witnesses about Austin can prove: Early in the spring of 1839, when the trees were covered with green leaves, and the earth with grass, and varie-gated flowers which perfumed the air with their fragrance, when the forest resounded with the " native wood-note wild," of feathered songsters, and everything alive seemed to enjoy existence, a band of 500 Indians attacked the settlements near Austin, just located in the hunting grounds of the Comanches.

They first attacked, about 10 o'clock in the morning, the house of Mrs. Coleman, near the Colorado river, sixteen miles below Austin. She was in the garden at the time with her little son, Thomas, aged about seven years, and on the approach of the Indians, she called her little boy and ran into the house. Mrs. Coleman out-running her son, arrived at the house first, when looking around for him, an Indian pierced her through the neck with an arrow; she then entered the house and assisted another son, thirteen years old in barring the door.

There were also in the house her two daughters, about nine and eleven years old, and an infant son, who took refuge under the bed. After barring the door, Mrs. Coleman, with the maternal instinct of defending her young ones, seized a rifle, and seating herself in a chair, with the weapon on her knees, drew the deadly arrow from her neck, and almost instantly thereafter, fell from the chair and expired, covering the floor with her blood. The boy seized the gun, and as the Indians approached, fired and shot their chief, who fell dead on the door steps, and then reloading, fired twice more, killing another Indian and wounding a third, when one of the savages thrust his spear through a hole in the side of the house, and pierced the brave boy through the body. He fell near the bed where his sisters and brothers lay concealed, when the eldest took his head in her lap. While bleeding to death he said to the poor little ones: "I will not groan to let them know I am wounded" Then with his expiring breath he said to them: "Father is dead, mother is dead, and I am dying, but something tells me God will protect you." The Indians then broke open the door, but hearing voices under the bed, and fearing more deadly bullets, after piercing the dead bodies with their spears, by thrusting them through the door, retired, taking with them little Thomas, but leaving the other three defenseless children terribly frightened, but unharmed.

A few hours after, when relief came, they crawled out from their place of concealment, and in giving their mother a farewell kiss, wet their clothes in her blood. The Indians next attacked Dr. Joe Robertson's residence, about 500 yards from Mrs. Coleman's, and captured all but one of his negroes, but the doctor was fortunately on a visit with his family, and thus escaped. After robbing the place, they next went to what was afterwards known as Wells' fort, where three families, of Mrs. Wells, John Walters, and G. W. Davis, resided, but just before arriving at the house, sixteen frontiersmen deployed in the front and stopped them, but returned before the Indians, taking the three families, mounted behind them, to Fort Wilbarger. The Indians were on foot, and turning off from the last place attacked, to Wilbarger's creek, camped for the night, and buried their dead, while the frontiersmen divided, a few remaining to watch the Indians, and the rest scattering as couriers over the country to raise men to fight them. By daylight, eighty men were assembled at Wilbarger's, and General Ed. Burleson assuming command, marched to meet the Indians, leaving a detail of five to protect the women and children.

General Burleson came up with the Indians about one o'clock, in the open prairie, near Brushy creek, twenty miles northeast of Austin, when, dividing his men into two parties, one of which Captain Jones Rogers led, and he the other, they charged the Indians, who took position in the bend of a ravine covered with scrubby elm and cactus.

The Indians at first retired before the galling fire of Burleson's men, but recovering, they charged, and forced Burleson and his party back upon the same ground. The contest lasted from 1 o'clock till night, when the Indians retired from the field of battle, beating their drums, rattling their shields, and singing their war songs, carrying with them their dead and wounded, supposed to be about eighty warriors.

Burleson lost four killed, viz: Jacob, his brother, Rev. James Gilleland, John Walters, Edward Blakely, and several wounded. Jacob Burleson was killed in front and his body fell into the temporary possession of the Indians, who cut off his hands, scalped him, and cut out his heart, which they took off with them. Wearied and exhausted from marching, fasting and fighting, Burleson returned to Fort Wilbarger the next day after the battle, bearing the bodies of his dead, when a more painful scene was never witnessed: the bereaved wife wept for her husband, the mother for her only son, and brothers and sisters for their brothers. One incident occurred which equals or surpasses anything of the kind recorded in Grecian or Roman history. On arriving at the fort, the bodies of the dead were laid out, preparatory to their funeral obsequies, in a room by themselves. Mrs. Blakely, on starting into the room to take a last look at her son, was stopped and informed that he was shot in the face, and so mangled and disfigured that the sight would be so horrid and painful that she must not go in. She claimed and demanded her right as mother to take a last look at her son. It was granted; and going into the room, she kneeled by his dead body, wiped the blood and brains oozing out from off his forehead, kissed him, and for a moment rested her head upon his manly breast, and then rising, pale and calm, she exclaimed, with tearless dignity: " His father and brother died in defense of their country, and now he is dead — my only living protector! But if I had a thousand sons, and my country needed them, I would cheerfully give them up." God grant this mother and son the ineffable joys of paradise, and inspire all Texans with the same transcendent virtue and patriotic devotion.

Sometime in 1842, Captain Jack Hays, with fifteen men, including Ad. Gillespie, Sam Walker, Sam Luckie, and the famous story-teller, Kit Acklin, fought his celebrated and most desperate battle with Yellow Wolf, and eighty Comanche warriors, at the Pinta trail crossing of the Guadalupe, between San Antonio and Fredericksburg. and. after a hand-to-hand contest and two charges, defeated them, killing and wounding about half their number, with a loss of one killed and three wounded, but without taking much spoils. Hays' report of the efficiency of the five-shooters used in these battles caused Mr. Colt to produce the six-shooter, and to engrave on the cylinder the ranger on horseback, charging Indians.

Before or after this engagement, a ranger named James Dunn, whose hair was remarkably *red*, was captured by the Comanches and led away a hopeless prisoner. to their camp. Strange to say. the murderous. bloodthirsty savages neither tortured, killed, or ate him alive, which he thought they would do, but actually took a fancy to him. treated him with great kindness, and, as Jim afterwards related, came within an ace of killing him with kindness, or, rather, drowning him in Rio Frio while attempting to wash the red (paint) from his hair.

On the evening of the 1st of January, 1843, after attending a public meeting in Austin, Captain Alexander Coleman and William Bell started in their buggy for a ride. followed by Joseph Hornsby and James Edmondson on horseback. Just as Hornsby and Edmondson mounted the spur of Robertson's hill, east of Austin, where George L. Robertson now resides, they saw Coleman and Bell jump from their buggy, cross the fence, and run for dear life across the field southeast of them, pursued by about thirty Indians. They saw the Indians capture them both, kill Bell, and about to kill Coleman. when, after a moment's consultation they resolved. though unarmed, save with a single-barreled pistol between the two. to stampede the Indians and rescue their friend

Coleman, or perish in the attempt. In their flight, Bell and Coleman had separated, and the pursuing Indians did the same, many of them leaving their horses at the fence when they entered the field, and it so happened that when Hornsby and Edmondson, charged them at full speed, yelling terribly, and discharging the single-barreled pistol in their midst, that they were frightened, left Coleman at liberty, but almost naked, and took to their heels, no doubt thinking that Hornsby and Edmondson would immediately be followed by more Texans. Coleman did his best running back to town, and raised the alarm, while his liberators hung on the rear of the retreating Indians for two and a half miles, yelling and hallooing, until assistance joined them, when a little battle took place, wherein three savages were killed and their horses and accoutrements captured.

One night, John Wahrenberger, a Switzer, and gardener of Colonel Louis P. Cook, Secretary of the Navy, returning home with a bag of meal on his shoulder, fell in with a party of Indians at the head of the avenue, near the Alhambra. He fled, and gained the residence of Colonel Cook, who then lived where Colonel A. H. Cook now resides, but received three arrows in his meal sack and one in his arm. As the poor fellow reached the door, he fell exhausted, and fainted, while Colonel Cook fired on his pursuers, and wounded one so badly that their trail was easily traced the next day by the blood on the ground.

One night, as Col. James S. Mayfield, Secretary of State, was returning home from a party with a young lady, Indians shot at and wounded him.

For some time after the capitol was removed to Austin, Indians were very troublesome, making frequent raids on the settlements, and killing and robbing without mercy. On one occasion Captain Billy Wilson, with a party of young men, including Colonel Jack Baylor, who relates the story, pursued them for three days without rest or food, and overtook them on the head of the Yegua, near Austin. Just before the Indians, who were retreating at their utmost speed, reached the timber, one of them, to facilitate his speed and escape death, being left behind, cut loose a large piece of raw meat, and letting it fall to the ground, continued his flight. Colonel Baylor and his companions saw this operation, and being exceedingly hungry, stopped, lighted a fire, cooked and commenced eating the captured meat, when Captain Wilson, who rode a safe rather than a swift horse. and was behind, came up and saw them devouring the captured property, and he being hungry himself, exclaimed: "Great God! that meat is poisoned! You'll all be dead in fifteen minutes! Run down to the creek and drink as much water as you can to kill the poison!" Baylor and his young Indian hunters heard and obeyed their chief, but as they returned to the spot, they beheld their commander as he was swallowing the last particle of the captured meat, and who, wiping his mouth with his sleeve, exclaimed, with a cunning smile, " Well, boys, we will all die together, I have *histed in* what you left."

In May, 1834, the Kiowa Indians made a descent on the settlements of northern Texas, on Glass creek. killed and wounded Judge Gabriel N. Martin, the brother-in-law of T. G. and G. W. Wright, and carried away to their stronghold in the Wichita mountains, his little son, Mat. W. Martin, then eight years old. After burying the husband of his only sister, who was almost distracted by his death, Captain T. G. Wright. with three volunteers, John Ragsdale, Thomas McCowin and Hardy. a negro, who had lived with the Kiowas, and spoke their language, bid good-bye to their friends and struck out over the boundless prairie to hunt the murderers of Judge Martin, rescue little Mat. and return him to his grief-stricken mother.   It was arranged that when the little party should find the camp of the Indians, Captain Wright, with Ragsdale and McCowin, should conceal themselves in the thicket, while Hardy should enter alone the camp of his old associates, and, while pretending to rejoin them, find the little boy, and when opportunity afforded, with him leave the camp of the Kiowas, seek the hiding place of his friends, and with them and little Mat. return as best they could to the settlements.   For days and weeks they traversed the prairie and cross-timbers, but before they neared the village of the Kiowas, these bold and death-daring frontiersmen most fortunately fell in with General Leavenworth, of the United States army, who, with a detachment of infantry and cavalry, was seeking the same Indians, by the order of the government, to treat with them for the delivery of other captives then held by them.   Captain Wright and his party joined the command of General Leavenworth, and all of them being good woodsmen, were of great service in finding lost horses and killing game.   The weather was hot, the prairie dry, and water very scarce, while the Indians fled before and hung around their rear, refusing to stop even for a white flag, or to hold any communications whatever with them.   From bad water, exposure, anxiety of mind, or some other cause, General Leavenworth sickened and died, when Captain Wright and his party, with twelve soldiers, were detailed to carry back his body to Fort Wichita, from whence it was afterwards taken to Delhi, New York, for final interment.   As a soldier and officer General Leavenworth was admired

for his many excellent qualities, and his untimely death
was sincerely mourned by his whole command. Captain
Wright and his party returned from Fort Wichita to the
little army under the command of the next senior officer,
Captain Dean, with which he and his party passed
through the cross-timbers, suffering much, after pressing
the juice from wild grapes to quench their thirst, which
not only relieved them but had an exhilerating effect,
similar to wine. After much suffering and hardships
they came to a country abounding in water and game,
when they luxuriated upon roast turkey, venison and
buffalo steaks, besides a variety of fresh-water fish, and
honey, found abundantly in the hollow trees. But it was
some time before they found the village of the Kiowas;
in the course of time, however, after scouring the
country all round where the trail disappeared, they discovered an Indian on the prairie, when two select men,
on swift horses, were ordered to catch him. The race
was short. for, when the Indian saw his pursuers gaining
on him, and losing all hope of escape, dismounted, and
leveled his gun at them, whereupon they also dismounted
and advanced upon him without presenting their guns,
but making signs to him not to shoot, which he did not
do, and the two horsemen came up to him without harm
and induced him to visit their camp. The Kiowas had
been at war with the Osage Indians, and when this Kiowa
entered the camp of the white men, to his great joy and
astonishment, *his only sister* (who had been captured by
the Osages in one of their battles with the Kiowas, and
had been ransomed or purchased by the United States,
in order to present her as a token of friendship to her tribe)
ran up to him, and falling on his neck, wept for joy. The
objects of the expedition having been explained to this
Indian, he piloted Dean's command to the place where

'the trail gave out on the bank of a creek, up that creek several hundred yards through the water, to a plain road on the opposite bank, which led to their village, where a treaty was soon concluded, and many liberated captives ran to the arms of their kindred and friends. Little Mat. again made glad the heart of a fond mother and other relations and friends, while Captain Travis G. Wright still lives and enjoys that sweetest and most exquisite pleasure which always comes home to the hearts of those who delight to make others happy.

The Indians continued to molest the frontier settlers from the time they became hostile until they were finally subjugated and driven from the country, which was about the year 1878. Sometimes they were not so bad, but again they would scourge the frontier from the Rio Grande to Red river; homes would be desolated. and sometimes whole settlements would be destroyed. Some settlers would give it up in despair and move east, never more to face the red man; but others would remain and fight it out until the rangers would come to their assistance, who were always ordered out by the governor under these circumstances, and when the frontier became quiet again, and the Indians driven out, the rangers would be disbanded, and return to their homes.

In 1858, the following appeared in the Seguin *Mercury*, published by William Dunn, who is the present sheriff of this county, (Guadalupe), at this date, 1883:

" The following gentlemen have been authorized by Governor Runnels to raise volunteer companies in their respective counties, under the Texas regiment bill, which provides for the raising of 1,000 mounted men for the defense of the Texas frontier; and which his excellency will receive and tender to the president in response to his contemplated requisition: Colonel John S. Ford, of Travis; Captain Henry McCulloch, of Guadalupe; Captain William Tobin, of Bexar; Captain E. A. Palmer, of Harris; Cap-

tain E. R. Hord, of Star; A. Nelson, of Bosque; Major A. M.
Truitt, of Shelby; Major E. A. Carroll, of Henderson; General
J. H. Rogers, of Cass; Colonel Sam Bogart, of Collin.

"In the above list of names we find that of our fellow citizen,
Captain H. E. McCulloch. We feel confident that should the
Captain comply with the call made upon him and others, and
undertake the raising of a company, he will rally to his standard
many brave hearts and willing arms, that have in former times
served with him in defense of our then much exposed and unprotected frontier. This county need entertain no fears concerning the valor of her sons; for, at the battle of Escondido, they
won laurels which time will not soon pluck from their brows,
and far more worthy to be worn than the showy plume or gilded
epaulet. Here is a capital chance afforded to those who wish
to display their martial courage on 'the tented field' in sangui-
nary combat with the 'redskins.' Captain McCulloch is well
versed in Indian warfare, and to say that he is at the head of a
company, is sufficient. He needs no passport to entitle him to
command, but his universal acknowledged bravery, and consum-
mate knowledge of border warfare, of which none that know him
can doubt. The post of colonel of the proposed regiment could
not be bestowed upon one more deserving,' and one to whose
qualifications so eminently fit him for that position."

The most of these companies, I think, were raised.
Colonel John S. Ford took the field, and penetrated
far into the western wilds, and fought the Comanches in
their stronghold. It was his company of rangers that
fought such desperate battles with the noted chief, "Iron
Jacket," in two engagements in the same day. Ford's
men killed fifty-seven of Iron Jacket's warriors, but the
famous chief escaped unhurt, although he engaged the
rangers at close quarters, and led the charge in person.
Some of the best riflemen in the command tried in vain to
bring him down, and it was the general belief among the
rangers that he must be encased in an iron jacket, as his
name implied. One of the rangers offered to bet that
if ever he came within range of this chief again, that he

would kill him. Not long after this Colonel Ford was again on the track of the celebrated chief. He trailed him far into the mountains, until one evening the scouts dashed back and reported Indians in force just ahead, on a little creek. Ford arranged his men in proper order and advanced. As they neared the creek, a small detachment was sent ahead to find them, and the main body moved slowly up in perfect order, for well they knew what desperate charges the Comanches would make, led by Iron Jacket. They left the hills, entered the valley, and were nearing the timber on the creek, and still nothing could be seen of the enemy. Everything was calm and still, the advance guard cautiously advanced, and was assured by the scouts that the Indians were near, and so they were. All at once they came bounding up the creek bank, hundreds of them, and with such yells as would almost make the stoutest hearts quail, and, bounding like a deer in front of this host of painted demons, was Iron Jacket, but he had to contend with Ford's invincibles who had often made him and his braves fly before them. The advance of the rangers delivered their fire with great coolness and precision, and fell back towards the main body, who were hurrying to the front with loud cheers, but Iron Jacket was seen to fall at the first discharge from the advanced scouts. The battle soon became general, and the Comanches fought bravely around their fallen chief, and made desperate endeavors to carry him off, when they saw the battle was going against them. but they fell so fast that they finally abandoned the attempt, and gave away on all sides. The route was complete, and great numbers of the Indians were slain. When the combat was over, and they approached the great chief, they found he was not dead, only having both legs broken. The ranger who

5

wanted to make the bet that he would kill the chief, was in front for that purpose. When the Indians made their appearance, he waited for a good chance, and then fired both barrels of his shot-gun at once, loaded with buckshot. He aimed to strike about the knees, with the above result. On examining the body he was found to be encased from the throat nearly to the knees in a Spanish coat of mail, resembling the scales on a fish, but more pointed and lying close to his body. In rubbing downward with the hand it was smooth, but in passing the hand upward, the scales would turn up. It was carried to Austin and placed in the capitol, where I saw and examined it. I have often sat, when a boy, and listened to one of Ford's rangers tell about these battles.

CHAPTER VII.

MAJOR VAN DORN'S GREAT BATTLE WITH THE COMANCHES IN 1858—DEATH OF LIEUTENANT VAN CAMP.

JUST previous to the time that Colonel Ford commenced operations against the hostile Indians in the west, Major Earl Van Dorn, with his command, were in the northwestern part of the State, vainly endeavoring to bring the Indians to battle, who were in large force, but the wily savages for some time avoided a general engagement, but finally, on the morning of the 1st of October, 1858, a decisive battle was fought in the Wichita region. Van Dorn's official report of this battle was first published in the San Antonio *Herald*, and republished in the Seguin *Mercury*, bearing date October 20th, 1858, by William Dunn, publisher, which is as follows:

"By the arrival, last night, of an express from the Wichita expedition, the department here received the following official report of a most brilliant engagement with the Comanches, in which *fifty-six warriors were left dead on the field*. The battle took place near the Wichita village, on the morning of the 1st of October.

"Having been permitted, at a late hour last night, to copy the report of this signal victory, we lay it before our readers at the earliest possible moment, in an extra, and, also in our regular weekly edition, our daily having already been struck off.

"That the news is most glorious, it is needless to announce, though accompanied with the sorrowful news of the loss of a gallant young officer, and the wounding of several others, among whom is the intrepid leader of the expedition, Major Van Dorn.

"The vital blow at the supposed invincible Comanche nation, in their mountain fastness, signally demonstrates the wisdom of

our department commander in organizing this expedition. But
we cannot dilate now on the valuable results which we anticipate
from this judicious measure in subduing the savages on our
frontier. The report of Major Van Dorn is characterized by great
good taste, and is as follows:

> " HEADQUARTERS WICHITA EXPEDITION,
> "CAMP NEAR WICHITA VILLAGE,
> "October 5th, 1858.

" CAPTAIN:—I have the honor to make the following report of
the operations of my command since the 25th ult., the date of
my last report. The stockade work in progress of construction
at that date, was completed on the 29th, and preparations were
being made to move towards the Canadian river the following
morning, when two of our Indian spies came in and reported
a large Comanche camp near the Wichita village, about ninety
miles due east of the depot. Upon receipt of this information, I
had all the stores, draught mules, and extra horses, moved
at once into the defensive enclosure, and marched for this point
with the four companies of cavalry and Indian allies. After
making a forced march of ninety odd miles in thirty-eight hours,
during the last part of which we were continually in the saddle
for sixteen and a half hours, including the charge and pursuit, we
arrived at this camp on the morning of the 1st inst.

" I had been in hopes of reaching a point in close proximity to
the enemy before daylight, and had made disposition for an
attack, based on information received from the spies, but as daybreak came upon us some three or four miles off, and I found
them very inaccurate in their information, I moved the companies up in columns with intervals of a hundred yards, and moved
in the direction of which the camp was said to be, sending instructions to the captains to deploy and charge whenever it was over
the crest of the hills, in advance of us. After marching with this
information about two miles, at an increased gait, the sound of
the charge came from towards the left, and in a moment the
whole command poured down into the enemy's camp, in the most
gallant style, and we soon found ourselves engaged on a warmly
defended battle field. There being many ravines in and about
the camp that obstructed the easy operation of cavalry, and gave
good shelter to the Indians, it was more than an hour before they
were entirely beaten out or destroyed, during which time there

were many bloody hand-to-hand engagements, both on the part of the officers and men.

"The friendly Indians, I ordered, in approaching the camp, to stampede the animals, and get them out of the way. This order they effectually carried out. Delawares and Caddos also entered into the fight with the troops, and did effective skirmishing, in the neighboring hills and ravines.

" We have gained a complete and decisive victory over the enemy. Fifty-six warriors are left dead on the field, and it is presumed that many are lying in the vicinity, as many were, doubtless, mortally wounded, but enabled to escape on their horses from the battle field. How many were wounded is not known. Over 300 animals were captured, and about 320 lodges burned. The supply of ammunition, cooking utensils, clothing, dressed skins, corn and subsistence stores, were all burned or appropriated to the command. Those who escaped, did so with the scanty clothing they had on, and their arms, and nothing is left to mark the site of their camp but the ashes and the dead. I regret that I have to report that two Indian women were accidently killed, their dresses only concealed, not indicating their sex. Two Wichita Indians were accidently killed, being in the Comanche camp. The number of Indians has been variously estimated from 300 to 500. I think there were over 400. The victory has not been achieved without loss on our side. Lieutenant Cornelius Van Camp, one of the most promising and gallant young officers of our regiment, or of the service at large, fell, pierced through the heart by an arrow, whilst charging the enemy's camp, and died as the brave alone should die. In his loss we feel our victory to be a dear-bought one. The following is a list of the killed and wounded, as furnished me by the captains:

" A " Company — Wounded: Brevet Major Earl Van Dorn, severely; Corporal Joseph P. Taylor, dangerously. " K " Company—Wounded: Private Smith Hinkley, slightly. "H" Company—Killed: Privates Peter Magar and Jacob Eckard; missing, supposed to be killed, Private Henry Howard; wounded, Sergeant C. B. McLelland, slightly; Corporal Bishop Gordon, slightly; Bugler M. Abargast, slightly; Private C. C. Alexander, severely. " F " Company—Wounded: Sergeant J. E. Garrison, mortally; since died; Private C. C. Emery and A. J. McNamara, severely, and Private W. Frank, slightly.

"Mr. J. T. Ward, sutler to the command, and Mr. S. Ross, in charge of the friendly Indians, were also wounded, the former slightly, and the latter quite severely.

"I am greatly indebted to all the officers of the command collectively, for the energy, the zeal, the ability, and gallantry, which they gave me in achieving this success, that I feel it impossible to name one as being more distinguished above the others. I am equally indebted in the same manner to all the non-commissioned officers and soldiers of my command, who, under all the circumstances of the forced march, and the battle, proved themselves to be soldiers worthy of the name. Their gallantry, personal daring and fearless intrepidity, are the admiration of their officers, but they find themselves unable to discriminate where all were brave. The officers present were, Captains Whiting, Evans, Johnson, Lieutenants Phifer, Harrison, Porter and Major, and Assistant Surgeon Carswell. Captain Evans killed two, Lieutenant Harrison two, Lieutenant Phifer two, and Lieutenant Major three Indians, in hand-to-hand encounters, during the battle. Mr. S. Ross and Mr. Ward charged with Captain Evans, and did good and efficient service, and were highly spoken of by all the officers, for their bearing, during the engagement. In fact, I am indebted to all the command.

"I regret that my wounds have prevented my writing this report at an earlier date. I have requested Lieutenant Lowe, at Fort Belknap, to copy this, and send it to you in proper form.

"I am, sir, very respectfully, your obedient servant,
[SIGNED]   "EARL VAN DORN,
"Brevet-Major-Captain Second Cavalry, Commanding.'"

CHAPTER VIII.

"THERE was a gallant Texan,
    They called him Mustang Grey,
When quite a youth, he left his home,
    And went ranging far away."

AT an early day, when the greater part of Texas was one vast wilderness, with no human inhabitants except roving bands of Indians, a great many high-spirited young men, who were fond of adventure, left the old States, and turned their faces towards Texas, as place where they could gratify their longing for a wild life on the border. Among those who came at an early date was Mabry Grey, known throughout Western Texas as "Mustang Grey." He was a handsome young man, and was scarcely grown when he made his appearance in the west. He was of slight build, with a mild yet fiery blue eye. The way he got his appellation of "Mustang," was from a circumstance which happened while he was hunting buffalo on the plains. In a chase after a large herd of buffalo, he became separated from his companions. His horse fell with him, and Grey was thrown to the ground. He quickly regained his feet, but his horse being frightened at the huge buffalo that were charging around him, sprang to his feet, and, before Grey could secure him, dashed off across the prairie, and was seen by him no more. Grey remained for some time on the spot, watching the buffalo as they faded from sight in the distance, and anxiously scanning the prairie for a sight of his companions; but the herd had become separated in the chase, and the balance of the hunters had followed the other portion, it being the largest. Grey finally went back the way he came in the pursuit, hoping that before night he would be able to rejoin his companions; but night came, and he was still on the boundless prairie with no one in sight. Tired, and almost exhausted, he threw himself on the ground and tried to sleep, but anxiety and thirst kept him awake most of the night. By dawn he was again on his way, and shortly came upon a wounded buffalo, which had taken refuge in a small thicket. As he still carried his gun and ammunition, he soon dis-patched it, cut out as much as he wanted of it, and went in search of water. Seeing a small clump of trees not far off, he went to it, and found a pond of water, and, after quenching his thirst, raised a fire, and cooked and ate a portion of the buffalo meat. While here, he discovered that this pond was a watering place for Mustangs. His first thought was of trying to secure one of them, but then he had no rope, and abandoned that idea. When the Mustangs came to water, he secreted himself and watched. There was some beautiful ones among them, and he longed to be on one of their backs, even if it was wild. He had but little hope of crossing the dreary plains on foot. He had deviated from his course so much in the search for water that he had become completely, as the saying is, turned around. The prairie is somewhat like the sea, nearly all places look alike along its even surface, except, occasionally, a small clump of trees, or a pond of water, at long intervals, breaks its sameness. Grey knew that hunters often perished for water on these vast plains, even when mounted, and what chance had he on foot, and not a very good hand to walk at that. Finally, he thought of a plan that he immediately set about carrying out, and that was to go and skin the buffalo which he had killed, plat him a lariat out of the hide, and try to secure one of the Mustangs when they came to water. After he had made him a good long and stout lariat, he mounted a tree under which the wild horses had to pass when they came to drink, and patiently awaited their coming. He adjusted a noose in one end of the rope, and took the precaution to fasten the other to a strong limb, for fear the Mustang would jerk him out of the tree when caught. When the Mustangs came, Grey had no trouble in dropping the noose over one's head. Then the fun commenced; the frightened animal reared, kicked and plunged, but all to no purpose; he had him fast. The others hastily stampeded, and were soon hid behind a cloud of dust on the prairie. After the Mustang became somewhat accustomed to the sight of him, and the pressure of the lariet around his neck, he became more docile, and Grey finally mounted him with the rope still tied to the limb, but the Mustang set off at full speed, and when the rope tightened, it jerked him back so suddenly, that Grey was thrown. After this, he worked with him until he could go up to his head and fasten a loop around his nose, so that he could hold him when he attempted to run. He then fastened his gun to his back, turned the horse in the direction he wanted to go, and mounted. The Mustang set off at full speed across the prairie, with his head down, and Grey could not hold him. As there was nothing for him to run against, or a bluff to run from, Grey remained on him until he was completely run down and subdued. For several days Grey traversed the prairie. He often suffered for water and food, but was lucky enough, one day, to ride into the camp of his companions, who were greatly rejoiced to see him, for they had, after a long search, given him up as lost.

Not long after this Grey became commander of a company of rangers, with no pay except the spoils taken from the enemy. They scoured the country between San Antonio and the Rio Grande, and fought many desperate battles with the Indians. Sometimes they would cross over into Mexico, where horses were cheap, buy up a lot, and trade them off to good advantage in Texas. In one of these trading expeditions Grey became the owner of a splendid iron-grey horse, to which he became greatly attached, and would not sell him under any circumstances, although offered large sums for him. On one occasion, as Grey and his men were returning from Mexico on their way to San Antonio, they fought a bloody battle with the Comanches near the Nueces river. Grey had between thirty and forty men with him at the time. The main body were considerably in advance of Grey and two or three others, who were riding leisurely along some distance in the rear, when suddenly they heard sharp firing in front. Grey immediately put spurs to his horse, and exclaimed, "Come on, boys; there is trouble ahead." He soon arrived upon the scene, and found his men dismounted, and having a terrible fight with a large band of Comanches. Some of them were about giving way under the furious charge of the Indians, who outnumbered them five to one, but seeing their commander dash up, raised a yell, and fought with redoubled fury. The fight was long and obstinate; nearly one-third of the rangers were killed and wounded. Some of them were Grey's best men, who had been with him from the first. The Comanches lost many of their bravest warriors, and finally fled before the unerring rifles of their foes. In the last charge the Indians made, and while fighting at close quarters, Grey's horse was killed from under him, and he received an arrow in his right arm, and, at the same time, Robinson, one of his best. men, was killed by his side. After the fight was over Grey was found by the side of his dead horse. In his grief at the loss of his gallant steed, he seemed perfectly oblivious. to his own wound, until reminded, by one of his men, that he had better have it attended to, as the arrow was still sticking through his arm near the shoulder. " All right, boys;" says he " some of you extract the arrow, and take poor Robinson's sash there, and bind up the wound. Poor fellow;" says he, looking at Robinson, who lay near, " he would willingly give it to me if he was alive." Grey was furious against the Comanches, and vowed vengeance on them at no remote period; and, as he had lost so many men and horses in the fight, concluded to go into camp near the battle ground, where the wounded could be taken care of; and sent some men on to San Antonio to get horses and recruits, and then, as soon as possible, follow the Comanches to their homes and fight them again. As soon as Grey's wound was dressed, a small party set off to carry out the orders of their chief. As they were about starting, and Grey was telling them what kind of horses to get, he said: " Be very particular now, in getting me a horse. I want a strong, heavy-made one, as much like my Grey Eagle, here, as you can get it. I want one that has nostrils that you can ram your fist in." Grey gave the men that were a decent burial. All the rangers stood around the killed. graves with uncovered heads, and fired a salute over each.

After the return of the party with horses and men, and after the wounded had sufficiently recovered, Grey set out in search of the Comanches. He had a splendid horse but said he was not equal to the other. The Indian village was found near the head of the Nueces river. It was a complete surprise, but the Indians fought well, and several more of Grey's faithful followers bit the dust; but they were finally driven out, and the villages burned. Grey was satisfied now, and returned to the settlements to recruit up and rest. When not on the frontier, he spent most of his time in San Antonio, but sometimes going down to Seguin and and remaining for some time. Many old settlers can recollect seeing him there on several occasions. To show what power some men have over the minds of others. I will relate an incident which occurred in San Antonio. There used to be a noted gambling house there, called the "Bull's Head." One night, a terrible racket was heard at this place, and Grey, who was on the plaza, asked some one what that row was he heard. "They are having a big fight at the Bull's Head," remarked a man who had just come from there in somewhat of a hurry. Grey set out down there at once, saying, "he would go and stop it;" and, strange to say, that in a few moments after this man entered the furious and excited crowd, everything was calmed down.

Mustang Grey died in Mexico. A few of his faithful followers remained with him to the last. These were his last commands to them: "Boys, when I am dead, bury me in *Texas soil*, on the banks of the Rio Grande." When all was over, these sorrowing comrades set out with his remains to carry out his last wishes, to bury him in the soil he loved so well. His grave may still be seen by the traveler, in a wild secluded spot, with lofty mountains around, and the turbid waters of the Rio Grande rolling ceaselessly by it.

> "And no more he'll go a ranging,
>   The savage to affright,
> He has heard his last war-whoop,
>   And fought his last fight."

CHAPTER IX.

"THE deeds of our fathers in times that are gone;
Their virtues, their prowess, the fields they have won,
Their struggles for freedom, the toils they endured,
The rights and the blessings for us they procured."

INDIAN RAIDS IN GUADALUPE AND COMAL COUNTIES—
DEATH OF JESSE LAWHON AND YOUNG MCGEE—INDIAN
FIGHT ON THE CHICON—DEATH OF RUBE SMITH AND
PETE KETCHUM—BIG FOOT WALLACE'S FIGHT WITH
INDIANS ON THE DRY SACO—RAIDING ON THE ATAS-
COSA—DEATH OF HERNDON.

As LATE as 1855, the Indians still continued to raid the
counties joining Guadalupe, especially west and northwest. About 1853, they made a raid into Guadalupe
county, and killed Parson McGee's little son, on the
Cibilo, while he was hunting horses in company with one
of his uncles. I think it was his uncle, but am not certain.
The poor little fellow was riding a mule, and had no
chance to escape from the savages. He was the first one
to discover them, and called out to his companion, who
was in advance, to "look there, what ugly men were
coming." He was soon roped and dragged to the
ground, fearfully tortured, and finally killed and scalped.
His companion, who was well mounted, made his escape.
The writer of this was a small boy at the time, and can
recollect what an excitement it created among the people.
A company of young men were raised in and around
Seguin, and was called the Guadalupe Guards, but such
was the rapid flight of these small bands of well-

mounted Indians, that it was almost impossible to come up with them. But this party were followed and overtaken by some settlers, and in the fight which ensued, Hal. Holland, a brave and gallant young man, was killed.

In 1855, they made a raid into Comal county, on Curry creek, and killed Mr. Jesse Lawhon. We get the account of this affair from the *Texan Mercury*, bearing date, July 21, 1855, and published by R. W. Rainey, Seguin, Guadalupe county, Texas. The particulars were given by the Hon. William E. Jones, and are as follows:

"Mr. Editor:—It is the painful duty devolving on me to communicate to you the particulars of an Indian outrage just committed in this neighborhood. On Saturday morning last, Mr. Jesse Lawhon, who has been living with me for nearly two years, in the capacity of overseer and manager of my farm and stock, went out, accompanied by one of my negro men, to drive up oxen. About 11 o'clock the boy ran home afoot, and barefooted, and wet to the hips, and told me he feared that Mr. Lawhon had been killed by Indians. That Mr. Lawhon and himself were riding together in search of cattle, and while descending a hill into the valley of one of the branches of Curry creek, near the foot of the mountains, they were attacked by five Indians, who emerged from the bed of the creek, and rushed upon them at full speed. They did not discover the Indians until within forty or fifty yards of them. Mr. Lawhon wheeled and ran in the opposite direction, while the boy dashed towards home. A large Indian, mounted on an American horse, pursued the boy. On arriving at the creek, his horse plunged into it and fell; he jumped off and ran up the bank, when an Indian fired at him, the ball striking the ground beyond him. He then saw the other four pursuing Mr. Lawhon very closely on the hill, and, jumping into the channel of the creek, made his escape and saw no more.

"He stated from the beginning that one of the party was a white man, and the other four, Indians, naked, and armed with guns. The white man was dressed in dark clothes with a white hat. He saw most distinctly the one that pursued him. After he had shot at him, and being not more than twenty feet from him; thinks he cannot be mistaken in saying that he was an Indian and not a Mexican. The boy has often seen Indians in Texas, and has mixed a good deal with Mexicans, and, as his statements are thus far the only evidence of the character of the party which we have, I have thought it proper to give them more fully than I should have done under other circumstances.

"In the meantime the alarm had been given in the settlement, and a party of men repaired to the scene, taking the boy along with them. On arriving there, the Indians had left, and Mr. Lawhon could not be seen, but the statements of the boy being all substantially confirmed by the horse tracks and other signs on the ground, they proceeded to search for him. His hat was found near the starting point; his saddle, with the stirrups and skirts cut off, was found on the retreating trail of the savages, about one mile off. Then they found the trail of his horse from the place where he was attacked, and followed it until they found his dead body in a thicket. He had been shot through the heart with a large ball, and his body and face otherwise bruised and cut. A blunt arrow was found by his side. He was wholly unarmed and compelled to trust to his horse for safety; and the horse he rode, although large and strong, was not fleet. He had evidently made a desperate struggle to save his life. From the point at which he first discovered the Indians, he had turned westward in the direction opposite to that which they came, but soon being overtaken by his pursuers, he wheeled, by a short circuit, and leaping a large ravine, passed the place from which he had started, crossed the creek at the point from which the Indians had first issued, and ran up the hill on that side in the direction of home. Being overtaken again by his savage pursuers, he dashed back again into the creek valley lower down, and here among the small thickets and brush, he seems to have been surrounded and hemmed in an angle made by the creek, impassable here, it being a perpendicular bluff. Wheeling again, he burst through the Indians and regained the elevated ground, followed by the whole pack, and once more faced home. After running four or five hundred yards across the heads of ravines, he appeared to have been again overtaken, when, in utter desperation, he plunged down a bluff thirty feet high, and nearly perpendicular, part of the distance his horse tearing up the rocks and crushing the brushwood in his course down. At the foot of this bluff he landed in one end of a long thicket, and, possibly, might have escaped, if he had abandoned his horse. None of the Indians followed him down the bluff, but the horse tracks indicated that a portion of them turned the point of the bluff and met him as he emerged from the point of the thicket, and shot him. Mr. Lawhon was an industrious and most worthy citizen—sober, moral and of unimpeachable integrity—universally esteemed by all, neighbors and acquaintances. He was about twenty-five years of age, of manly person, and gave the highest promise of usefulness to his country and honor to his family. He left a wife and two small children, who were in his life-time, dependent on him for their maintenance."

From 1850 to 1860 the settlements extended rapidly west of San Antonio into the great stock region; from this place south to the gulf, west to the Rio Grande, north and northwest to Red river. The staked plains were one vast grazing ground, comprising millions of acres of ground unoccupied except in a few localities by stock men. No crops could be raised that would pay a farmer, and the settlers were all engaged in the stock business, raising cattle, horses and sheep; but they had to fight the red man at every step, and many a lonely grave can be seen, between San Antonio and the Rio Grande, that marks the footsteps of the pioneer. Up to the breaking out of the war between the North and South, settlements had been made on the Medina, Atascoso, Hondo, Saco, Frio, Nueces, Sabinal, and other streams. The most of these were bold, running streams, and afforded one of the finest stock regions in the United States. The climate was mild, the country healthy, game was in abundance on every side, and the streams stocked with fish. The only time it was unhealthy was when the Comanches were on the war path. Among the settlers on the Hondo, in 1862, were Rube Smith, Jerry Bailey, the McCombs', Monroe Watkins, William Mullins, Manuel Wydick, John Brown, Nathan Davis, Howard Bailey, Fountain Tinsley, Peter Ketchum, Parson Newton, and others. About the middle of June, 1862, the Indians made a raid down the Hondo valley, and killed Rube Smith, the particulars of which and the pursuit and fight with the Indians I learned from Mr. Jerry Bailey and Nathan Davis.

The evening before the Indian raid, Smith and Bailey had agreed to ride in the woods together on the next day, and Bailey was to come to Smith's house early in the morning, and start from there. Accordingly, early the next morning, Bailey repaired to Smith's house, and was informed by his wife that Rube had gone after his horse, and would be in directly, as they had heard the bell at daylight, and he could not be far off. Bailey waited for some time, and, becoming somewhat uneasy at Smith's protracted absence, said he would walk over that way, and see what was detaining him. He had proceeded but a short distance from the house when he heard some one running near him, who seemed, from the noise he made, to be nearly out of breath. Stepping behind a tree, until the runner came in view, Bailey saw it was another one of his neighbors, named Manuel Wydick. He at once hailed him, and asked him what was the matter. Wydick came up and, in broken accents, for he was nearly out of breath, told him that he thought Rube Smith was killed by Indians; that he heard them running him and heard Smith calling to him, for they had just separated. He said Smith was only armed with a small single-barreled pistol, which he heard him fire as he was calling to him.

Bailey, being well-armed, the two then turned in the direction of the running, heard by Wydick, and soon came upon fresh horse-tracks, which cut up the earth in

6

such a manner as to plainly show they had been running, and they were soon convinced they were on the right trail by seeing Smith's track in the loose soil among the horse-tracks. After going a short distance further, Bailey found Smith's stock book (containing brands, accounts of sales, etc.) which had fallen from his pocket in this desperate run for life. Shortly after, they found where the Indians had roped him, the prints of his hands being plainly seen in the soil where they pulled him down; but he regained his feet and ran a short distance further, but was again thrown down and caught on his hands; but then it seems they gave him no chance to rise, but dragged him on the ground for some distance, then stopped and lanced him, for here they found considerable blood; but could nowhere see the body of Smith. They then separated and began the search for the body, for the ground had become rough, and the trail was hard to keep. But at length Bailey found him under some bushes, and announced the fact to his companion, who was not far off, and soon came to the spot. Bailey proposed then to stay and watch the body of Smith while Wydick should go and inform his family of his sad fate, and alarm the settlement. This was done, and assistance soon came and carried the bloody and mutilated settler's remains to his grief-stricken family.

Nathan Davis and Lewis McCombs were also near by, and heard the firing. A dog, belonging to James McCombs, was lying by the body of Smith when found.

It was then agreed that all the families should be brought to Smith's house, some of the men should remain for their protection, and the balance go in pursuit of the Indians.

This was soon accomplished, and nine men mounted their horses and announced themselves as ready to start in pursuit. Jerry Bailey, being the oldest, was chosen commander, and the little band of settlers set out, and were soon upon the trail. We will here give the names of the party: Jerry Bailey, William Mullins, Manuel Wydick, Nathan Davis, West McCombs, Lewis Mc-Combs, Sam McCombs, Monroe Watkins, aud John Brown.

The trailing was slow and tedious, for in their retreat the Indians generally travel through the roughest ground so as to delay pursuit as much as possible.

The first night out they encamped on the trail. The next day the Indians were overtaken, but they outnumbered the white men nearly four to one, and seemed so defiant that it was thought advisable to send a runner after some rangers, who were about twenty-five miles away, the balance of the party to keep the Indians in sight, and delay them as much as possible, until the re-enforcements could come up. Accordingly, Lewis McCombs and John Brown set off in quest of the rangers.

The Indians remained some time in the position which they had chosen for the battle, and several shots were exchanged, without effect. The enemy, seeing they were not going to be attacked, again moved off, closely followed by their pursuers. The day passed off, and again the pioneers encamped on the trail of the red men.

Early next morning the pursuit was renewed, and seeing that the Indians would make their escape before the re-enforcements could come up, they determined, if they caught up with them again, to hazard a battle, each one vowing to stick together. With this resolution, they traveled on the trail as fast as possible, and again came up with the Indians, who, at sight of the settlers, commenced yelling loudly and preparing for battle.

They took a position in the thick timber, among the rocks and bushes, and awaited the charge from the whites.

Bailey advised the men to make a quick run, and gain a point of timber, near the position of the Indians. This was agreed to, and they all set off at once, greeted by loud yells from the Indians, who began running from tree to tree as they saw the white men boldly advancing upon them. But instead of keeping on to the timber, all except Bailey wheeled to the left and dismounted behind some large rocks. Bailey kept on into the timber, dismounted, and tied his horse.

The Indians commenced the fight by one of their number stepping out and, at the distance of sixty yards, leveling his Enfield rifle and firing at Bailey, but missed his mark. Firing then commenced rapidly on both sides, each party covering themselves as best they could. Bailey fired both barrels of his shot gun, and hastily commenced reloading, at the same time shouting to Wydick, who was the nearest to him, for all of them to come over there, as the Indians were closing in on him, and if he attempted to leave the spot, he would be killed. Bailey, therefore, still remained at his tree.

It was a perilous undertaking for the men to attempt to gain the position of Bailey, for they would have to run through open ground exposed to the fire of the Indians at close range. It was equally as perilous for Bailey to go to them. The Indians (some of them were under cover near the spot where he stood), could rise up and be upon him before he could untie his horse. It was all he could do to keep from being hit behind his tree, as the arrows constantly zipped past him when he would expose any part of his body. But his neighbors and companions, who, like him, had became involved in this unequal contest, were brave men, true and tried.

Davis took command, and it was agreed to mount and run the gauntlet to Bailey. When they made the dash, they were greeted with a volley of bullets and arrows which wounded several horses and killed the one rode by Davis; but they gained the point of timber in which Bailey was posted without losing a man. Here they fought a regular border battle, every man to his tree and every man look out for himself. The nearest Indians, who had so closely besieged Bailey, were driven back with the loss of some of their number. The chief of the band had taken his position about sixty yards from the whites, and when he wished to discharge an arrow stepped from behind a tree into a small opening a little larger than the size of his body where he could plainly see the white men behind their trees. He would then discharge his arrows at any one who was the most exposed, and step back in time to avoid the bullets that always greeted his appearance. This was kept up for some time, until he finally hit Nathan Davis, the arrow striking him in the right shoulder and the spike coming through on the opposite side, near the shoulder blade.

Bill Mullins went to him at once and endeavored to extract it, but was compelled to cut the arrow below the spike-head and pull it through, the men at the same time loading and firing as fast as they could, to keep the Indians under cover while this was being performed. The poor horses suffered terribly, being hit very often. Davis becoming very sick after the arrow was extracted, lay down behind a tree, and turned deathly pale, and for some time it was feared that he had been shot with a poisoned arrow, but it was only the shock of the iron spike tearing through the flesh and sinews, and he soon recovered, and again took the front encouraging the boys by word and example, to stand their ground and keep a bold front. In the meantime William Mullins told the men if they would stop firing at the chief when he made his appearance, he would kill him. Of course, this they all agreed to do, for this chief had already got one of their men down and wounded several horses. Mullins then took his gun, a Mississippi yauger, and squatting behind a small tree, rested his gun on it, and drew a close bead in the centre of the opening, about breast high to a man, where the chief stood in the act of discharging his arrows; his eye was sure and his finger on the trigger, and the moment the body of the chief filled the opening, he fired, and the Indian fell dead in his tracks, shot through the heart. When the settlers saw this they gave a loud yell and charged, and never stopped until they came to the body of the fallen chief, the wounded Davis among the balance.

The warriors vainly endeavored to carry off their dead chief, but were shot by the settlers before they could accomplish it. The Indians fell back and kept closely under cover about a hundred yards off, occasionally firing when opportunity offered. One of the settlers drew his knife, and cutting to the skull around the crown of the head of the dead chief, told the wounded Davis to pull off the scalp, which he did by twisting the long black hair round his left hand, placing his foot against the shoulder of the Indian, and thus braced, giving a strong pull, when the scalp came off with a loud pop. It was then placed on a stick and held up so the Indians could see it They replied by placing Rube Smith's hat on a stick and holding it up to view. This was the winding up of the fight. The Indians moved off under cover and continued their retreat towards the mountains, secreting the most of their dead before starting. Several of them were afterwards found in the rock water hole near by. The settlers returned to their homes without further incident. The most of the men engaged in this fight are still alive. Old man Bailey lives near the Atascosa post-office, on the International road. The McComb boys still live on the Hondo, or near there. Nathan Davis lives in Guadalupe county, fifteen miles south of Seguin, near the county line. This fight took place on the Chicon, just above where it empties into the San Miguel.

On one occasion, Pete Ketchum, one of the Hondo settlers, left home one morning to hunt cattle up the valley. Some time during the day his horse returned home covered with sweat and blood, and his breast, legs and shoulders terribly lacerated. Ketchum's family were alarmed, and the neighbors were soon notified and a party set out in the direction from which the horse came, to search for the missing man. After a long and tedious search, he was found in the hills near the Hondo river, killed and scalped. He was lying beneath a mesquite tree, with a rock under his head. He had run his horse through a dense thicket of mesquite chaparral or pears, which accounted for the lacerated condition of his horse. Slowly and sadly his neighbors carried him home to his bereaved family and buried him, one more victim to the savage hate. Nearly a year afterwards Mr. Bailey, in passing near the spot where Ketchum was killed, found his hat.

About this time, the Indians made a raid in the Sabinal valley, and carried off a grey mule belonging to old man Tucker. A small band of settlers collected and pursued the Indians until the trail led into a dense brake of young cedar. Here the scout who was leading the party, cautioned the men to be very quiet, and go slow, as signs indicated that the savages were close at hand. He then advanced, carrying his rifle in his right hand, ready for instant use, and keeping a sharp look out ahead. Suddenly he raised his rifle and fired, at the same time dashing forward and telling the men to charge. They soon came upon the body of one Indian lying doubled up on the ground. It seems that he was somewhat behind the balance, for they scattered at the report of the gun, and could not be found. Only a glimpse of some could be seen as they dashed off through the brake. On the return of the party to the spot where the Indian lay, they found he was not dead, only having a broken back. He fastened his snake-like eyes on the white men as they gathered round him, and said, "Bob shela, bob shela," which means, "good friend, good friend." One of the young settlers drew his pistol, and with the remark, "D—n such friends as you are," shot him dead. Near the spot where the Indian lay, stood old man Tucker's mule, the red skin having been shot off him. Years after this, Mr. Adam Wright, who was one of the party, passed this spot while hunting deer, and says the bones of the Indian which lay scattered around were red.

Not long after this, in the fall of '61, the Indians came down in force and raided the Chicon valley, the home of "Big Foot" Wallace, the famous scout and Indian fighter. The news soon spread, and about forty men were in arms in a short time. Wallace was chosen commander. Among the men from Hondo, were Lewis McCombs, Nathan Davis, Fountain Tinsley, John Retus, John Watkins, Roe Watkins, and others. The most of these men were hardy frontiersmen. The sharp crack of rifles, and the yelling of Comanches, had no terrors for them; these were things they had become long accustomed too, but they fought the savage in his own way, making no unnecessary exposure of their person. When fighting with riflemen at close range, under the leadership of such a man as Wallace, they felt confident as to the final result against vastly superior numbers. At that late day the Indians had become almost as well armed as the white men, carrying both rifles and revolvers, in the use of which they had become very skillful.

The trail of the Indians was large and rapidly followed. Wallace and his party overtook them in the mountains on the Dry Saco. Nathan Davis was spy and scout that day, and located the Indians. The Indians took a position on one of the high hills overlooking the Saco valley, and awaited the onset of the enemy. Their position was a strong one, the hill being covered with cedar and large rocks. Their force also greatly exceeded that of the white men. The fight commenced by the advance scouts being fired on as they entered the brake, near the foot of the hill. The Indians were mostly concealed, and the scouts, after some firing, fell back to the main body, who were advancing as fast as the nature of the ground would admit.

Among the foremost scouts who received the first fire of the Indians, were Lewis McCombs and Nathan Davis.

Wallace dismounted his men at the foot of the hill and commenced ascending on foot, deploying to the right and left through the rocks and trees, routing and driving the Indians who were posted near the base of the hill. The Indians finally concentrated near the crest of the mountain, among the huge rocks and dwarf cedar, where they could pour down their shots upon the advancing settlers. Imagine this scene on the border, in this far western country. The settlers bounding from rock to rock, and from tree to tree, the ringing of rifles, the "whirr" of bullets as they glanced from huge boulders, mingled with the almost deafening yells of the Comanches, which echoed far up these dark cañons for miles around.

Wallace, with a portion of his men succeeded in getting within thirty or forty yards of the Indians, and halted under the overhanging rocks, which greatly protected them from the bullets of the enemy, and here, for the space of an hour, they kept up the fight, firing as opportunity offered. Each party kept closely under cover for it was rifles against rifles, at short range, and the commander knew that with his inferior force, he could not risk a hand-to-hand fight. The balance of the men were just below, keeping a sharp look-out, and often got good shots at the Indians who would expose themselves in trying a shot at the men with Wallace, who were directly under them. One square inch of the swarthy body of a savage was enough for these trained riflemen. The Indians, seeing they could not dislodge the white men, commenced silently to withdraw and scatter off through the dense brakes and cañons. When Wallace discovered this he withdrew his men from the hill back to the horses, for he was unable with his force to pursue them any further.

Several of his men were wounded; Davenport severely. The casualties were small on both sides, owing to the manner in which they fought among the rocks; but the body of several dusky warriors were seen among the rocks where they had fallen, and where they were left to decay. After the Indians left the mountains, the settlers took a circuitous route and ambushed them in a mountain pass; but the premature discharge of a rifle prevented them from killing many of them, but captured 140 head of horses which the Indians were driving off. It was supposed by some that renegade white men were with this band of Indians. Fountain Tinsley, who was in the fight, says during its progress he fired at a man

wearing a white shirt, but as his face was hid he could
not tell whether he was a white man or an Indian.

W. W. Wallace received his name of "Big Foot"
from the Mexicans, while a prisoner in their hands, after
the disastrous battle of Mier, in Mexico. When they
arrived at Perote, the Mexicans concluded to buy shoes
for their prisoners, but could find none in the place that
were large enough for Wallace, and they called him
"Big Foot," which has stuck to him ever since. This
old scout and Texan still lives on the San Miguel, in
Western Texas.

About this time, or just previous, the Indians made a
raid into Kerr county, high up on the Guadalupe river,
and atfer committing some depredations retreated back
through the Guadalupe mountains. A young man named
Spencer Goss, collected seven or eight of his neighbors,
and followed them. As the trail was through a rough
and broken country, they went on foot, trailing the
Indians as long as daylight lasted, then camping and
resuming it again as soon as it was light enough to see
it. They went on this way until near the head of the
river, when, finding a bee tree, they stopped and cut it,
stacking their guns around a tree close by, while they
were engaged in eating honey. The Indians in the meantime had discovered that they were pursued, and had
placed themselves in ambush near the spot where they
had stopped to cut the bee tree, and seeing the unguarded
situation of the settlers, crept up near them, and making
a sudden dash, secured their guns. The young men
sprang to their feet and rushed upon the Indians, but it
was too late. They were shot down in their tracks
without any chance of defending themselves, except
Spencer Goss. This young man had a large revolver
buckled around him, which he instantly drew and com-

menced firing upon the Indians, killing one at every
shot; but he soon fell, wounded in three places, and
being able to raise up, grasped the butt of his revolver
with both hands, discharged the balance of his shots,
taking deliberate aim, and dropping an Indian each fire.
By this time his companions were either all killed or
scattered, and taking advantage of the confusion occa-
sioned by the pursuit, by the Indians, of his two comrades
who had got clear of them, Goss rolled off a steep
bank into the gully unperceived, for he had killed all ot
those who had assailed him. Although his wounds were
very painful, he succeeded in crawling some distance
from the bloody battle-ground, and then stopped to rest
and listen. Finding that the Indians had not discovered
his trail, he began to entertain hopes of making his
escape, and redoubled his exertions to place as much
distance between him and the savages, before night, as
possible, for then he knew he could travel, and the
Indians would be unable to trail him. Suffice it to say
that Goss, after much suffering and many days alone and
badly wounded, in the mountains, he arrived at his
father's house, and finally recovered. His two companions, who escaped the Indians, were also badly
wounded; one of them so badly in the thigh, that
it was with great pain and difficulty that he could
walk. He made him a crutch out of a forked stick,
and with this help, was able to hobble along, living
on berries, black haws, etc., and after many days,
was fortunate enough to reach home. In the meantime,
a party had repaired to the scene of the conflict, and
brought back the dead. The other wounded man,
Adams, was never seen; being wounded, the supposition
was, he died in some lonely spot among the mountains,
with no one to soothe his last moments. Years after-

wards, some men, while hunting, found the skull and several bones of a man at no great distance from this battle-ground, and, also, near by, was found a leather purse with twenty-five cents in silver it, and it was thought that these remains were those of the missing pioneer.

CHAPTER X.

DURING the years 1860, '61 and '62, the Indians were
numerous on the western border towards the Rio Grande,
committing many murders, carrying off stock, etc., but
in a fight with the settlers on the Saco, the chief, Lone
Wolf, was killed, which somewhat checked them in that
quarter; but along the San Miguel, Atascosa, and other
streams, they were almost constantly on the move.
Among the settlers in and around the little village of
Pleasanton, then just starting on the banks of the Atascosa, were O'Brien, Herndon, N. B. Tucker, Calvin
S. Turner, Anderson, and others.

On one occasion the Indians ran O'Brien into the
village, shooting three arrows into his back.

About the same time, Herndon and Napoleon Tucker
went out on a cow hunt together. When they were fixing
to start, Herndon took down his pistol, and drawing it
from the scabbard, remarked, "that it had but three
loads in it, but he had seen no Indians yet, and supposed
he would not this time;" and, buckling it around him,
mounted his horse, his wife at the same time telling him
he had better stop and load his pistol.

They had proceeded about three miles from town and were riding through an open black-jack country, when Tucker remarked that there was a crowd of cow hunters under the trees ahead of them. Tucker at this time had never seen any Indians, but as soon as Herndon saw them he checked his horse and said, "Them are Indians, and we have got to run for it," at the same time turning his horse around. The Indians, when they saw that the white men had discovered them, came out from among the trees and gave chase. Tucker was mounted on a splendid horse, and could easily make his escape, but Herndon was on a cow pony and soon saw that escape with him was impossible, and urged Tucker to abandon him, as the Indians were close upon them. "Go," says he, "carry the news to town; it is no use for both of us to be killed;" and, drawing his revolver, looked back over his shoulder at the pursuing Indians, who were close at hand and yelling furiously. Tucker, thus urged, let his horse out, and was soon beyond danger. He then held up and looked back. Herndon was completely surrounded, and he saw him fire his three shots at close quarters. The Indians seeing Tucker halt, some of them again pursued him. Seeing he could do his friend no good, Tucker set out like the wind towards Pleasanton, where he arrived in a short time and gave the alarm. A crowd was soon gathered, and under the guidance of Tucker, set out to search for the body of the unfortunate Herndon, and, if possible, to overtake and fight the Indians. They had proceeded about a mile from the village when they espied two men on the prairie running at full speed towards them. Not knowing whether they were white or red men, they drew back behind a small thicket until they should come up. As they neared the spot they discovered that the foremost man was Anderson. He was leaning forward in his saddle and running at full speed, and seemed to be trying to escape from the one in the rear, for no others were in sight behind them. One man said the hindmost one was an Indian, and raised his gun to fire, but was prevented by some one who seized his gun barrel, and told him to hold, that they were both white men running from the Indians. About this time the Indian, for such it proved to be, discovered the party by their loud talking, and knowing that it would not be safe to pursue Anderson any further, adjusted an arrow, and leaning forward on his horse, sent it with terrible force, striking Anderson square between the shoulders, and he about eighty yards in advance, and both running at full speed on good horses. Anderson was a brave man, but was entirely unarmed, and knew that his only chance of safety was in flight. The Indian, as soon as he discharged the arrow, wheeled his horse while still on the run, and dashed off across the prairie and made his escape. The reason he so completely fooled the settlers and passed them without being shot, was the fact that he had on Herndon's hat, coat, pants and boots. He had done it on purpose, to get near some cow hunter on the prairie. The Indians had not molested them for some time in this settlement and citizens became careless, and very often would not encumber themselves with arms while hunting stock. Anderson, after receiving the arrow, sank down in his saddle and remained on his horse until he arrived in Pleasanton. A surgeon being in town, he was quickly called, and extracted the arrow as soon as possible; but it had remained in there so long, the sinews, with which the spike was wrapped, relaxed, and left it in his body when the arrow was withdrawn. It had penetrated so deep the surgeon would not attempt to cut it out. This sealed the fate of Anderson, for it gradually wore his life away, and he died about twelve months afterwards. After the Indian had shot Anderson and turned off across the prairie, the settlers pursued him, but he was not overtaken. They then went to the spot where Tucker last saw Herndon, and after a short search, found his body about two hundred yards from there. It was lying at the root of a tree entirely naked, and black with powder which had been shot into it. The Indians were entirely successful in this raid, killing two white men, wounding a third, and getting away without losing a man, unless Herndon killed some, but none were found, and, likely, his pistol balls were knocked off by shields.

During these years the Indians raided the San Miguel country. On one occasion, James Winters, while going to some place with women and children in his charge, saw five Indians at no great distance off, and leaving his charges in the road, pursued the Indians for some distance, but could not come up with them.

Shortly after this, a large force made a raid and committed depredations in the neighborhood where Winters lived. A small band of settlers soon collected, including himself, West, Davidson, Kirg, Ward, and five or six others. Winters was impatient to get off, and without waiting for further re-enforcements, set out in pursuit of the redskin marauders. They soon struck the trail and followed hard upon it nearly all the day, and overtook the Indians in the evening on Black creek, who, numbering about forty, immediately stopped at sight of the whites and prepared for battle. Seeing their force numbered about four to one, Winters was eager for the combat, and dismounting, swapped for the fastest horse in the crowd, saying he intended to catch them this time, and mounting, urged the men to follow him,

7

and charge. They were all brave men, but still they hesitated to engage the savages against such fearful odds. They moved up nearer, however, and some of the Indians began to move off. Winters thinking probably they were going to run, told the boys to come on, and dashed towards them, drawing his six-shooter and carrying it in his hand. The men urged him to come back, but he did not heed them, and never checked his horse until he ran in among them. They closed around him, and the men who had stayed back on the rising ground, could see him fighting desperately among them. In a short time they saw that he was unhorsed, but still fighting on foot. He carried a brace of revolvers, and they could see the Indians falling around him. At this juncture, Ward, who was a brother-in-law of Winters, could stand it no longer, and, drawing his pistol, put spurs to his horse, and dashed up to within thirty paces of where they were fighting. A part of the Indians then commenced discharging arrows at him, but his shots were so rapid and deadly that their aim was uncertain in their attempts to shoot and dodge his bullets at the same time ; but he saw that Winters had fired his last shot, and was lying prone on the ground. As his revolver was now empty, he wheeled his horse and attempted to save himself, but as soon as he turned his back to them he was shot between the shoulders with an arrow, but his horse being quick, he was soon out of range, and the Indians did not follow him. When he came to where his companions were, he told them to draw the arrow from his back as quickly as possible. They attempted to do so, but pulled and jerked at it for some time before it would come, and when it did, the spike which had penetrated a bone, remained behind. In this condition he had to ride a long distance back home. When he arrived there a doctor was sent for, and when he came, Ward was placed upon his back, and the surgeon had to cut away some of the flesh before he could get a hold upon it with a pair of pincers, and when he did so, he told Ward to hold against him, and commenced pulling. Ward was a large stout man, but before the spike came loose, it raised him clear of the bed, but it was finally extracted, and the wound carefully and skillfully dressed, but it was a long time before Ward recovered. The party who went back to recover the body of Winters, say it was a bloody battle ground; the blood pools around his body showing that not less than seven or eight Indians were killed by Ward and Winters.

As we have now followed the pioneers from the coast almost to the Rio Grande, we will conclude this part of the work by relating an incident which occurred near the Rio Grande, which was then raided by the Apache Indians. We take it from the *Daily San Antonio Express*, bearing date, January 25, 1883:

"Colonel Albert C. Pelton, whose beautiful twenty thousand acre ranch is out toward the Rio Grande, near Laredo, has been the "Peter the Hermit" of the Texans for years. He has believed that he held a divine commission to kill Apache Indians. Colonel Pelton came to Texas in 1844, a common soldier. By talent and courage he rose to the rank of colonel, finally, in 1867, he commanded Fort Macrae. That year he fell in love with a beautiful Spanish girl near Abequin, New Mexico. Her parents were wealthy and would not consent to their daughter going away from all her friends to live in a garrison. The admiration of the young couple was mutual, and parental objections only intensified the affection of the lovers. The nature of the Spanish girl is such that once in love she never changes. Finally, after two years of courtesy and devotion, Colonel Pelton won the consent of the beautiful Spanish girl, and they were married.

"Then commenced a honeymoon such as only lovers shut up in a beautiful flower-environed fort can have. The lovely character of the beautiful bride won the hearts of all the soldiers of the fort, and she reigned a queen among the rough frontiersmen. One day, when the love of the soldier and his lovely wife was at its severest, the two, accompanied by the young wife's mother and twenty soldiers, rode out to the hot springs, six miles from the fort, to take a bath. While in the bath, which is near the Rio Grande, an Indian arrow passed over their heads. Then a shower of arrows fell around them, and a band of wild Apache Indians rushed down upon them, whooping and yelling like a band of demons. Several of the soldiers fell dead, pierced with poisoned arrows. This frightened the rest, who fled. Another shower of arrows, and the beautiful bride and her mother fell in the water, pierced by the cruel weapons of the Apache. With his wife dying before his eyes, Colonel Pelton leaped up the bank, grasped his rifle, and killed the leader of the savage fiends. But the Apaches were too much for the Colonel. Pierced with two poisoned arrows, he swam into the river and hid under an overhanging rock. After the savages had left, the Colonel swam the river and made his way to Fort Macrae. Here his wounds were dressed, and he finally recovered, but only to live a blasted life — without love, without hope — with a vision of his beautiful wife, pierced with poisoned arrows, dying perpetually before his eyes.

" After the death of his wife a change came to Colonel Pelton. He seemed to think that he had a sacred mission from heaven to avenge his young wife's death. He secured the most unerring rifles, surrounded himself with brave companions, and consecrated himself to the work of revenge. He was always anxious to lead any and all expeditions against the Apaches. Whenever any of the other Indians were at war with the Apaches, Colonel Pelton would soon be at the head of the former. One day he would be at the head of his soldiers, and the next day he would be at the head of a band of Mexicans. Nothing gave him more pleasure than the sight of dead Apaches. He defied the Indian arrows and courted death. Once, with a band of the wildest desperadoes, he penetrated a hundred miles into the Apache country. The Apaches never dreamed that anything but an entire regiment would dare to follow them into their camp in the mountains. So when Colonel Pelton swooped down into their camp with ten trusty followers, firing their Henry rifles at the rate of twenty times a minute, the Apaches fled in consternation, leaving their women and children behind. It was then that there darted out of a lodge a white woman. "Spare the women," she cried, and then fainted to the ground. When the Colonel jumped from his saddle to lift up the woman he found she was blind. "How came you here, woman, with these d——n Apaches?" he asked. "I was wounded and captured," she said, "ten years ago. Take, oh take me back again." "Have you any relatives in Texas?" asked the Colonel. "No; my father lives in Abequin. My husband, Colonel Pelton, and my mother, were killed by the Indians." "Great God, Bella! is it you, my wife?" "Oh, Albert, I knew you would come?" exclaimed the poor wife, blindly reaching her hands to grasp her husband.

"Of course there was joy in the old ranch when Colonel Pelton got back with his wife. The Apaches had carried the woman away with them. The poison caused inflammation, which finally destroyed her eyesight."

When I saw the Colonel he was reading a newspaper to his blind wife, while in her hand she held a boquet of fragrant cape jessamines which he had gathered for her. It was a picture of absolute happiness.

CHAPTER I.

" AND now for scenes where nature in her pride,
    Roared in rough floods, and waved in forests wide,
    Where men were taught the desert path to trace,
    And the rude pleasures of the mountain chase."

INCIDENTS IN THE LIFE OF AN OLD TEXAN — COMING TO
TEXAS — SCOUTING AND HUNTING — FIDELITY OF AN
INDIAN — MASSACRE OF THE PEDDLERS — SETTLERS
TRAILING THE INDIANS—FIGHT ON THE BLANCO—THE
SHAWNEES—SETTLING ON THE GUADALUPE.

WHEN the Mexican government held out extraordinary
inducements for immigrants to settle up the vast region
of Texas, many came from the States, and each of those
who came with families, received a league of land for
their headright. Among those who came at an early day,
is the subject of this sketch, Andrew J. Sowell. For the
benefit of the connection, who, in after years, may wish
to know something of their people, I will state that the
Sowells came from the Highlands of Scotland, into
England, and from there, at an early day, to the colonies
in America, and when the war of the revolution broke
out, John Sowell, then a young man, and great grandfather of the present generation in Texas, was living in
North Carolina. He had five sons, Newton, Shadrach,
Lewis, John, and William. At one time during the
war he was caught and severely beaten by the Tories
and left for dead in the public road, but was picked up
by a market man and carried home, and restored. His
sons removed from North Carolina and settled in Ten-

nessee; and some of them soon after joined General Harrison's army, and were in the battle of Tippecanoe. They also served in the Blackhawk war, and were in the battle at Macanaw Island, in which Lewis was killed. They served under Jackson in the war with the Creek Indians, and were in the battle of Horseshoe Bend. They were all stout, athletic men except John, the father of Andrew, the subject of this sketch. During the charge at the Horseshoe battle upon the works of the Indians, which consisted of felled trees, brush and sand bags, Shadrach became entangled in a tree top, and the Indians seeing this, made an attempt to kill or capture him, but he succeeded in avoiding their blows, and in killing three of them with the butt of his gun.

About this time, Sam Houston, then a young lieutenant, sprang upon the works and drew his sabre, but was instantly shot with an arrow which penetrated deep into his thigh. It was soon extracted by a soldier, and Houston was ordered back to the rear by General Jackson, but remained but a short time. Binding up the wound with a silk handkerchief, he returned to the battle ground, and led a forlorn hope against the log fort near the river. In the charge he received two rifle balls in the shoulder, and was carried off by his men. He afterwards commanded the Texas army and won the famous battle of San Jacinto, which gave independence to the young republic.

When the war of 1812 broke out, all four of the Sowell brothers joined Jackson's army, and were in the battle of New Orleans. Arms were hard to procure, especially rifles. One company was in need of thirty, and John Sowell being a gunsmith, was taken from the ranks to make them, which he did, and they rendered good service at New Orleans.

Andrew Sowell was born in Davidson county, Tennessee, in sight of the Hermitage (General Jackson's residence), in 1815, and emigrated to Texas with his parents in 1829, and settled at Gonzales, on the Guadalupe river, about a mile below its confluence with the San Marcos. He was the elder of five brothers—the others being William, Lewis, John and Asa. His father, John Sowell, being a gunsmith and blacksmith by trade, on arriving at his new home, on the banks of the Guadalupe, and after building a dwelling house, set up a shop and commenced to work at his trade, making and repairing guns, blacksmithing, etc. Andrew's mother was the fifth white woman to cross the San Marcos river. The boys were quite different in their tastes. Andrew and John loved the woods, and the other boys turned to books. Lewis brought a fine library with him from his old home in Tennessee. As there was not much to employ a young man about home in those days, Andrew was frequently absent, hunting, fishing, and exploring the country; and he and his brother John soon became excellent scouts and hunters.

After the Indians became hostile, Andrew would never miss a chance, if it was in his power, to follow them when they made a raid into the settlements. The Indians were friendly at first, and often came to the shop and watched the old man at work, and looked upon him as a great man. They would pick up all the old scraps of iron they could find lying about the place, and bring them to him; and, on one occasion, brought in their paint sacks and wanted to paint him, saying he was "Big Chief."

When the Hodges moved into the settlement, they made a trip to San Antonio to buy land. Andrew and several other young men went with them as guards. They carried $4,000 in silver loaded on mules. At that time the Indians were hostile, and the Mexicans were not to be trusted.

It was about this time that two of the Moore children were lost. They went out in the evening to drive up the cows, and, not returning at night, the alarm was raised, and men scoured the woods all night, shouting, firing guns, etc., but morning came and still they had no tidings of the lost children. The search was continued for several days, but proving unsuccessful, they gradually gave it up, and all went home except Andrew, who still continued to search the woods far and near for sixteen days, when he too gave it up as hopeless. Whether they were carried off by Indians, or perished for want of food, or were slain by wild beasts, no one could tell. No tidings ever reached the bereaved parents of the fate of the lost ones.

Very often during the settlement of this country, men would leave home to be gone only a short time, and never be heard of again. One man, living on the Guadalupe river, went out one morning to hunt, and when night came without his return, his family became alarmed ; neighbors came and remained through the night, firing guns at short intervals, thinking it likely he had lost his way, but their worst fears were confirmed next morning when his dog returned horribly mangled and scarcely able to walk. As there were a great many wild beasts in the woods, such as bear, panther, Mexican lions, etc., they concluded he had been killed by some of these, or so badly hurt as to be unable to return home, and the condition of the dog verified this belief. Several parties set out and made diligent search for days, but could find no traces of the lost hunter. They would probably have been more successful if the dog had been able to accompany them.

Amid such scenes as this, Andrew passed his time

until he was about seventeen years of age, when, in the latter part of the spring of 1832, he had his first Indian fight.

About fifteen miles west from Gonzales, in the Guadalupe valley, lived a settler named Castleman. One evening, just before sundown, there stopped at his house a French peddler, named Greser, accompanied by ten Mexicans. He had a large lot of very costly goods which he was going East to sell. Not being acquainted with the country, he stopped to inquire of the settler where he could find a suitable camping place with good water and grass. Castleman informed him that there was a large pool of water not far from the house, and pointed towards it, but at the same time remarking: "You had better camp here by my yard. I have plenty of wood and water, and you can get all you want. The Indians are very hostile now, and might attack you before morning; there is no telling. You will be safe here, for my house is surrounded by strong palisades; and, in case of danger, you can come inside, and I will help you to defend yourself and property." The Frenchman thanked him very politely for his proffered assistance, but declined it, saying they were well-armed and would go down and camp by the pool of water. Castleman made everything secure for the night and retired. Just before daylight next morning, he was awakened by the firing of guns and the yelling of Indians in the direction of the Frenchman's camp. He instantly sprang out of bed, and hastily clothing himself, unbarred a small window, and looked out. Day was just beginning to dawn, and the fight by this time was raging at the peddler's camp. The Mexicans seemed to be making a stout defense. The loud reports of their escopetes, (a short, large-bored Mexican gun), continuously ringing out on the morning air, mingled with the loud yells of Indians. The sun arose, and still the Mexicans kept them at bay. Castleman stood at the window with his long rifle, and several times thought of trying to get to them, but it was too hazardous, and he could only watch and wait to see how it would terminate. The Indians would make a charge and then draw off; occasionally wait for some time before renewing the contest. The Mexicans were hid from view, but he could see the Indians nearly all the time moving from place to place, and they seemed to be very numerous. About a hundred and fifty yards from the house stood a large tree that Castleman had tacked a white piece of paper on, to serve as a target when he felt disposed to rifle practice. This paper caught the eye of an Indian as he was scouting around, and he came to the tree to see what it was. The settler instantly raised his rifle, as this was too good a chance to be lost. He had often hit a small bit of paper at that distance, and was certain he could bring down the Indian, but his prudent wife laid her hand on the rifle and told him to desist, that if he killed one of them the Indians would be almost certain to attack the house when the fight was over, but otherwise they might go off and not molest them. The Indian in question did not long remain as a mark for the pioneer, for as soon as he discovered several bullet holes in it, and around the paper on the tree, he turned and looked towards the house, and taking in the situation at a glance, ran behind the trees, and using it for a cover, beat a hasty retreat. The Mexicans now seemed to be reduced in numbers, as their shots were not so rapid, and about 10 o'clock the Indians made a combined charge and closed in on them from all sides. Their guns were all empty, without time to reload; a short hand-to-hand fight, and all was over. After securing all the goods that they could carry, the Indians rode in single file past Castleman's house and shook their lances at it. He counted eighty as they slowly filed past. But very few of them had fire-arms. They were armed with bows, lances, and tomahawks.

As soon as Castleman was convinced they were gone, he went and examined the battle ground. It was a terrible scene. The Mexicans had built a breastwork out of bales of goods, saddles, etc., and inside of this little square they lay, horribly mutilated and drenched in blood. The Indians had thrown their dead in the large deep pool of water near by. Castleman then mounted his horse and set out for Gonzales, where he soon arrived and told the news. It spread rapidly, and, before morning, twenty-seven men were in their saddles and on the way to Castleman's ranch. Among this number were the following names, which I obtained from Mr. David Darst, who was a boy at that time and saw them start: J. C. Darst, Dan. McCoy, Mathew Caldwell, Ezekiel Williams. B. D. McClure, John Davis, Malone White, Jesse McCoy. Wash Cottle, Almon Dickinson, (afterwards killed in the Alamo), Dr. James, H. C. Miller, A. J. Sowell, and Castleman. The names of the rest I could not obtain.

They selected McClure as commander, and pushed rapidly forward, and soon arrived at the scene of the fight. The trail of the Indians was plain, and the pursuit commenced up the valley of the Guadalupe.

After crossing Darst creek, some twenty-six miles from Gonzales, just below where the residence of the late Colonel French Smith now is, the Indians amused themselves by unwinding thread across the level flats on the west side of the creek. They would secure the end of the thread, and then throwing the spool down, let it unwind after them as they traveled, very likely, tying it to the tails of their horses. I expect they were greatly astonished at the length of it. This thread greatly aided the settlers in trailing them. They did not seem to apprehend pursuit.

After passing through this part of the country they gradually bore to the northwest, passing near the head of Mill creek, and then across the York's creek divide.

The pursuing party would camp as soon as night came, put out guards, and be off again as soon as they could see the trail in the morning.

The second night out, Andrew Sowell left the camp and remained some time alone on a ridge, listening, and while doing so, his quick ear caught a far-off sound like Indians singing; and, after waiting some time longer, he was convinced that such was the case. Hastening to the camp, he informed the captain of the facts, and advised going on some distance further and sending scouts ahead, and if it proved to be the Indians, to attack them at day-light. But the commander seemed to think it was coyotes that Andrew had heard: and he sent out a short distance from camp himself and listened, but could hear nothing, and coming back said: "Andrew, I guess you are mistaken, I can not hear anything, and none of the scouts have heard it; let's turn in and be after them in the morning." "All right," said Andrew; "but I think I heard Indians singing straight ahead of us, but a long way off."

By daylight next morning they were again on the move, and after traveling about two miles, came to the Indian camp on a high ridge, which overlooks the place where San Marcos now stands; at the head of the river of the same name.

· About the center of the camp, a pole was sticking in ground, and the grass tramped down around it, where the Indians had performed the scalp dance the night before.

As they always sing when engaged in this merry-making, it proved beyond a doubt that Andrew was right in his assertions the night before. Although the distance was two miles, the Indians being on a ridge, the sounds floated a long ways on the still night breeze. "You were right, Andrew," says the leader, "we would have caught them here, had we taken your advice; but they cannot be far ahead, and we may get them yet before they reach the mountains, unless they started as early as we did. In that case we can not do it, as the foot of the mountains are not more than two miles off. "They might have started three hours before day," remarked some one, "and in that case, they are nearly to the Blanco."

These conjectures only lasted a few minutes and they were off again, every one looking ahead anxiously, expecting a sight of the Indians; for the country was tolerably open ahead for two or three miles; but all in vain.

That night the company camped in the brakes of the Blanco river, without sighting the red men. The next morning was very foggy, and they moved with great caution. They knew from the signs they must be very near the Indians.

As they were going down into the valley of the river the fog lifted, and presently they heard the yelling of an Indian on a mountain across the river. He had been placed there as a look-out. and was giving the alarm of the approach of the whites to his comrades in the valley below.

The captain seeing that his party was discovered, ordered a rapid advance. But they soon entered a dense cedar brake bordering the river, and an order to dismount was given. The horses were turned loose in the brake, two scouts were sent ahead, and the balance followed on foot. Finally they came to a narrow opening near the river, where three or four men could walk abreast.

At this juncture the scouts were seen running back closely pursued by several Indians. The captain and others sprang into the opening and raised their rifles, but could not shoot without endangering the lives of the scouts, who were directly between them and the pursuing Indians, who now began to adjust their arrows. As they ran, the hard-pressed men, taking in the situation at a glance, sprang to one side in the brush, when the captain fired first, killing the foremost Indian. Several more shots were fired in quick succession, and another Indian fell partly across the body of the first as he came running up. A third had his bow stick shot in two while he was in the act of discharging an arrow. The remaining Indians fled back towards the river, yelling loudly. The whites charged and were met by a re-enforcement. The fight then became general, but the Indians soon gave way, and retreated back to the river and commenced crossing. While the first fight was going on some of the Indians were trying to convey the goods across the river, and they partly succeeded in so doing. Owing to the rough nature of the ground, the men scattered along the bank and fought from cover, as the Indians greatly outnumbered them. The Indian could not long stand the sure aim of the deadly rifles. They soon gave way and commenced rapidly to cross the river. Several were killed in the water; and some, after they had crossed to the other side of the stream.

As fast as they got clear of the rifles they disappeared in the dense brakes beyond the river, and were followed no further, as the men knew they scattered after a defeat, so as to prevent pursuit.

Three times during this short but bloody fight Andrew's gun missed fire at short range, when he was almost certain to get one, and not until the Indians had crossed the river did he get his gun to fire. He noticed an Indian who had just got out of the water, going up the bank on the opposite side, and once more he hastily primed his gun, and before the Indian could get to cover, "dumped his carcass" with a large rifle ball in the back.

The fight now being over, they began to sum up the casualties, which stood thus: None killed, some wounded and one missing. They at once commenced a search for the missing man, thinking he was killed somewhere in the brush, but their hunt was of no avail, they could not find him, and fearing their horses would wander too far off, they went to secure them before searching any more for the missing man; but while they were gathering up the horses, he came to them without hat or shoes, looking as wild as a buck. When asked what he had been doing, he said he had been running and darting about through the brush ever since the fight commenced; that the yelling and firing was more than he could stand. He had no idea what he had done with his shoes. They were afterwards found on the bank of the river, near the edge of the water, as if he had an idea of crossing. The men forebore to tease him much, as they saw from his torn feet and tattered looks that he had suffered worse than any man in the company.

They were fortunate enough to collect all of the horses, selecting as many costly goods as they could carry, left the balance on the banks of the river, and returned without further incident to Gonzales.

A party was afterwards made up and returned to the scene of battle, and carried off the balance of the goods, which, however, were somewhat damaged by the rains.

One morning, not long after this, Andrew's brother, William, had a difficulty with a man named Morrison. Andrew stepped between them to stop it, and turned his face towards his brother. entreating him to desist. Morrison, who had drawn a pocket knife, and was holding it in his hand, open, reached over Andrew's shoulder and stabbed William in the neck; and then, mounting his horse, rode off towards the West. Andrew assisted his brother to get home, but he soon bled to death.

I will state here an incident of the fidelity of an Indian for a friend. A portion of the Shawnee tribe of Indians had come to Gonzales from Arkansas, on a hunting expedition after beaver, which they heard abounded in the streams of Texas. They camped near the town for some time. William had employed one of them to help him do some work about the place. He treated him very kindly, and often gave him nice presents of such things as an Indians delights in. The Indian therefore formed quite an attachment for him, and said he would never leave him, not even to go back to his tribe. When William died the Indian mingled his tears freely with those of the bereaved family, and in broken English cursed the man who killed his friend, often repeating the words, "He kill my friend; me kill him." No one had taken particular notice of the poor Indian, or his threats; but next morning they were somewhat surprised to see him rigged out, as if for a journey, with a well-filled quiver of arrows, knife and tomahawk in his belt, and the war-paint on his face. He went round to every member of the family, presenting his hand, and saying, "good bye." Some one asked him where he was going; he pointed towards the West with the same words he used the night before, "He kill my friend; me kill him;" and turned and walked off, and that was the last they ever saw of the Shawnee Indian. Some time after that some men coming in from Mexico, said the body of Morrison was found near the Rio Grande with an arrow stuck deep in his breast.

While the Shawnees were camped here, they often made long trips to the unexplored West, and came back with beaver skins. They hated the Comanches, and often fought with them, while on their trips.

On one occasion they were attacked by a large body of Comanches, near the head of the San Antonio river. There were but twenty-seven of the Shawnee warriors, yet they were armed with rifles and were splendid shots. One of their number, a boy about sixteen years old, stood behind a tree and killed twenty-one Comanches, and was just raising his rifle to get the twenty-second when he was shot in both legs, and fell. The Comanches charged, and the Shawnees came in a body to his rescue; and here, around the fallen young brave, the hardest battle was fought — fighting hand-to-hand with war clubs and tomahawks; but the Comanches were beaten off, and the Shawnees made a hasty retreat to Gonzales, carrying all of their wounded with them. They made a great pet of the wounded young warrior, who had so distinguished himself in the battle, telling the white men they would make a big chief out of him when they got back to their tribe.

On one occasion, one of them came in to old man Sowell's shop and asked him to fix his gun, which was out of repair. "Fix it good, too, Mr. Sowell," says he, "for we are going on a hunt, and if we meet the Comanches, we will fight them; they killed one of my brothers, and I want to kill some of them." The Indian's name was John, and he could speak good English. The gun was fixed, and the Indians went on a hunt, and one evening discovered a camp of Comanches. The chief concealed his warriors until night, and then advanced close to the hostile camp, and at daylight next morning made the attack. John was amongst the foremost as they rushed into the camp, when suddenly a squaw dashed out of a wigwam and drove a lance nearly through his body. He fell dead from his horse, without firing his gun; killed by a squaw, when he was so sanguine of avenging his brother's death. The Comanches made but a poor fight, and soon scattered. Several of them, however, were killed.

The Sowell league was located on the Guadalupe river, just below where the town of Seguin is now situated, in what is now called the Steward Bend; but the old man did not immediately move on to it. However, in 1832, he moved from Gonzales, and settled six miles below the present town of Seguin, at the mouth of a small stream, now known as Sowell's creek. The boys cleared up a small piece of land and raised some corn in 1833. This place at that time was a paradise for the hunter, and Andrew was nearly always in the woods. He became a good bee hunter as well as a good game hunter, and kept the table supplied with honey, venison, turkey, bear, fish, etc., which were in abundance. They had brought some cows up with them, and with plenty of milk and butter, living was cheap. The house was built on the bluff of the Guadalupe river, overlooking a beautiful valley; on the west, the creek emptied into the river just above the house, on the west side; and often on bright moonlight nights, when the family were sitting in the yard, enjoying the cool gulf breeze blowing from the South, they could see bear crossing the open flat between the creek and river bottoms.

One night, a panther came up near the house and

attempted to carry off a pig; but the dogs and the boys ran it so close, that it was compelled to drop it, and take refuge in a tree, in the creek bottom, a short distance from the house. It was so dark that they could not see it in the thick bottoms, and a bright fire was made under the tree, when it could be plainly seen. Andrew raised his rifle and shot it dead; but as it did not fall, he then concluded to climb the tree and shake him out. When he got on to the limb where he was, it bent, and the panther slid down towards Andrew; in trying to avoid a collision, he lost his footing and fell, landing in the fire. He was not much hurt or burnt, and laughed it off. The panther was a large one, and fell with a heavy thud to the ground.

On the river below them were Tumilson, Montgomery, Dickinson, Baker, and some others.

One evening, Mrs. Baker was coming up to old man Sowell's place, accompanied by several dogs, when a large animal suddenly confronted her; she was greatly frightened, and set the dogs on it, one of which was instantly torn to pieces. Out of breath, nearly, she ran on to the house, and told the circumstances. The boys repaired to the spot and found the slain dog, but could not find the animal. The next day, Jim Tumilson killed a tiger, near the spot, which, from her description of the animal, must have been the same.

On one occasion, while the boys were clearing a piece of land near the bluff of the river, one of them, in splitting a large elm log, while the sap was up, the bark slipped from one-half of the cut, making a shell nearly as large as a small canoe; and for amusement, pushed it off the bluff: it slid down until one end went into the water, and then hitching on something, remained in that position. Next morning, while they were again at work, the hunting dogs collected on the bluff and commenced barking furiously at something, apparently in the water. William Sowell, a boy about five years old, grandson of the old man, was sent to see what the dogs were barking at; he ventured up, and looking over, came running back, saying it was an awful ugly thing. Lewis grabbed his gun (for they always kept their arms near), and ran to the spot, and discovered it to be a large alligator, which had crawled up on the bark which they had pitched in the day before, and was sunning himself. Lewis raised his rifle, and aiming at its eye, fired. The alligator, with a terrible contortion. slid back, throwing up water in every direction; blood was mixed with water as he sank.

Andrew had many mishaps and adventures while hunting alone in the woods. One time, having shot a turkey-gobbler, and only breaking its wing, concluded he would run it down, being long-winded and fleet of foot. The chase led towards the river bank, and Andrew bent all his nerve to catch it before it arrived at the water's edge, and when near it, was running at top speed, and so was the turkey; and fearing he would lose the game, made a frantic effort to catch hold of it, but, unfortunately, just at that critical moment, his foot struck a root, and he was precipitated head-first into the river. The turkey at the same time wheeled around and made good its escape before the unlucky hunter could get out, who, with dripping garments and muttered curses, went back in search of his rifle.

At another time, while hunting near the bank of the river, he saw a half-grown deer drinking in some tall coarse grass that grew on the water's edge, and, throwing up his rifle. was just in the act of firing, when, with a terrible splash, the deer was knocked into the river by an alligator, and was seen no more.

Again, while hunting in the thick timber, he saw a large buck standing behind a tree, with its head and shoulders only, exposed. He saw it would take a close shot to hit him in the right place, in fact, he would have to just graze the bark on the tree. Having taken a careful aim, he fired, but struck a little too far to the right. and the ball glancing, killed another deer about thirty steps to the left, one that he did not see when he fired.

At one time, while living in the Blanco river, he concluded to go up the river, one night, to a turkey roost; and arriving at the spot, saw a large cypress tree near the bank of the river, which was tolerably steep. Getting under the tree, he raised his gun to shoot a large one, but there was a limb in the way, and he stepped a little to the left, with his gun still in position; but the limb was still in the way, and he kept stepping to the left until he stepped off the bank into the Blanco river. He went straight down, with his rifle pointing up; the water was over his head, and he went to the bottom. and it was with great difficulty that he got out. The bank was steep and nothing but small bushes to hold to. He finally hung on with one hand until he could pitch his rifle out on the bank, and then succeeded in getting out himself, and picking up his gun, started for home, madder, he says, than he ever was before in his life. He also gained a great reputation as a bee hunter, and after he moved to Seguin, when that place was first settled, found a great many in the river bottom near town. Some of the settlers were not as expert at the business as he was, and got so they would look for Andrew's marks on the trees instead of looking for the bees, and very often, when he would take his wagon after a load of honey, his trees would be cut. But as they were so sly about it, he could not find out who the marauders were, so he concluded to play a trick on them, and quit marking bee tree, which, instead of saving them, led to their loss.   Accordingly he went into the bottom near the river, where the trees were extra large, and marked three or four of the largest he could find.   In a short time these were cut; but they had their labor for their pains; for they found no honey. He often found bee trees under peculiar circumstances. On one occasion, he was running a bear at almost full speed, and ran under a stooping tree which bent over until the top was near the ground, which had a hollow in the end of it; in stooping to dodge this, he noticed that bees were working in and out of it.   He went on and got the bear, and then returned and secured the honey, having got a bear and a bee tree in the same run.   At another time, while lying down, drinking water out of the Guadalupe river, he saw the shadow of bees in the water, and looking up, saw them working in and out of a knot-hole in a cypress tree, over his head.   The largest number of bee trees he ever found in one day, was twenty-seven, on the Blanco river.   One old settler said that Andy Sowell was the best bee hunter he ever saw.   " I will tell you," said he, " what I will bet he can do.   You may put him in a barrel and roll him through the woods, and he will find a bee tree by getting a glimpse occasionally through the bung hole."

Such was the life he spent while living at this place. As yet, they had not been molested by Indians ; although there was no other white family living above them, on the Guadalupe river.

One day, while the men were all away from the house, a large bear came out of the bottom and ran through the yard, doing no harm, but frightening the women and children.

At one time, Indian tracks were seen in the vicinity,

and shortly after, a small band of Indians made their appearance, but professed friendship. The settlers had their doubts, and kept close watch upon them. They camped about, on the river, a few days, and then disappeared, and at the same time two horses were missed from the neighborhood, and accordingly Andrew, Montgomery and three others went in quest of them. At the mouth of Mill creek they found the missing horses in possession of two Indians. They were surrounded, and they gave them up, making no show of resistance. Their arms were taken from them, and they were escorted to the house of Dickinson, for trial, it being the nearest. Dickinson was gone and they carried the Indians in the house until they could come to some agreement as to their disposal. It was finally decided to kill them, and picking up their guns, carried them out in the yard for that purpose, but Mrs. Dickinson commenced screaming, and told them for "goodness sake" not to kill them in her yard. The men thought this would look a little too bad, and concluded to take them across the hollow and dispatch them in a little grove of timber on the ridge. As they walked along, Montgomery was on the right of the largest Indian. They knew their fate and commenced talking in a low tone in the Indian dialect. Andrew was narrowly watching them as they conversed, and, although not understanding any thing they said, he thought from their looks they were planning mischief, and warned Montgomery to keep a sharp lookout, and not to walk too near that large Indian. "All right;" said Montgomery, " I am watching him ; and if he makes a move, I will plug him." These words had scarcely left his lips, when the Indian, with a motion as quick as a flash, drew a long knife from some where about his person, and plunged it to the hilt in Montgomery's breast; who, without a groan, sank to the earth and expired in a few seconds. Both Indians then made a leap and ran. Three shots were fired almost simultaneously, and the Indian that killed Montgomery fell dead before he had gone a dozen paces; but the men in their hurry and confusion, shot one of their own number, wounding him severely in the leg. In the meantime the other Indian was running at top speed, and was about to make his escape; one of the party snatching up Montgomery's gun, ran a few steps, and dropping on one knee, made a rest out of his elbow by placing it on his knee, took steady aim at the flying Indian, who was at least 150 yards off; but at the report of the gun, he fell, and soon expired. The bodies of Montgomery and the wounded man were conveyed home, but the bodies of the Indians were left to decay where they fell. This took place in the live oaks just south of where the Patterson farm now is.

This occurrence somewhat alarmed the settlers, for they were a long way from the settlements below, and fearing a general outbreak, as they still continued to skulk near by, there was some talk of breaking up the settlement and moving back.

One evening, while some of the small boys were out hunting cows, they saw an Indian hide himself ahead of them, and they ran home and told the news, but no depredations were committed at that time.

In 1834, the old man moved back to Gonzales, and resumed his trade, that of gun making, which was in demand in this frontier country, and commanded a good price. In the meantime emigrants still continued to come and settle in or near Gonzales.

About this time, the Indians made a raid and stole several horses near town; Andrew's among the number.

Those having horses, mounted, and started in pursuit. Andrew, and several others, who had lost their horses, concluded they would take it afoot, and go a nearer way to a point some twelve miles from town, where the Indians were in the habit of passing as they went out on a raid. They made good time, and getting near the place, on a hill, where they could look over in to a creek bottom, stopped, and resting a few moments, heard firing in the bottom ahead of them. The horsemen who were trailing the Indians, had caught up with them, and were engaging them. They started on a quick run and soon entered the bottom, but the fight kept receding from them, as the Indians were running and the mounted settlers pursuing. They used every exertion to overtake them and assist in the fight, but the firing, whooping and yelling, kept always just ahead. They finally came upon a dead man, named Davis, and being exhausted, the footmen stopped by his body until the return of the pursuing party. Several Indians were killed. One lay near the body of Davis, who was killed by him after he had been shot. Davis was a brave and true pioneer, and it was with heavy hearts and sorrowful faces that his comrades picked him up and bore him back. It was late in the night when they arrived at Gonzales, bearing their bloody burden. The house in which they laid out Davis, was still standing a short time ago.

CHAPTER II.

JAMES BOWIE—ORIGIN OF THE BOWIE KNIFE — FIGHT AT
GONZALES—MARCHING TO SAN ANTONIO— BATTLE OF
MISSION CONCEPCION — THE GRASS FIGHT — SKIRMISH
AT THE POWDER HOUSE—CAPTURE OF SAN ANTONIO—
DEATH OF MILAM— TRAVIS ENTERS THE ALAMO—THE
SIEGE.

JAMES BOWIE, the noted Indian fighter and gold
hunter, often came through Gonzales, on his way East,
after a prospecting tour in the mountains. He generally
had twenty or thirty men with him, all good Indian
fighters, and they often had fearful encounters with the
Comanches and other hostile tribes, while exploring
the country in the far West.

In one of these fights Bowie made a thrust at an
Indian when they were at close quarters, and his hand
slipped over the blade of his butcher-knife, cutting him
severely. This mishap suggested the idea of a guard
between the blade and the handle, and he determined to
have one made that way. Accordingly, selecting a soft
piece of wood, he made a pattern of the kind of knife he
wanted, and the next time he went to Gonzales, he went
to Mr. Sowell's shop, and showing him the pattern,
asked him if he could make one like it. The old man said
he thought he could; and selecting a good piece of steel,
proceeded to shape one like the pattern, and after it was
finished, presented it to Bowie for inspection. He was
greatly pleased with it, and paid a handsome price for the
work. The old man then asked Bowie if he might name

the knife. " Oh yes ; Mr. Sowell, certainly," said Bowie, " give it a name." " Well then," said the old man, " I will name it in honor of you ; we will call it the ' BOWIE KNIFE.' " It afterwards became a famous knife, and gained a world-wide reputation. The gunsmith made a great many of them afterwards, and a Texan did not think he was fully armed unless he had one of them.

Bowie afterwards became a famous leader in the war for independence, and commanded the Texas forces at the battle of Mission Concepcion, below San Antonio. He was killed in the Alamo when that fortress was stormed by the Mexicans.

In 1836, the war-cloud began to rise in Texas, which was soon to spread over and darken this fair land. The Mexicans becoming jealous of the Americans, and alarmed at the numbers which continued to flock to this country, determined to drive them out before they became any stronger. General Cos landed at Capauo with 400 men, and marched to San Antonio, and openly proclaimed the object of his mission ; which was to over-run Texas, establish custom houses, disarm the people, and drive out all Americans who had come into Texas since 1830. And it was commenced by Captain Castanado being sent to Gonzales, with 200 men, to carry away a small cannon which the Government of Mexico had furnished the people of Gonzales to defend themselves against the Indians, if the town was attacked. The people of Gonzales refused to give it up, and sent to Bastrop, San Felipe and elsewhere for assistance.

The people obeyed the call with alacrity, and soon a force of 180 men were assembled at Gonzales. The Mexicans had taken a position on the west side of the river, and on the evening of October 1. 1835, the

Texans moved out to engage them, under the command of Colonel John H. Moore.

Andrew Sowell and all of his brothers who were able to bear arms, were in the ranks. The small cannon, which was the bone of contention, was carried along by the Texans, to help rout the Mexicans. Old man Sowell, knowing that the ammunition for the cannon was scarce, picked up a lot of iron scraps, which were lying about his shop, such as pieces of horse-shoes, chain-links, etc., and put them in a sack, and told the boys that if it came to a fight, that when he heard a discharge from the cannon he would come with his scraps to load with, when the balls gave out.

About 7 o'clock in the evening, the Texans crossed the Guadalupe river, made such disposition of their forces as they thought best, and sent out scouts to learn something of the enemy. A thick fog arose during the night, and about 4 o'clock in the morning, as one of the Texas scouts was riding about over the prairie, he saw a mounted man close by his side, and thinking it was one of their own scouts, leaned over towards him, and said in a whisper, "Have you made any discoveries yet?" The reply was a stunning report of an escopete almost in his face; the ball barely grazed him, and his face was burnt black with powder. His horse sprang suddenly to one side, and he was thrown heavily to the ground, where he lay for some time in an almost senseless condition, but was finally able to get up and rejoin the command. This shot, which was fired by one of the Mexican pickets, alarmed them, and they immediately formed in line of battle, on a high mound. The Texans then advanced until within 350 yards of the enemy, the advance scouts came into collision with them, and, after a few rounds, retired to the main body, closely pursued by a small detachment of Mexicans.

The little cannon was then opened on them, and the entire force of the enemy fell back to another position, and the Texans advanced. Castañedo then desired a conference, which was granted, and he inquired of them why the attack by the colonists. The Texans referred him to his orders, which commanded him to take, by force, the cannon which had been presented to the citizens of Gonzales for their defense, and told him he was an instrument of Santa Anna, who had overturned the rights of all the States, except Texas, and they were going to fight for their privileges to the last; and thus terminated the conference without an adjustment. The Texans again opened fired on them with the cannon, and advanced rapidly towards the Mexicans, but they fled in disorder towards San Antonio, leaving quite a number of men killed and wounded. The Texans had none killed, and none fatally injured.

Dr. John T. Tinsley, while riding near the bank of the river after the Mexicans crossed, saw one halted on the opposite bank. The doctor rode up to a tree, and laying his rifle against it, fired at the Mexican, but did not bring him down, but must have hit him, for he beat a hasty retreat, and the doctor heard him say " carajo!" (a Mexican oath), as he disappeared in the timbered bottoms.

The Texans remained masters of the field, and, having collected the spoils of the victory, returned in triumph to Gonzales.

On the way back, some of them met old man Sowell coming as fast as he could with his iron scraps on his back, but the battle was over, and they were not needed. He was up very early that morning, probably not having slept any through the night, such was his anxiety about the result of this midnight march of his sons and neighbors. He had just taken his seat at the breakfast table,

9

although it was very early, when the boom of the little cannon was heard across the prairie. "There!" says he, "there it goes!" and jumping up from the table, gathered his sack and started for the scene of action.

Mr. David Darst, who was there, says that Mr. Sowell afterwards made wrought-iron balls to fit the cannon.

Morphis says:

"Thus commenced the memorable contest for liberty and struggle for independence in Texas, which in the development will call forth a tear of sympathy from the generous, for the misfortunes and calamities of those who suffered and died in it, and a word of applause and admiration for its victorious survivors, who in the end so wisely and heroically constructed upon the ruins of Mexican misrule and domination, the beautiful fabric of Anglo-American republicanism. The ball of revolution had been put in motion, and increased, by going."

News of the battle at Gonzales spread like lightning through all the settlements. Houston and Rusk, Austin and Johnson, Bowie and Travis, hastened to the scene of conflict. Goliad was taken by planters from old Caney, under the command of Captain George Hollinsworth. Stephen F. Austin was elected commander-in-chief of the Texas forces. Andrew Sowell joined Austin's command and marched with him to San Antonio.

On the 20th, Austin arrived at the Salado, five miles east of San Antonio, and sent in a flag of truce to General Cos, who refused to receive it, and threatened to fire on a second one, if sent. Austin then removed to the San Antonio river, ten miles below the city, and remained some time waiting for re-enforcements.

On the 27th, he sent Colonels Fannin and Bowie to hunt a suitable camping place near the enemy. They encamped near Mission Concepcion, in a bend of the river. Andrew was with the party, under Bowie.

The Mexicans came from San Antonio during the night and surrounded them. Next day a bloody battle was fought, known in history as the battle of Mission Concepcion. The Mexicans sustained a heavy loss. The Texan loss was slight. Bowie and Fannin had but ninety two men in this fight, against a large portion of the Mexican army. The Texans had the advantage of the banks of the river, while the Mexicans had to advance partly through open ground. They succeeded in planting a brass six-pounder in eighty yards of the Texas force, but it was charged and captured by a portion of Bowie's men. Andrew was in the charge, and said the Mexicans worked the cannon until they were close upon them, and were shooting them down with their rifles, before they broke and fled. They left about 100 men killed and wounded on the battle-field, including many officers.

In about an hour after this fight, the main army, under Austin, arrived. "Had it been possible," said Bowie, "to have communicated with you, General Austin, and brought you up earlier, the victory would have been conclusive, and San Antonio would have been ours before sundown." But the force under Fannin and Bowie were completely surrounded, and all communications with the main army cut off.

After the battle, Austin camped with his army on the battle-field, until the 2nd of November.

The next day, after the battle, General Cos sent in a flag of truce to General Austin, requesting permission to bury the dead, which was granted. An agreement was also entered into between the two commanders, whose forces were on the opposite sides of the river, that their men would not ambush one another when they came down to the river to water their horses. Both sides were bound to do this. As the river was narrow, it would be very dangerous for either side to go to water unless an agreement of this kind was entered into.

Everything was quiet for a while, but finally some of the men became restless and longed for a more active life, and a change of programme.

One day, Jesse McCoy came to where Andrew Sowell was sitting somewhat alone, chafing under the monotony and inactivity of a camp life, and said: "Andy, don't you want to shoot at a Mexican?" "Yes," said Andrew, jumping up, "by Gonny, yes; where is one?" "Follow me," said McCoy, "and I think you can have that exquisite pleasure." The two men then slowly walked off down the river with their rifles, as if squirrel hunting. After proceeding some distance, McCoy stopped, and pointing across the river, said: "Do you see that trail over there coming down to the water's edge?" Andrew said he did. "Well, I have been scouting about down the river here for three or four days, and I have noticed that two Mexicans come down there every day to water their horses. I know it is against orders to shoot them, but this is too good a chance to lose, and as it is now about their time of day to put in an appearance, we will secrete ourselves here behind these bushes, and try them a whack anyhow." They had not long to wait; they heard voices across the river in the bottom, and presently two gay young Mexican soldiers come down the bank and rode their horses into the stream, still continuing their conversation. McCoy moved a little and raised his rifle, remarking in a whisper, "Now, Andy; you take the one on the right." Both rifles cracked simultaneously. A cry of terror from the Mexicans, and both horses wheeled and dashed up the bank. One of the Mexicans came near falling from his horse, but hung on, and both were soon out of sight. "That is what I call poor, shabby shooting," remarked McCoy, as the Mexicans disappeared. "We ought to have dumped both of their carcasses right there in the water. But it was all one of them could do to carry off the lead he got. Let's go back to camp."

Next morning a flag of truce was sent in by the Mexican commander, stating that two of his men were badly wounded by riflemen from the east side of the river, and at the same time demanding the culprits according to agreement. The Texan commander told the officer that brought the flag, that he had no way of finding out who the guilty parties were. The Mexican said he thought he could find them if the men were formed in line. This was accordingly done, and the keen-eyed Mexican officer went down the line closely watching the features and actions of every man as he passed them. Andrew and McCoy stood and looked the Mexican straight in the eye as he passed, never once glancing at each other, although standing close together. The officer finally gave it up and went back. It is doubtful whether it would have done him any good or not, even if he had succeeded in detecting them. There were too many brave men there with trusty rifles to see two of their comrades turned over to the tender mercies of the treacherous Mexicans, although they had done wrong.

From this place, the Texans moved up north of the city, and camped near the head of the river. They were daily expecting troops from Mexico to re-enforce those in San Antonio. Scouts were kept out on the hills to watch through the day, as the Texan commander wanted to cut them off from the city on their approach. Men were also sent out at night, away from the noise of the camp, to listen alone on the prairie, so as to detect any signs of the approach of a body of troops.

One night, Andrew was sent out on this kind of service,

and had remained an hour or so, when he heard the jingle of a large pair of Mexican spurs. He raised himself up and listened a few moments, and the horseman seemed to be coming near the spot where he stood. Satisfied that it was a Mexican, for he was going in the direction of San Antonio; he cocked his rifle, and waited for a chance to shoot. It was pitch dark, and he had to guess where to aim by the sound of the spurs. When the Mexican got opposite him, about forty yards off, he leveled his gun and fired. A loud "Waugh" from the Mexican, and the clatter of horses feet, and the jingling of spurs, proved to him that his shot was ineffectual.

A few days after this, Andrew participated in what is called the "Grass Fight." Deaf Smith, a noted scout, came in and reported that he thought he had discovered the long looked-for re-enforcements coming in on the west side of the city. The troops were immediately put in motion to intercept them; but it proved to be a party sent out to cut grass with which to feed the cavalry horses. They had the grass put up in small bundles and carried on jacks. A detachment of Mexican soldiers were with them as guards. The Texans charged, and a running fight commenced; but re-enforcement was sent out from the city, and a very lively battle was fought, in which about fifty Mexicans were killed, while the Texans had only two men wounded and one missing. Andrew says when the firing commenced, the jacks carrying the hay, set out in a gallop for San Antonio, braying at every jump.

While the troops were encamped here, parties of them were continually riding around the city, watching every chance to shoot Mexicans; and some times would go within rifle shot of the walls of the Alamo; and all were anxious to storm the town.

On one occasion, a small force secreted themselves

behind the powder house hill, and sent some of their best riders to annoy the Mexicans and endeavor to draw them out. This ruse was successful. They ventured so near the town they were charged by a company of cavalry. The Texans fled towards the powder house, hotly pursued by the enemy, but as they neared the crest of the ridge, were greeted by a shower of rifle balls, which turned them; and they, in turn, were chased back; Andrew being one of a small party that pursued them close to the walls of the fort.

After this fight, Andrew with a great many others, left the army and returned home, as they were not prepared with suitable clothing for a winter campaign; consequently he missed the chance of going into San Antonio with old Ben Milam; for the city was stormed by Milam, Bowie, and others, and General Cos surrendered in his absence; but the victory was dearly bought. Many were killed and wounded. Among the former was the brave and patriotic Milam himself.

Pleasant McAnnelly, of Guadalupe county, was present when Colonel Milam was killed. He says Milam had just got to their position at the Veramendi house, on Soledad street, and seeing a great many balls lying about, which had been shot through the doors by the Mexicans, made some remark about them, and stooped to pick one up. Some one said, "Look out, Colonel;" and at the same moment a ball struck Milam in the head, and he fell forward. Several men sprang to him, and lifting him up, bore him into a room. As they passed through the door, Mr. McAnnelly says he saw his head drop to one side, and blood running from his temple; he knew then Ben Milam was killed.

A short time before, Franklin Harvey was killed near the same place where Milam fell.

" But where, O where's the hallowed sod,
　　Beneath whose verd the heroe's ashes sleep.
Is this the cold neglected mouldering clod
　　Or that the grave at which I ought to weep?

" Why rises not some massy pillar high,
　　To grace a name that fought for Freedom's prize;
Or, why, at least, some rudely-etched stone, nigh,
　　To show the spot where matchless valor lies."

Colonel Travis then took command and entered the Alamo, with about 200 men. Among these were Colonels Bonham, James Bowie, and David Crockett, the famous hunter and humorist, and ex-congressman from Tennessee.

At this time, Santa Anna was President of Mexico, and commander-in-chief of her armies. When the news of the capture of San Antonio reached the City of Mexico, Santa Anna took the field in person, with about 8,000 men, and on the 23rd of February, arrived in San Antonio with a considerable part of this force under his immediate command, and demanded the surrender of the Alamo, which was refused. He then began to invest the place.

On the 2nd of March, 1836, the Declaration of Independence was made and signed at Washington, on the Brazos, and on the 4th, the Convention made General Sam Houston Commander-in-Chief of the Texan Army.

As soon as possible, Andrew equipped himself and joined Travis, at the Alamo; but in a short time was sent back to Gonzales in company with another man, (Lockhart, I think), to secure some beeves, and drive them to San Antonio, for the use of the garrison during the siege.

CHAPTER III.

"It was on one Domingo morning,
  Just at the break of day,
That holy Sabbath morning
  When Christians went to pray.

"The tocsin bugle sounded
  The final overthow,
Of Freedom's sons surrounded
  In the fatal Alamo.

"The bugle sound, no quarter!
  Though countless numbers fall.
Like famished dogs of slaughter,
  They swarmed upon the wall.

"And across the lonely prairies
  There comes a wail of woe,
From Guadalupe's azure tide
  To the fatal Alamo."

STORMING OF THE ALAMO—FLIGHT OF THE SETTLERS—
BURNING THE BODIES OF THE SLAIN TEXANS—A MEXI-
CAN ACCOUNT OF THE DEATH OF BOWIE—THE ALAMO
MONUMENT — EXTRACT FROM A SPEECH OF HENRY
MCCULLOCH.

WHILE Andrew and his companion were engaged in
gathering beef cattle to drive to San Antonio, the Alamo
was stormed by Santa Anna's army, and its brave defenders massacred; the wife of Lieutenant Dickinson, with
her infant daughter, and the negro servant of Colonel
Travis, alone escaping the terrible butchery. Andrew
was just preparing to start when Mrs. Dickinson arrived

with the fearful news.   Everything was thrown into the wildest disorder and confusion in Gonzales, for Mrs. Dickinson had reported that the exultant and victorious Mexican army was then marching on that place, and before morning, nearly all the families in and around Gonzales, had left, (The Darst family remained until after daylight), fleeing towards the coast in wagons, on foot, on horseback, and, in fact, just any way they could go.   Andrew Sowell and his brother, Asa, then a boy of about thirteen years old, went out in the night and hunted up a yoke of oxen, and hitching them to a wagon, put in a few clothes, bedding, provision, etc., and the family rolled out.

General Houston was there with about 300 men.   He had got this far on his way to relieve Travis.   He remained at Gonzales with his army until the people had proceeded some distance in their flight.   He sent messengers to settlers that lived some distance from the town, warning them to flee.

It was truly a melancholy sight to behold the terror of the women and children wailing, in their dire bereavement; for many of the gallant men and boys who fell at the Alamo were from Gonzales.

Mrs. Dickinson relates one touching incident that she witnessed while the Mexicans were storming the walls. When the storming party advanced, she had retired to the inner room of the fort, and sat there, pale and trembling, with her baby hugged close to her breast, while the conflict was raging, almost deafened by the cannon shots which shook the walls around her.   While here, Albert Fuqua, of Gonzales, a boy about seventeen years of age, came where she was with both jaws broken by a bullet. He looked pale and haggard, with the blood flowing from his mouth.   He made several attempts to tell her something, but she was unable to understand him. He then held his jaws together with his hands and tried to communicate with her, but was unable to do so. He then shook his head and went back on the walls where the fight was still raging.

The final assault was made on Sunday morning, March 6, 1836. The Mexicans advanced in solid columns with bugles sounding "*No quarter!*" and the black flag flying. The brave men under Travis who manned the walls, knew their doom was sealed, as they watched the

(Storming of the Alamo.)

almost countless numbers of Mexicans advancing to the assault; but with a firm grip, each man grasped his rifle, and stood at his post, determined to sell his life as dearly as possible.

There were 180 Texans in the fort. Captain G. C. Kimble, with thirty-two men from Gonzales, run the gauntlet and entered the Alamo a short time before the final struggle, but, alas! only to die with those whom they came to rescue. Hundreds of the Mexicans were killed in attempting to scale the walls. As fast as the ladders were placed and filled with Mexicans, strong men would throw them off, while the deadly crack of rifles kept them continually dropping from the ranks, while a line of officers was formed in the rear with drawn sabres, urging them forward, and threatening to cut the first man down that attempted to come back. A great many of the Mexicans were shot square in the crown of the head, as they advanced close to the walls.

After the massacre of Fannin's command, at Goliad, Doctors Shackleford and Barnard, who were spared on account of their profession, were sent to San Antonio, to take charge of the officers there who were wounded at the storming of the Alamo. Dr. Barnard says:

" Yesterday and to-day, (April 21), we have been around with the surgeons of the place to visit the wounded; and a pretty piece of work ' Travis and his faithful few ' have made of them. There are about 100 here now of the wounded. The surgeons inform us that there were 400 brought into the hospitals the morning they assaulted the Alamo; but I should think from appearances that there were more. I see many around the town who were crippled there; apparently 200 or 300 such; and citizens inform me that 300 or 400 have died of their wounds. We have two colonels, one major, and eight captains, under our charge, who were wounded in the assault."

Mrs. Dickinson says in her account of the storming of the Alamo:

" I knew Colonels Crockett, Bowie and Travis, well. Colonel Crockett was a performer on the violin, and often during the siege, took it up and played his favorite tunes. I heard him say several times during the eleven days siege, ' I think we had better march out of here and die in the open air; I don't like to be hemmed up.' A Mexican woman deserted us one night, and, going over to the enemy, informed them of our inferior numbers."

In another place she says:

" The struggle lasted more than two hours, when my husband rushed into the church where I was with my child, and exclaimed:

' Great God, Sue! the Mexicans are inside our walls! All is lost! If they spare you, save my child!' Then with a parting kiss, he drew his sword and plunged into the strife that was raging in different parts of the fortification.

"Soon after he left me, three unarmed gunners, who had abandoned their useless guns, came into the church where I was, and were shot down by my side. One of them was from Nacogdoches, and was named Walker. He spoke to me several times during the siege about his wife and children with anxious tenderness. I saw four Mexicans toss him up in the air, as you would a bundle of fodder, with their bayonets, and then shoot him. At this moment a Mexican officer came into the room and addressed me in English, asking me if I was Mrs. Dickinson. I answered, yes. 'Then,' said he, 'if you wish to save yourself, follow me.' I followed him, and, although shot at and wounded, was spared. As we passed through the enclosed ground in front of the church, I saw heaps of dead and dying.

"The Texans, on an average, killed between eight and nine Mexicans each. One hundred and eighty-two Texans and 1,600 Mexicans were killed. I recognized Colonel Crockett lying dead and mutilated between the church and two-story barrack building, and even remember seeing his peculiar cap lying by his side. Colonel Bowie was sick in bed, but as the victorious Mexicans entered his room, he killed two of them with his pistols before they pierced him through with their sabres. Colonels Travis and Bonham were killed while working the cannon. The body of the former lay on top of the church. In the evening the Mexicans brought wood from the neighboring forest and burned the bodies of the Texans, but buried their own dead in the city cemetery, across the San Pedro."

And thus perished the heroes of the Alamo, of whom the poet says:

" Gashed with honorable scars,
    Low in Glory's lap they lie.
Though they fell—they fell like stars,
    Streaming splendor through the sky."

But they were terribly avenged on the bloody field of San Jacinto, where 732 Texans made the prairies ring with the battle cry of " Remember the Alamo! " and Goliad! as they rushed like a whirlwind on the glittering ranks of Santa Anna's army.   They were avenged, but in the words of the poet:

> " The muffled drums sad roll has beat
> The soldier's last tattoo;
> No more on life's parade shall meet
> That brave and gallant few.
>
> " On Fame's eternal camping ground
> Their silent tents are spread,
> And Glory guards with solemn round
> The bivouac of the dead."

Colonel Travis wrote several appealing letters for aid, and sent them east, while being besieged.   In one of them he says:

" This call may be neglected, but I am determined to sustain myself as long as possible, and die like a soldier who never forgets what is due to his own honor and that of his country.   Victory or death!

" W. BARRETT TRAVIS,
" Lieutenant-Colonel, Commanding."

It was this appeal from Travis which brought the gallant Kimble to the Alamo with thirty-two men.

In another letter, written on the 3rd of March, he says:

" From the 25th to the present date, the enemy have kept up a bombardment from two howitzers (one, a five-inch and a half, the other, an eight-inch), and a heavy cannonade from two long nine-pounders, mounted on a battery from the opposite side of the river, at the distance of 400 yards from our walls.   During this period the enemy have been busily employed in encircling with entrenched encampments, at the following distances: In Bexar, 400 yards west; in Laveletta, 300 yards south; at the powder house, 1,000 yards east by south; on the ditch, 800 yards north.   Notwithstanding this, a company of thirty-two men from Gonzales, made their way to us on the morning of the 1st instant, at 3 o'clock, and Colonel J. B. Bonham, a courier from the same place, got in this morning at 11 o'clock."

And further on, he says:

" I sent an express to Colonel Fannin, which reached Goliad on the next day, urging him to send re-enforcements. *None have yet arrived*. I look to the *colonies alone, for aid*. Unless it arrives soon, I will have to fight the enemy on his own terms. I will, however, do the best I can under the circumstances. And I feel confident that the determined spirit and desperate courage heretofore evinced by my men, will not fail them in their last struggle. A blood-red banner waves from the church of Bexar, and in the camp above us, in token that the war is one of vengeance against rebels. * * * The bearer of this will give your honorable body a statement more in detail, should he escape through the enemy's line. *God and Texas! Victory or Death!*"

As I am not writing a history of Texas, of course I can not go into all the details of the war of independence, which has been so often given by much abler pens than mine. My purpose is to give enough of it so that the readers of this little book, who are not familiar with the history of Texas, may have a correct idea of the condition of the settlers at that time.

And, although Andrew Sowell escaped the massacre at the Alamo, by being on detached service, yet he left such a short time before the fall, his name was engraved on the monument erected to the memory of those brave and gallant few who fell. I take the following in regard to this, from the " American Sketch Book," published at Austin, in 1881 by Mrs. Bella French Swisher:

" Mr. A. J. Sowell is perhaps the only man living that lived to see a monument erected to his memory, by his country for his self-sacrifice, and for his country's freedom. His name is said to appear among the fallen at the Alamo. Mr. Sowell was born in Tennessee, came to Texas in 1829, and soon after his arrival, entered the Texas army; was with Bowie in the battle at the Mission, near San Antonio. He was in the Alamo, but a short time before the fort was surrounded by the Mexican forces, Mr. Sowell, and one other, was detailed and sent out after beef to supply the fort, but before they had time to procure the beef, the fort had been surrounded; and no country has ever lost a grander, and nobler, and braver set of men, than Texas lost at the fall of the Alamo."

The Alamo monument was made from stones taken from the floor of the Alamo fort. One of the inscriptions on it is: " The blood of heroes hath stained me." After its completion, it was offered to the State for sale; and, strange to say, the passage of the bill was opposed by some members of the Legislature. In connection with this, we take the following from the Seguin *Mercury*, bearing date, April 7, 1858:

" From an eloquent speech of our State Senator, Captain H. E. McCulloch, delivered in the Senate the 22nd of July last, on the bill for the purchase of the Alamo monument, we make the following extract:

" 'I will relate a circumstance which occurred in my presence, with one of these mothers of our country; and, sir, I shall never never forget my feelings upon that occasion, and can scarcely control them now sufficiently to speak. She was the mother of one whose youthful blood was mingled with that of Travis, Crocket, Bowie, and others, to water the tree of liberty which sprang up on their graves; the blood that bought our country, (Texas), and made us free.

" 'In the fall of 1842, General Wall, a Mexican general, at the head of a band of Mexican robbers, (for I can call them by no milder name), some 1,200 or 1,500 strong, led, in part, by heartless traitors — and when I say that, I mean what I say, and will name Colonel Juan N. Seguin, who now lives on the San Antonio river, and Captain Antonio Perez, who is dead, as the leaders I refer to — made a descent upon San Antonio, when the district court was then in session, and overpowered and took the place, making prisoners of all the Americans that were there, robbing and plundering the town, and spreading alarm through a sparsely populated and defenseless country, causing the settlers to leave their homes and flee to places of safety. Women were flying, and men whose hearts beat high for their country, were gathering together and hurrying to meet and drive back the dastard foe; I was sent forward by my captain, the noble and lamented Matthew Caldwell, to get every man on or near the road, to join us; and calling at the residence of one, who, when young and able to perform his part, had rendered good service to his country; to see if I could get some one at that place; I told him my business, and said: ' I know you are too old to go now,' and asked him if there was any one who could be spared to go. He hung his head, evidently struggling between his feelings as a parent and love for his country. The only son he had old enough to bear arms and take the field in defense of his country, was standing impatient for the answer, when the mother spoke and said: ' John might be spared from home a few days very well.' ' But,' said the old man, the tears filling his eyes, ' we lost William at the Alamo; can we see John go, too? ' The mother looked him full in the face, and in a firm, mild voice, said: ' 'Tis true, that William died at the Alamo, and we have no son to spare, but we had better lose them than our country.' He went, and like a true son of a noble mother, who had voluntarily offered him, if need be, upon the altar of her country, he stood amid the clangor of arms and din of battle, side by side with the descendants of the heroes of the Alamo, and other citizens of the country, numbering 202 men, till victory perched upon our standard—till the Lone Star waved in triumph over the battle-field of the Salado. Such, sir, are specimens of the widows and descendants of the men whose names are inscribed upon that monument, and it is with pride and pleasure I discharge my high duty to them and my country, by casting my vote for the bill, and I hope it will pass.' "

A bill has also recently been passed by the Legislature appropriating a sum for the purchase of the Alamo, and also for the battle-field of San Jacinto.

From the Houston *Daily Post*, bearing date, March 1, 1882, we get the winding-up scene at the Alamo after the battle. The sketch was written by W. P. Zuber, of Iola, Grimes county. The facts were furnished him by a Mexican fifer, who was in the assault, and is as follows:

10

"This sketch is an account of the burning of the bodies of the heroes of the Alamo, after the storming of that fortress by the forces of Santa Anna, on the 6th of March, 1836, and includes the murder of Colonel James Bowie. The facts were related to me by the Mexican fifer, Apolinario Saldigua, who was then but sixteen years old, and who was an eye-witness of the scene. He was known in Texas by a contraction of the Christian name Polin, pronounced *Poleen*, accenting the second syllable. I knew him during several years, and feel that I can safely vouch for him as a truthful boy.

"After the fort (the celebrated church of the Alamo at San Antonio) had been stormed, and all of its defenders had been reported to have been slain, and when the Mexican assailants had been recalled from within the walls, Santa Anna and his staff entered the fortress. Polin being a fifer, and therefore a privileged person, and possibly more so on account of his tender age, by permission, entered with them. He desired to see all that was to be seen; and for this purpose, he kept himself near his general-in-chief. Santa Anna had ordered that no corpses should be disturbed till after he should have looked upon them all, and seen how every man had fallen. He had employed three or four citizens of San Antonio to enter with him, and to point out to him the bodies of several distinguished Texans.

"The principal corpses that Santa Anna desired to see, were those of Colonel W. Barrett Travis, Colonel James Bowie, and another man, whose name Polin could not remember. I asked Polin if the other man's name was Crockett, to which he replied: 'May be so; I can't remember.'

"On entering the fort, the eyes of the conquerers were greeted by a scene which Polin could not well describe. The bodies of the Texans lay as they had fallen, and many of them were covered by those of Mexicans who had fallen upon them. The close of the struggle seemed to have been a hand-to-hand engagement, and the number of slain Mexicans exceeded that of the Texans. The ground was covered by the bodies of the slain. Santa Anna and his suite, for a time, wandered from one apartment of the fortress to another, stepping over and upon the dead, seemingly enjoying this scene of human butchery.

"After a general reconnoitering of the premises, the Dictator was conducted to the body of Colonel Travis. After viewing his form and features for a few minutes, Santa Anna thrust his sword through the dead man's body, and turned away. He was then conducted to the body of the man whose name Polin could not remember. This man lay with his face upward, and his body was covered by those of many Mexicans who had fallen upon him. His face was florid, like that of a living man, and looked like a healthy man asleep. Santa Anna also viewed him for a few moments, thrust his sword through him, and turned away.

"The one who had come to point out certain bodies, made a long but unsuccessful search for the body of Colonel Bowie, and reported to Santa Anna that it could not be found.

"Then a detail of Mexican soldiers came into the fort. They were commanded by two officers, a captain and a junior officer, whose title Polin could not explain to me; but whom I shall for convenience call the lieutenant. They were both quite young men, very fair, and handsome, and so nearly alike in complexion, form, size and features, that Polin judged them to be brothers; the captain being apparently a little older than the other. Polin did not remember to have ever seen them before; was confident that he never saw them afterwards; and did not learn their names.

"After the entry of this detail, Santa Anna and his suite retired; but the two officers, with their detail, remained within. The two kept themselves close together, side by side. Polin was desirous to know what was to be done, and remained with the detail; and to enable himself to see all that was to be seen, he kept himself near the officers, never losing sight of them.

"As soon as the Dictator and suite retired, the detail began to take up the Texans and to bring them together, and lay them in a pile. I had learned from other prisoners that the Mexicans, at the same time, performed the additional work of rifling the pockets of the slain Texans.

"The two officers took a stand, about the center of the main area. The first corpse was brought and laid as the captain directed. This formed a nucleus for the pile. The bodies were brought successively, each by four men, and dropped near the captain's feet. In imitation of the general, the captain viewed the body of each Texan for a few moments, then thrust his sword through him, and then, by a motion of his sword, directed the four men who had brought him, to throw him upon the pile, which pantomime was instantly obeyed.

"When the Texans had all been thrown upon the pile, four soldiers walked around it, each carrying a can of camphene from which he spurted the liquid upon the pile. This process was continued until the bodies were thoroughly wetted; then a match was thrown upon the pile, and the combustible fluid instantly sent up a flame to an immense height.

"While the fluid was being thrown upon the pile, four soldiers brought a cot, on which lay a sick man, and set it down by the captain; and one of them remarked, 'Here, captain, is a man who is not dead.'' 'Why is he not dead?' said the captain. 'We found him in a room by himself,' said the soldier. 'He seems to be very sick, and, I suppose, he was not able to fight, and was placed there by his companions, to be in a safe place, and out of the way.' The captain gave the sick man a searching look, and said, 'I think I have seen this man before.' The lieutenant replied, 'I think I have, too,' and stooping down, he examined his features closely. Then, raising himself up, he addressed the captain: 'He is no other than the infamous Bowie.' The captain then also stooped, gazed intently on the sick man's face, assumed an erect position, and confirmed the conviction of the lieutenant.

The captain then looked fiercely upon the sick man, and said: 'How is it, Bowie, that you have been found hidden in a room by yourself, and have not died fighting, like your companions?' To which Bowie replied, in good Castilian: 'I should certainly have done so, but you see I am sick, and can not get off this cot.' 'Ah, Bowie,' said the captain, 'you have come to a *fearful end* — and well do you deserve it. As an immigrant to Mexico, you have taken an oath, before God, to support the Mexican government; but now you are violating that oath by fighting against the very government which you have sworn to support. But this perjury, common to all your countrymen, is not your only offense. You have married a respectable Mexican lady, and are fighting against her countrymen. Thus you have not only perjured yourself, but you have also betrayed your own family.'

"'I did,' said Bowie, 'take an oath to support the constitution of Mexico; and in defense of that constitution am I now fighting. You took the same oath, when you accepted your commission in the army; and you are now violating that oath, and betraying the trust of your countrymen, by fighting under a faithless tyrant for the destruction of that constitution, and for the ruin of your people's liberties. The perjury and treachery are not *mine*, but *yours*.'

"The captain indignantly ordered Bowie to shut his mouth. 'I shall never shut my mouth for your like,' said Bowie, ' while I have a tongue to speak.' 'I will soon relieve you of that,' said the captain.

"Then he caused four of his minions to hold the sick man, while a fifth, with a sharp knife, split his mouth, on each side, to the ramus of the jaw, then took hold of his tongue, drew out as much of it as he could between the teeth, out of his mouth, cut it off, and threw it upon the pile of dead men. Then, in obedience to a motion of the captain's sword, the four soldiers who held him, lifted the writhing body of the mutilated, bleeding, tortured invalid from his cot, and pitched him alive upon the funeral pile.

"At that moment a match was thrown upon the funeral pile. The combustible fluid instantly sent up a flame to an amazing height. The sudden generation of a great heat drove all the soldiers back to the wall. The two officers, pale as corpses, stood gazing at the immense column of fire, and trembling from head to foot, as if they would break asunder at every joint. Polin stood between them, and heard the lieutenant whisper, in a faltering and broken articulation: 'It takes him — up — to God.'"

"Polin believed the lieutenant alluded to the ascension, upon the wings of that flame, of Bowie's soul to that God, who would surely award due vengeance to his fiendish murderers.

"Not being able to fully comprehend the great combustibility of the camphene, Polin also believed that the sudden elevation of that great pillar of fire was an indication of God's hot displeasure toward those torturing murderers. He further believed that the two officers were of the same opinion, and thus he accounted for their great agitation. And he thought the same idea pervaded the whole detail, as every man appeared to be greatly frightened.

"For a time, Polin stood amazed, expecting that the earth would open a chasm through which every man in the fort would drop into perdition. Terrified by this conviction, he left the fort as speedily as possible.

"On a subsequent day, Polin entered the fort again. It was then cleansed, and it seemed to be a comfortable place. But in a conspicuous place, in the main area, he saw the one relic of the great victory — a pile of charred fragments of human bones."

The writer, a short time ago, while going through the Alamo, looking at its dark and gloomy walls, came across two little boys looking for the grave of Crockett. The little boys were under the impression that the old hero was buried on the spot where he had fallen.

> " What solemn recollections throng,
>   What touching visions rise,
>   As wandering these old walls among,
>   I backward turn my eyes,
>   And see the shadows of the dead flit round,
>   Like spirits when the last dread trump shall sound."

CHAPTER IV.

SANTA ANNA PURSUING HOUSTON—BATTLE OF SAN JACINTO—INCIDENTS OF THE BATTLE—SANTA ANNA'S SADDLE—MANNER OF HIS CAPTURE—AN ATTEMPT ON HIS LIFE—A PERILOUS VOYAGE ON THE GULF—THE MASSACRE AT GOLIAD.

AFTER the families had all left the vicinity of Gonzales, General Houston followed in their rear with his little army, leaving a few men in Gonzales with orders to burn the place on the approach of the Mexicans; but the men became restless, and thinking the Mexican army would soon be there any way, fired the place, and left before they came in sight. When they did come, they passed down on the south side of the river, learning from the scouts, perhaps, that the place had been destroyed.

While Santa Anna was pursuing Houston, a strong force under General Urrea, was marching against Fannin at Goliad.

At the burning of Gonzales, the settlers lost all their possessions, except a few things they could carry with them in their flight. One man afterwards told old man Sowell: "I set fire to your house myself." Every thing was consumed, including a fine library belonging to his son, Lewis, who brought it with him from Tennessee.

Andrew accompanied his parents to the coast, and saw them safely on board of a vessel, in company with a great many fugitives like themselves, the captain sailing out into the gulf with them. Andrew then hastened back to join Houston's army, but arrived too late to participate in the battle of San Jacinto, which had just been fought when he arrived, but had the satisfaction of learning that the Mexican army had suffered a total defeat and that Santa Anna himself, was a prisoner. The battle was fought on the 21st of April, 1836, near the San Jacinto river, something over 200 miles east of San Antonio. The Mexican army numbered upward of 1,600 men, while that of Houston was only 783.

The rout of the Mexican army commenced at 4:30 o'clock, and from that time until night put an end to the

(The Battle of San Jacinto.)

pursuit. It resembled a slaughter more than a battle. At the breastworks, before the rout commenced, the contest was fierce and bloody. The Texans fought with clubbed rifles, breaking a great many of them off at the breech. The best troops that Santa Anna had, was the famous Tampico regiment, that fought with great bravery. The most of them were either killed or captured.

General Santa Anna was captured the next day after the battle. He had thrown off his uniform and was lying in the tall grass on the prairie when found by the scouts, who were scouring the country, bringing in prisoners. Mr. Sylvester thus relates the manner of his capture, which was published in the Texas Almanac, in 1858:

"Mr. Sylvester, in company with two others, were scouting near Vince's bayou, when, turning out from the road, some deer were seen at a distance. 'Boys,' said one, 'stop here until I get a shot at those bucks.' Then riding cautiously through the skirts of the timber, at a proper distance from the deer, he dismounted and tied his horse, and keeping his eye on the deer, crept towards them. All at once, he observed their heads and tails up, as usual when about to start, and suddenly they leaped off. As their heads were turned from him, he knew that something else had caused their alarm. He returned, and mounting his horse, beckoned for his companions to come up, and told them something had frightened off the deer, and he would see what it was; and starting off, they came to the spot, and after looking about, discovered a man lying in the grass. They rode up to him and ordered him to get up. Manifesting fatigue, he appeared unwilling to rise. One of them then said, 'Boys, I'll make him move,' and leveling his gun at the same time. 'Don't shoot, don't shoot!' said the others; and getting down from his horse, one of them gave him a kick, saying, 'Get up; get up!' The man then slowly arose. As none of them understood Spanish, they could not talk to him; but they saw plainly he was a Mexican officer, though entirely unknown to them. One of them gave him his horse to allow him to rest, while the other two rode by his side, till they got within a half mile of the camp, when he was made to dismount; the one who walked on foot now resuming his saddle, proceeded alone with the prisoner to the camp, the other two returning to scout through the prairie."

The reason why Santa Anna was not at once recognized, was the disguise of his dress. He had on a glazed leather cap, a striped jacket, (volunteer roundabouts), country-made, coarse cotton socks, soldier's coarse white linen pants, bespatted with mud. His fine linen bosom shirt, and sharp-pointed shoes, were all that did not correspond with a common soldier's dress.

When the scout, with his prisoner, arrived at camp, the

latter requested to be conducted to General Houston, who was then lying under a tree in the shade, suffering from a wound which he received in the battle. When the prisoner was presented to him by the scout, he (the prisoner) advanced close to the Texan commander, and said, in Spanish: "General Houston, I surrender myself to you, sir, Antonio Lopez De Santa Anna, Commander-in-Chief of the Mexican Army."

This announcement created great excitement in the camp, and several attempts were made upon the life of the Mexican Dictator. Santa Anna's saddle was also brought into camp; a very fine one, being richly silver-mounted. It was put up for sale, and was bid in by Colonel Lamar for $300.

The enemy's loss in the battle was 630 killed, among whom were one general, four colonels, two lieutenant-colonels, five captains, and twelve lieutenants. The wounded were 208; five colonels, three lieutenant-colonels, and seven captains. The prisoners were 730. Officers captured besides Santa Anna, were one general and five colonels. There were picked up, 600 muskets, 300 sabres and 200 pistols, on the battle-ground. Our loss was very small, only twenty-five killed and wounded. Several hundred mules and horses, and $12,000 in specie, were also taken by our men.

When Andrew arrived in the camp, the men were all in high spirits, and many tales were told of the battle. When the Texan army was advancing across the prairie to engage the Mexicans, who stood with a bold front in open view on the plain, with banners waving and bugles sounding, while flashily-dressed officers galloped to and fro on gaily-caparisoned steeds, with their sabres glittering in the sun, two brothers were riding close together in the line of the advancing Texans. When they drew near this glittering array of flashing sabres and waving banners, Dick, the youngest, who was only about seventeen years old, began to show the white feather, and told his brother he did not think he could stand it, and began to look to the right and left, as if he was about to dodge out. "Dick," said his brother, sternly, "if you run, I will shoot you;" and the stripling thinking his brother was in earnest, said he had rather be killed by a Mexican than his brother, spurred up his horse, when the charge was sounded, and dashed into the fight.

While the contest was raging around, Dick fired at a Mexican that was beginning to run, and brought him down, and, leaping from his horse, drew his knife and began stabbing the already dead Mexican; for he had made a center shot. Some one asked him after the battle why he had stabbed the Mexican after he had killed him. "By gosh," said Dick, "I was afraid he would get up."

One old man was seen going into battle carrying two rifles, and being asked why he did this, said the Mexicans had killed two of his brothers at Goliad, and he was going to have two of them, and fearing he would not have time to reload after the first fire, he was going prepared for it.

One man was seen to come out of the fight with his gun-stock broke off, and the bloody barrel grasped in his hand. He seemed to be perfectly furious, and rushed upon a gang of prisoners, and commenced braining them right and left, still shouting his battle cry of, "Remember the Alamo." He was immediately disarmed and placed under guard.

Andrew found his brother, John, here, who had gone on with Houston's army from Gonzales, and had participated in the battle.

One day, while Santa Anna was being kept in a small log cabin, a man came through the camp, and said if he

had a pistol he would go and kill Santa Anna.   " Say,
boys; who will lend me a pistol," he called out, " to go
and kill old Santa Anna with?"   John Sowell, who was
sitting near, reached round and pulled out a large holster
pistol and handed it to him.   He grasped it without a
word, and concealing it under his coat so that the guards
could not see it, set out on his bloody mission.   The men
waited and listened in anxious expectation.   Some said
he would not do it; that he was only gassing.   But these
conjectures were suddenly brought to a close by the crack
of a pistol, and the man came running back, exclaiming
that he had killed Santa Anna, and leaving the camp, ran
off towards the bottom.   He was subsequently caught
and brought back, and as he had failed to kill the Mexican general, he was only placed under guard.

When he presented himself at the door of the log
cabin, Santa Anna was sitting in a chair, leaning back
against the back wall of the cabin, with his face towards
the door.   The guards, thinking he only wanted to look
at the famous self-styled Napoleon of the West, did not
pay much attention to him, and, in fact, they did not have
much time, for he almost immediately drew the pistol,
and fired.   With the flash of the pistol Santa Anna
ducked his head, and the chair slipping, he fell to
the floor, and the man thinking he had made a dead shot,
threw away the pistol, and fled.   The ball struck a few
inches above the tyrant's head.

Washington Lonis, an infantry soldier, was shot in the
breast early in the action, and fell in the tall grass, and
lay there until after night, without being seen by his victorious comrades.   He suffered terribly from his wound,
and almost famished for water.   He heard the battle
receding from him; heard the shouts of victory, and the
voices of his comrades near him, returning from the pur-

suit; but he was too weak to call for aid, and lay there wallowing about in his blood, and almost delirious from the burning thirst that raged within. Some times he gave up all hope, and thought he must die for want of help with so many of his brave comrades near; but, then again, he would hear the sound of voices and hope would again revive, only to be disappointed as the sounds died away in the distance. It was now long after night, and he had been lying there since 4 o'clock, with a rifle ball in his breast, with not even enough strength to raise his head, but only to move it from side to side, and mutter low gurgling moans. At last he gave up all hope; he knew he could not survive until morning in this condition; his tongue was dry and thick, and he was almost choked with thirst; but, suddenly he heard a footstep near, which seemed to be passing the spot where he lay; his articulation was almost gone, but he uttered a faint moan. A few quick steps and Howard Baily and Frank Sparks bent over him. "Wash Lonis;" says Baily, 'poor fellow, he is almost gone." With a canteen of water he soon relieved the thirst of the wounded man. Baily being a strong man, carried him to camp in his arms, and by careful nursing, Washington Lonis recovered and survived the battle of San Jacinto twenty-five years, and died in Guadalupe county.

The vessel on which the parents of Andrew Sowell embarked, sailed out into the gulf and in a short time encountered a terrible gale; the ship became unmanageable, and for several days beat off before the wind toward the Mexican coast. The second day the captain became very uneasy, and paced his deck in gloomy silence, giving no satisfactory answer to questions asked by the frightened, anxious passengers, who saw from his looks and actions that some thing was wrong besides the storm, for the vessel was weathering it all right, although her course could not be changed as long as the wind blew from that quarter. The captain ate but little, and slept none; he was always up pacing the deck and looking ahead.

On the third day, just at sun down, the boom of a cannon was heard across the water. The captain started, as if struck by a bullet, and looked anxiously in the direction of the report, but said nothing, and when asked what that cannon-shot meant, only told them to wait. That night the wind changed and the captain turned the course of the vessel, and crowding on all sail, steered for the coast of Texas.

The next morning, the captain was cheerful and communicative, telling his passengers and crew that on the evening before he did not wish to alarm them, as he knew it would do no good; but, said he, "I can tell you now that we have made a very narrow escape. That cannon we heard yesterday evening at sunset, was fired in Tampico, on the coast of Mexico; and, if the wind had not changed before morning, we would have been in the hands of the Mexicans. I have been in Tampico and knew all the time where we were drifting. They always fire a gun, and lower the flag, in that place, just as the sun goes down. Heaven knows what our fate would have been, had we fallen into the hands of the treacherous Mexicans, since the war has assumed such a brutal aspect on their part; but we are all right now, and will soon touch the Texas coast again, and God grant that Houston and the brave boys with him, will defeat the tyrant, and drive him and his butchers from our soil."

In a few days they were sailing along the coast of Texas. One evening, a smoke was seen curling up from a small island near the main land, and a boat was dispatched to see what it meant. On landing, they saw a pale, haggard, half-starved looking man, trying to cook a sea-gull, which he had killed, on a small fire which he had kindled out of a few dry sticks. On their approach, he hastened to them ; and, asked who he was, and how he came there, he informed them that he was a fugitive from the massacre at Goliad, and had traveled several days without any thing to eat, and that he was almost completely exhausted, and half-starved, and he had come across to this place to hide from the Mexicans, who were scouring the country in every direction to recapture those who had escaped. He was taken on board, and, after being refreshed, he told them of the sad defeat, and subsequent massacre of Fannin and comrades. Fannin attempted to escape from Goliad after it was too late. He was overtaken on the prairie by a much superior force, and a desperate battle was fought which lasted far into the night. Being cut off from water, and his cannons becoming useless for want of water to cool them, Fannin surrendered under a promise of being liberated soon, and sent home. But the ever treacherous enemy, after they had disarmed this brave band, that numbered about 500, took them in a few days back to Goliad, and gave orders to shoot them. They scattered in various directions when the firing commenced, and some few made their escape. This wholesale slaughter was done by order of General Santa Anna.

In the next chapter will be given an account of the escape of four of Fannin's men, as it was published in the " American Sketch Book," in 1881.

CHAPTER V.

DILLARD COOPER'S REMEMBRANCES OF THE FANNIN MASSACRE.

"On the morning of the 27th of March, 1836, about daylight, we were awakened by the guards, and marched out in front of the fort, where we were counted and divided into three different detachments, We had been given to understand that we were to be marched to Capono, and from there shipped to New Orleans. The impression, however, had in some way been circulated among us, that we were to be sent out that morning to hunt cattle; though I thought at the time that it could not be so, as it was but a poor way, to hunt cattle on foot.

"Our detachment was marched out in double file, each prisoner being guarded by two soldiers, until within about half a mile southwest of the fort, we arrived at a brush fence, built by the Mexicans. We were then placed in single file, and were half way between the guard and the fence, eight feet each way. We were then halted, when the commanding officer came up to the head of the line, and asked if there were any of us who understood Spanish. By this time, there began to dawn upon the minds of us, the truth, that we were to be butchered, and that, I suppose, was the reason that none answered. He then ordered us to turn our backs to the guards. When the order was given not one moved, and then the officer, stepping up to the man at the head of the column, took him by the shoulders and turned him around.

"By this time, despair had seized upon our poor boys, and several of them cried out for mercy. I remember one, a young man, who had been noted for his piety, but who had afterwards become somewhat demoralized by bad company, falling on his knees, crying aloud to God for mercy, and forgiveness. Others attempted to plead with their inhuman captors, but their pleadings were in vain, for on their faces no gleam of piety was seen for the defenseless men who stood before them. On my right hand, stood Wilson Simpson, and on my left, Robert Fenner. In the midst of the panic of terror which seized our men, and while some of them were rending the air with their cries of agonized despair, Fenner called out to them, saying: 'Don't take on so, boys; if we have to die, let's die like brave men.'

"At that moment, I glanced over my shoulder and saw the flash of a musket; I instantly threw myself forward on the ground, resting on my hands.   Robert Fenner must have been instantly killed, for he fell with such force upon me as almost to throw me over as I attempted to rise, which detained me a few moments in my flight, so that Simpson, my companion on the right, got the start of me.   As we ran towards an opening in the brush fence, which was almost in front of us, Simpson got through first, and I was immediately after him.   I wore, at that time, a small, round cloak, which was fastened with a clasp at the throat.   As I ran through the opening, an officer charged upon me, and ran his sword through my cloak, which would have held me, but I caught the clasp with both hands, and tore it apart, and the cloak fell from me.   There was an open prairie, about two miles wide, through which I would have to run before I could reach the nearest timber, which was a little southwest of the place from where we started.

"I gained on my pursuers, but saw, between me and the timber, three others, who were after Simpson.   As I neared the timber, I commenced walking, in order to recover my strength, before I came near them.

"When he first started, we were all near together, but as Simpson took a direct course across the prairie, I, in order to avoid his pursuers, took a circuitous course.

"There were two points of timber projecting into the prairie, one of which was nearer to me than the other.   I was making for the furthest point, but as Simpson entered the timber, his pursuers halted, and then ran across and cut me off.   I then started for the point into which Simpson had entered, but they turned and cut me off from that.   I then stopped running and commenced walking slowly between them and the other point.   They, no doubt, thinking I was about to surrender myself, stopped, and I continued to walk within about sixty yards of them, when I suddenly wheeled and ran into the point for which I had first started.   They did not attempt to follow me, but just as I was

11

about to enter the timber, they fired, the bullets whistling over my head caused me to draw my head down as I ran.

"As soon as I entered the timber, I saw Simpson waiting and beckoning to me. I went towards him, and we ran together for about two miles, when we reached the river. We then stopped and consulted as to the best way of concealing ourselves. I proposed climbing a tree, but he objected, saying that should the Mexicans discover us, we would have no way of making our escape. Before we arrived at any conclusion, we heard some one coming, which frightened us so, that I jumped into the river, while Simpson ran a short distance up it, but seeing me, he also jumped in. The noise proceeded from the bank immediately above the spot where Simpson was, and I could see the place very plainly, and soon discovered that two of our companions had made their escape to this place. They were Zachariah Brooks, and Isaac Hamilton. In the fleshy part of both Hamilton's thighs were wounds, one made by a gun-shot and another by a bayonet.

" We all swam the river, and traveling up it a short distance, arrived at a bluff bank, near which was a thick screen of bushes, where we concealed ourselves. The place was about five miles above the fort. We did not dare proceed further that day, as the Mexicans were still searching for us, and Hamilton's wounds had become so painful as to prevent his walking, which obliged us to carry him. We remained there until about 10 o'clock that night, when we started forth, Simpson and myself carrying Hamilton. Brooks, though severely wounded, was yet able to travel. We had to proceed very cautiously and rather slowly.

" Fort La Bahia being southeast of us, and the point we were making for, was about where Goliad now stands. We proceeded in a circuitous route in a northeasterly direction. We approached within a short distance of the fort, and could not at first account for the numerous fires we saw blazing. We were not long in doubt, for the sickening smell that was borne towards us by the south wind, informed us too well that they were burning the bodies of our companions. And, here, I will state what Mrs. Cash, who was kept a prisoner, stated afterwards; that some of our men were thrown into the flames and burned alive. We passed the fort safely, and reached a spring, where we rested from our journey and from whence we proceeded on our travels.

But the night was foggy, and becoming bewildered, it was not long before we found ourselves at the spring from which we started. We again started out, and again found ourselves at the same place; but we had too much at stake to sink into despondency. So once more took our wounded companion, thinking we could not miss the right direction this time; but, at last when day began to break, to our great consternation, we found we had been traveling around the same spot, and were for the third time back at the identical spring from which we had at first set forth. It was now impossible to proceed further that day, as we dared not travel during the day, knowing we should be discovered by the Mexicans. We therefore concealed ourselves by the side of a slight elevation, amidst a thick undergrowth of bushes.

" By this time, we began to grow very hungry, and I remembered an elm bush that grew at the entrance of the timber where we were concealed, which formed an excellent commissary for us, and from the branches of which we partook, until nearly every limb was entirely stripped.

" About 9 o'clock that morning, we heard the heavy tramp of the Mexican army on the march; and they not long after that passed within a stone's throw of our place of concealment.

" It seems indeed, that we were guided by an over-ruling providence in not being able to proceed further that night, for as we were not expecting the Mexican army so soon, we would probably have been overtaken and discovered by them, perhaps in some prairie, where we could not have escaped.

" We remained in our hiding place the rest of the day, and resumed our journey after dark, still carrying our wounded companion. Whenever the enemy passed us, we had to conceal ourselves; and we laid several days in ponds of mud and water, with nothing but our heads exposed to view.

" When in the vicinity of Lavacca, we again got ahead of the Mexicans; and, after traveling all night, we discovered, very early in the morning of the ninth day, a house within a few hundred yards of the river. We approached it, and found the inhabitants had fled. When we entered the house, we discovered a quantity of corn, some chickens, and a good many eggs lying about in different places. Our stomachs were weak and revolted at the idea of eating them raw, so we looked about for some means of striking a fire, first searching for a rock, but failing to find one, we took an old chisel and ground it on a grindstone for about two hours, but could never succeed in getting the sparks to catch. We then concluded to return and try the eggs raw. We had taken one, and Simpson was putting on his shoes, which he had taken off to rest his feet, which were raw and bleeding, and had just got one on when he remarked: "Boys, we would be in a tight place if the Mexicans were to come upon us now." So saying, he walked to the window, when to his horror, there was the whole Mexican army not more than a mile and a half off, and fifteen or twenty horsemen coming at full speed within a hundred yards of us. We took up our wounded man and ran to the timber, which was not far off, Simpson leaving his shoe behind him. We got into the timber and concealed ourselves between the logs of two trees, the tops of which having fallen together, and being very thickly covered with leaves and moss, formed an almost impenetrable screen above and around us. We had scarcely hidden ourselves from view, when the Mexicans came swarming around us, shouting and hallooing through the woods, but did not find us. We heard them from time to time, all throughout the day and next night. The next morning, just before day, the noise of the Mexicans ceased, and we concluded they had left. Simpson then asked me to go with him to get his shoe, as it would be difficult for him to travel without it, and I consented to do so. We went out to the edge of the timber and stopped some time to take observations before proceeding further. Seeing nothing of the Mexicans, we proceeded to the house, found the shoe, and possessing ourselves of a couple of ears of corn, and a bottle of water, we returned to our companions. We had no doubt that the Mexicans had gone, so we sat down and drank the water and ate an ear of corn, when Brooks asked Simpson to go with him to the house, saying he would get a chicken, and we could eat it raw. They started, and had hardly got to the edge of the timber when I heard the sound of horses feet, and directly afterwards the Mexicans were to be seen in every direction. I was sure they had captured Simpson and Brooks. Soon I heard something in the brush near us, but did not know whether it was the boys or Mexicans, but it turned out to be the boys, who crept under cover, and, in a few minutes, four Mexicans came riding by, passing within a few feet of where we were lying, with our faces to the ground. After going into the woods a short distance they turned and passed out again, but it was not long after when six of them came riding quite close, three on each side of us, and leaning down and peering into our hiding place. It seemed to me they could have heard us, for my own heart seemed to raise me almost from the ground by its throbbings. I felt more frightened than I ever had been before; for at the time of the massacre, every thing had come on me so suddenly that my nerves had no time to become unstrung as they now were. The Mexicans passed and repassed us, through the day, so we dared not move from our hiding place. A guard was placed around us the following night, the main body having, no doubt, gone on, and left a detachment to search for us. I think they must have had some idea of our being some of Fannin's men, or they would scarcely have gone to that trouble. About 10 o'clock that night we held a consultation, and I told my companions it would not do to remain there any longer, as the Mexicans were aware of our place of concealment, and would surely discover us the next day. We all decided then to leave, and they requested me to lead the way out. I told them we would have to crawl through the timber and a short piece of prairie, until we crossed the road near which the Mexicans were posted; that they must be careful to remove every leaf and stick in their path, and to hold their feet up, only crawling on their hands and knees, as the least noise would betray us to the enemy. I was somewhat acquainted with the locality; for we were now not far from Texana, and I had some times hunted along these woods. Thus I led the way. Hamilton's wounds were so painful that we could move only slowly, and we must have been two hours crawling about 200 yards. When we at length passed the timber and reached the road, I stopped to make a careful survey of the situation. I could see the Mexicans placed along the road, about a hundred yards on each side of us. The moon was shining, but had sunk towards the west, which threw the shadow of a point of timber across the road, and concealed us from view. It would have been hard to discover us from the color of our clothes, as the earthy element with which they were mixed had entirely hidden the original fabric. We continued to crawl, until we reached a sufficient distance not to be discovered, when we rose up and walked. Although Hamilton had, with a great deal of pain, managed to crawl, yet it was impossible for him to walk, and his wounds had by this time become so much irritated and inflamed that he could scarcely bear to be carried. We traveled that night only a short distance, and hid ourselves in a thicket near a pond of water. Brooks had been trying to persuade me to leave Hamilton; but, although our progress was impeded by having to carry him, I could not entertain the idea for a moment. I indignantly refused, but still he would seize every opportunity to urge it upon me. He said it would be impossible for us to escape, burdened as we were with Hamilton. I could only acknowledge the truth of this, for it was a desperate case with us. The foe was around us in every direction. Brooks, finding that I was not to be persuaded, then attempted to influence Simpson.

"On the tenth day out, they took the bottle and went to the pond near by, for water. As they were returning, (I suppose Brooks did not know he was so near the place they left us), both Hamilton and myself heard Brooks urging Simpson to leave him. He told him if we remained with Hamilton, we would certainly lose our lives; but there was some slight chance of escaping, if we left him, and that Hamilton's wounds had become so much worse that he was bound to die, unless he could have rest; and, as we were doing him no good, and ourselves a great deal of injury by carrying him, it was our duty to leave him. Now Brooks had never carried him a step; Simpson and myself having done that; yet Brooks was the first who had ever proposed leaving him; and, although there was a great deal of truth in what he was saying, yet I felt quite angry with him, as I heard him trying to persuade Simpson. Hamilton did not say a word to them when they came in, but sat with his face buried in his hands a long time. At length, he looked up, and said: 'Boys, Brooks has told you the truth; I can not travel any further, and if you stay with me, all will be killed. Go and leave me, boys; if I have rest I may recover, and if I ever should get off safe, you shall hear from me again.' He spoke so reasonably, and we were so thoroughly convinced of the truth of what he said, after a brief consultation, we decided to depart without him. Hamilton had known Brooks in Alabama; he called him to him, and gave him a gold watch and $40 in gold, telling him to give it to his mother. We then bade Hamilton farewell, all of us shedding tears as we parted, but when we turned to go, my resolution failed me, and I could not find it in my heart to leave him. I said: 'Boys, don't let us leave him.' But Simpson and Brooks said that we could do neither him nor ourselves any good by remaining, and that they were determined to go. I told them I would remain with him, and do the best I could for him. So they started off without me; but Hamilton insisted so much that I should leave him, that I again bade him farewell, and followed and soon overtook the others. The reason that we started off in the day, was that it was raining quite hard, and we thought there would not be much danger in traveling, but we had not gone more than half way through the next prairie, when the weather cleared up, and we saw the whole Mexican army encamped at Texana, about two miles off; but they did not discover us, and we succeeded in reaching the timber on the Navidad. In the evening we walked out to a slight eminence which overlooked the prairie, to reconnoitre. While gazing across the prairie, we could see three men on horseback, but so indistinct were they, that we could not at first tell whether they were Americans or Mexicans. As they approached, we hid in the undergrowth; and as they passed, we saw that they were Mexican couriers returning to the command.

"At eight we again started forth, and coming out on the prairie, we discovered a road, which we concluded had been made by the refugees in their retreat from the enemy. During all this time we had nothing to eat but leaves and herbs, and the two ears of corn that we got at the house on Lavacca river.

"On the twelfth day, we reached the Colorado, at Mercer's crossing. As we were very tired, we sat down on the bank to rest a little, before attempting to swim over. While sitting there, a dog on the opposite side of the river began to bark. When we heard that well-known sound, our very souls thrilled with joy, and that was the first time since the awful day of the massacre that a smile had ever illuminated our faces. We looked at each other, and then burst into a great big laugh. We were all good swimmers, but I some times took the cramp while swimming, so we concluded to cross on a log. We procured a dead mulberry pole, and hanging on to it, one at each end, and one in the middle, we crossed over to the land of freedom, and a land where we found plenty to eat. After recruiting a little, we procured horses, with the intention of joining Houston's army; but before we reached there, San Jacinto had been fought and won.

"It was more than a year before I ever heard any thing of Hamilton.   He remained in the same place where we left him nine days, some times lying in the pond of water, which assuaged the pain of his wounds.   At the end of that time he was so much improved that he essayed to walk to Texana, and succeeded in doing so. He said the best eating he ever had in his life, was when he first entered Texana, and ate the meat from the rawhides the Mexicans had left.   The next morning he took a skiff, and made his way down to Dimmitt's landing.   He had scarcely reached there when he was taken prisoner by a Mexican soldier.   Not long after, other soldiers came in, and tying Hamilton on a mule, started for camp.   He suffered so much from his wounds that he fainted several times on the way.   Whenever this occurred, they would untie him, lay him on the ground, and throw water into his face until he revived, when they would again mount him on the mule and proceed on their way.   Hamilton remained in their hands for some time and gradually grew well of his wounds.   There was a Mexican who waited on him, who seemed much attached to him, and Hamilton was led to place much confidence in him.   One morning, this Mexican told him that if he wanted to live another day, he must make his escape that night, as he had learned that he and two other prisoners were to be shot before morning. Hamilton then arranged a plan for the escape of himself and two of his companions, which was a success, after many trials and tribulations."

CHAPTER VI.

EXPEDITION UNDER JOHNSON AND GRANT.

THE following sketch of the above named expedition, I take from the Seguin *Mercury*, bearing date, October 37th, 1858, and written by R. N. Brown, one of the survivors of this ill-fated expedition. It was written for the Texas Almanac, and is as follows:

"EDITORS TEXAS ALMANAC:—In compliance with your request I proceed to give you the facts in relation to the expedition under Colonel Johnson and Grant, which set out from San Antonio in December, 1835, and I do this more willingly because I have seen many erroneous statements in regard to this expedition. I arrived in San Antonio the second day after the capitulation of Cos, in company with Hugh and John H. Love, all of us Georgians, having come through from Nacogdoches. The Texans, who had aided in taking San Antonio, had all left for their homes, and we found there United States volunteers numbering some 460, who were then proposing an expedition to take Matamoras, and in three or four days after our arrival, the expedition was fully organized, and we joined it. Colonel Francis W. Johnson was elected to command, while Dr. James M. Grant was elected lieutenant-colonel, and Captain Robert Morris, of New Orleans Greys, was elected major; and, in his place, Captain William G. Cook was elected to command the Greys. Another company was commanded by Captain Pearson, who had been connected with a theatre in New Orleans, and another by Captain Lewelyn. I do not remember the commanders of the other companies. The whole number of men was about 400. The expedition soon set out for Goliad, leaving Colonel Neill in command of the Alamo, with some sixty men. I believe Travis and Crockett had not yet arrived. Major Bonham, of South Carolina, proceeded with us to Goliad, but returned to the Alamo, as he had received some

11*

appointment from Travis. Having arrived at the Cibolo, we learned that a convention had been called to meet at San Felipe, and we elected two delegates to represent us—one of them a Mr. Conrad. Having reached Goliad after a march of six or seven days, we there found Captain Philip Dimmitt in command of a company; and, in a day or two after, he raised the flag of independence, the first, I believe, that was ever unfurled in Texas. There were not then probably a dozen in our expedition in favor of that measure. When we set out from San Antonio we expected to join Colonel Fannin, who, we heard, had arrived at Matagorda bay with about 1,000 men. It was arranged to join him at Copano, to which place he was to proceed by steamer from Matagorda bay. Three or four days after our arrival at Goliad, General Houston and Colonel Hockley, with some five or six others, came there, General Houston then strongly proclaiming himself in favor of the expedition to take Matamoras.

After remaining in Goliad about a week, we proceeded to the Mission of Refugio, in order to be nearer to Fannin on his arrival at Copano, and General Houston and his half dozen companions followed us there. But after reaching that place he made a strong speech against the proposed expedition to Matamoras, and some of us then attributed his change of opinion in regard to that measure, to the fact that Fannin would be chosen to command the expedition. However, as this may be, Houston succeeded in detaching a large portion of the men who had joined us, so that we found only sixty-four left who were willing to go. With this small number, we proceeded to San Patricio, most of the New Orleans Greys having left, Captains Pearson and Lewelyn having only a part of their companies. As there were not probably half a dozen of us who lived to get back, I will give the names of all that I remember, namely: Colonels Johnson and Grant, Major Robert Morris, Daniel J. Toler, Dr. Hoyt, of South Carolina; Dr. Hart, of New Orleans; John H. Love, James M. Miller, nephew of Governor Miller, of South Carolina; Cass, of Philadelphia; Carpenter, of Tennessee; Francies, a creole of Louisiana; Langanheim, a German; Scurlock, and Jones.

"We received information from Fannin that he would be at Copano as soon as possible, but had been unavoidably detained in Matagorda bay, and he wished us to collect as many horses as possible, to enable him to mount his men. For this purpose, and in order to scour the country, we divided our men into two parties, one of which remained in San Patricio, under Colonel Johnson, while the other proceeded westward in search of horses, etc., under Colonel Grant. I went out with this party.

"Having reached Sal Colorado, about sixty miles from San Patricio, we fell in with some half a dozen Mexicans guarding some 300 or 400 head of horses that had been sent out there to be recruited for the service of Urrea's division of the invading army, then preparing to set out. We ascertained that Roderiguez, their captain, was encamped near by with a small force, and we made the men guarding the horses, whom we took prisoners, guide us to the camp of Roderiguez, which we reached by going in single file by a narrow path through a dense thicket of chaparral, and finally found the encampment in a small open space, surrounded on all sides by this chaparral. The tents were enclosed around by brush thrown up, and guarded by a sentinel. The sentinel, on seeing us, fired his escopete at me, as I was in the lead, but missed me, and then I shot him. We jumped over the brush at once, and making for the tents, took them all prisoners without firing another gun. This was just at daybreak. I took Roderiguez myself, though he surrendered only after much resistance. We then returned to San Patricio with our prisoners, sixty-seven in all, and several hundred horses. Colonel Johnson and Grant agreed to release the prisoners from close confinement upon parole, Roderiguez pledging his honor that they would not leave; but they all soon left, regardless of their parole.

"Our party started out on another expedition immediately, going north of the road to Matamoras. On the second day, a Mexican fell in with us, pretending that he wished to join us, and that he could bring with him a small company of mounted men. We suspected him for a spy, and our suspicions were confirmed in the morning, when we found he had left us during the night. Our guide had informed us that there was a party of some fifty Mexicans a little ahead of us, with several hundred horses, and we therefore made an early start, but when we came in sight of them, we found them moving off and driving their horses before them. We pursued them to the Rio Grande, where we overtook them, and as they were attempting to cross pell-mell, some of them were drowned. Having taken a considerable number of their horses, we returned on our way back to San Patricio, visiting the different ranches, getting all the horses we could, and buying them at a dollar a head. We' had reached the Agua Dulce, (Sweetwater), within some twenty miles of San Patricio, and, in high spirits, we made an early start from that place one morning, Colonel Grant, Placido Buenevidas and myself, being about half a mile ahead, to lead the horses, and the rest of the company following. We were passing between two large motts, when, suddenly, there came out from each of these motts, several hundred Mexican dragoons, who quickly closed in, surrounding both the horses and our party. Grant, Placido and myself, might then have made our escape, as we were well mounted and some distance in advance, but our first impulse being to relieve our party, we returned without reflecting upon the impossibility of doing any good against so large a number, for there were at least a thousand dragoons under the immediate command of Urrea himself. We then at once understood that Urrea had come in on the main road some distance below, or to the south of us; that he had been to San Patricio, and had probably slaughtered Johnson and his party. Placido wished to return with us, but Grant persuaded him to start forthwith to Goliad, and give Fannin information of Urrea's arrival. We had been absent from San Patricio some ten or twelve days. As Grant and myself approached to join our party, the dragoons opened their line, and we passed in. We at once saw that most of our party had already been killed, and we decided to sell our lives as dearly as possible. My horse was quickly killed with a lance, but Grant told me to mount Major Morris' horse, as Morris had just been killed. I did so, but without seeing any object to accomplish by it. Just at that moment the horses took a stampede, and broke the line of the dragoons, and Grant and myself finding ourselves the only survivors of our party, followed in the wake of the horses, the dragoons shooting after us, and wounding our horses in several places, but not badly. As we were flying, a dragoon rushed upon me with his lance set, but I knocked it to one side and shot him, holding my pistol against his breast; and scarcely stopping, I fled with Grant, the Mexicans following, and some of them occasionally coming up with us, and crying out to us to surrender and our lives would be saved. But we knew better, and continued to fly, but the number of those overtaking us became larger and larger, and after we had run six or seven miles, they surrounded us, when, seeing no further chance of escape, we dismounted, and determined to make them pay dearly for our lives. As I reached the ground a Mexican lanced me in the arm, but Grant immediately shot him dead, when I seized his lance to defend myself. Just as he shot the Mexican I saw Grant fall, pierced with several lances, and in a moment after, I found myself fast in a lasso that had been thrown over me, and by which I was dragged to the ground. I could do no more, and only regretted that I had not shared the fate of all the rest of my party.

"After Grant fell, I saw some ten or a dozen officers go up and run their swords through his body. He was well known to them, having lived a long time in Mexico. They had a bitter grudge against him.

"I was then lashed upon a horse and taken to the ground where the fight first commenced, where I saw most of our men lying dead. Among others whom I recognized, was one poor fellow named Carpenter, from Tennessee, who was fatally wounded but not quite dead. When it was discovered that he was alive, one of the dragoons was ordered to finish him. He dismounted and, while poor Carpenter asked to have life spared, he struck him on the head with his escopete, and thus ended his existence. I was then taken to San Patricio, and there confined in a small hut for seven or eight days, during which time I knew nothing of the fate of Colonel Johnson's command.

"On the second day of my confinement, I was approached by General Urrea's interpreter, who proposed to me that I should give a flag of truce to Colonel Fannin, and propose to him it he would surrender, he and his men would be sent safely back to the United States. The reason for making me this proposition, was double the fact of their having found letters about me from Colonel Fannin, with whom I had been on intimate terms, we both having come from the same section of the State of Georgia. I refused to accede to this proposition, assigning as my reason, that he required me to state what was not true; that the Mexican force under him were very large, and such as would overpower him; but I would certainly not have been the bearer of any proposition that would have been dishonorable to our army, or have prejudiced our cause. Urrea then said that I would have to be executed according to Santa Anna's orders. It was probably my indifference and recklessness of life, under the circumstances, that saved my life. I was then taken out to be shot, but was spared through the interposition of a priest and a Mexican lady, named Alvarez. After having been kept in San Patricio some seven or eight days, I was taken out of my place of confinement to be sent to Matamoras, where I was surprised to see some five or six of the men belonging to Colonel Johnson's command, brought out for the same purpose. They had been confined in another place, entirely unknown to me; and, as I then learned, were the only men of Johnson's command that had not been killed except Johnson himself, John H. Love, James M. Miller and Daniel J. Toler, who made their escape by a fortunate circumstance. An understanding had been had between the Mexicans and the few inhabitants of the town, that on the night when the attack on the town was to be made, the citizens should have lights burning in their houses, by which means they would be known and saved, while all the balance were to be slaughtered. It happened that on that night Johnson and Toler were engaged in writing to a very late hour, and their light, therefore, saved them till they had notice of the attack, and were thus enabled to make their escape.

"I was then marched with the other prisoners to Matamoras, being five or six days on the road; and, on our arrival, we were imprisoned and kept several days without food or drink. Soon after our arrival, we were informed that orders had been received from Santa Anna for our execution; but General Fernandez, commanding at Matamoras, to whom these orders had been sent, delayed the execution for the purpose of going through a mock trial. We were all taken out and questioned separately, taking near two days with each of us. We were then formally condemned and sentenced to be shot on the 6th of April, 1836. We had been in Matamoras from about the 1st of March. On the appointed day for our execution, we were all taken out, weak and greatly emaciated from the painful manner of our confinement and want of food. The sentence was read to us; but we were respited by the interposition of the priest and woman who had been residing in Matamoras. A large church had been commenced, but was left unfinished for the want of funds. It was by the promise of the money requisite to complete it, that the priest exerted their powerful influence in our behalf, but the money was promised merely for a respite for nine days, during which time, a messenger was to be dispatched to the City of Mexico, to try and obtain a reprieve. The messenger returned, having (much to our astonishment) obtained a commutation of the sentence of death to perpetual confinement from that time till the latter part of December following, subjected to every privation, half-starved, and only taken out of our close and filthy prison occasionally to sweep the streets, when we were always under a strong guard. We were barefooted and nearly destitute of clothing, and death was preferable to such a condition of wretchedness. Finally, myself and McNeely, of Louisiana, having been dvised that our friends had horses prepared for our flight, provided we would once escape from our confinement, determined we would use every exertion to get out, or die in the attempt. During the year, we had often asked for a privilege of sleeping in the prison yard, which was enclosed by a wall fourteen feet high. It was not until the latter part of December, that McNeely and myself finally prevailed on the officers to grant this privilege for one night. The time was propitous, as it was dark and rainy. A guard of twelve men alternated in watching over us. Near 12 o'clock, while were apparently asleep, I observed the guards with their cloaks or blankets, on their bayonets, over their heads, trying to protect themselves from the rain. We seized the opportunity, and glided unperceived to the wall of the quartelle, or enclosure. After exhausting our ingenuity in devising means to reach the top of the wall, it was finally decided that McNeely, who was a tall man, should place himself against the wall, close to the back house, which was not quite so high; and having done so, I sprang from his shoulders so as to reach the top, when he was able, by getting hold of my feet, to climb up my side. We then immediately jumped down the other side, but were discovered by the sentinel on the wall, who gave the alarm, and we only succeeded in making our escape by the darkness of the night. After groping about the remainder of the night without being able to find our friends, we secreted ourselves the following day, and the next night succeeded in procuring weapons, and then we proceeded up the Rio Grande to find a favorable point for crossing, traveling in the night and laying concealed in the day-time, till we reached a crossing a little below Mier early one morning where, seeing a canoe on the opposite bank, I swam over for it, and with it, we both crossed, swimming our horses. Before we reached the bank, we discovered a large number of Mexicans riding in pursuit of us, but fortunately we were unperceived by them, and made good our landing on the opposite bank. Having again mounted our horses, we pursued our way over the trackless prairie, as well as we could, but often lost our course, and it was not till after much exposure and several narrow escapes, that we finally arrived among our friends in Texas.

" We arrived at the Guadalupe, opposite Victoria, the latter part of December, or the first of January, during a fall of sleet, when the river was near an overflow, called to the opposite side of bank for somebody to bring the ferry-boat over for us, but Colonel Clark L. Owen, who was then in command of a company at that place, suspected a decoy by the enemy, and it was not till some time had passed, that he finally came over for us.

" I have given you all the leading events of our disastrous expedition under Colonel Grant, of which I was the only survivor, except Placido Buenvidas, who carried the first news of our slaughter to Fannin. I have omitted many events and details of suffering that would probably extend this communication too much for your use. It may be proper here to remark that Mr. McNeely is now a member of the legislature of Louisiana. The other prisoners who were with us, were finally released, by the influence of their friends, some four or five months after our escape. "Yours respectfully,

"R. N. BROWN."

CHAPTER VII.

RETURN OF THE SETTLERS TO GONZALES.

WE will now return to the vessel containing the fugitive families, which we left on the coast of Texas, after having taken on board the half-starved soldier from the Fannin massacre.

There were many sad and heavy hearts on board of that vessel when they again got under way and continued down the coast. Some had lost their loved ones at the Alamo, some at Goliad, and most all of them had sons, brothers, and friends, with Houston, and what might be their fate ere this, none could tell. The last news they had heard from them, they were being pursued by an overwhelming and victorious army under the dictator and blood-thirsty tyrant, Santa Anna, himself.

As the captain could hear no news concerning the movements of the armies, he at length concluded to sail for Columbia, on the Brazos, as being the place most likely to hear news from the seat of war.

On nearing the place, he saw a large vessel at the landing, with her decks crowded with men. The captain's heart sank within him at this sight, and turning to e anxious passengers who crowded around him, he said: "Texas is gone; Houston's army is embarking; t' v have been driven from the soil of Texas."

But what was their joyful surprise when, on coming up, they found out that the battle of San Jacinto had been fought, and the Mexican army had been totally defeated, and almost the entire army had been either killed or

12

captured, including Santa Anna himself, who was a prisoner. The men which they saw on board the vessel and taken for Houston's army, were Mexican prisoners.

Andrew Sowell and John here rejoined their parents, and there was great rejoicing at the meeting of friends and kindred after so many dangers and hardships. The Sowell family here went on board the vessel containing the prisoners, and remained several days. The old lady, who was somewhat hard of hearing, and could not hear an ordinary conversation, one day, while at the dinner table, asked who Santa Anna was, who sat near the head of the table, and was having some attention paid to him. On being informed that it was the Mexican general, Santa Anna, she arose from the table, saying she would not eat another bite while that old scamp was at the table, and she did not, but took her meals elsewhere, until Santa Anna was sent back on shore.

From this place, the Mexican president was sent to New Orleans, and from there to Washington City, and after peace was concluded, and the independence of Texas recognized, he was sent to Vera Cruz, and landed on the soil of Mexico, a somewhat humbled if not a better man.

Several families remained here at Columbia for some time, until the times became more settled. Among the number was old man Sowell : but finally they commenced moving back to their old homes on the Guadalupe and elsewhere, and, in 1838–'39, a great many had returned and again settled at Gonzales.

I heard of one incident connected with the sudden flight of the settlers on the approach of the Mexicans, which I will here relate. A family who were living some distance from Gonzales, were just sitting down to breakfast when one of the messengers which Houston had sent out arrived and told them of the fall of the Alamo, and the advance of Santa Anna. Without stopping to finish breakfast they hastily collected a few things and fled, and on their return more than a year afterwards, found everything as they had left it. The table was still set, and chairs around it, and mouldy bread and meat in the dishes, nothing having molested a thing.

Yoakum, in describing the flight of the settlers, says:

"On every road leading eastward into Texas, were found men, women and children, moving through the country over swollen streams and muddy roads, strewing the way with their property, crying for aid, and exposed to the fierce *northers* and rains of the spring. The scene was distressing indeed; and, being witnessed by the small but faithful army of Texas, whose families and wives they were, thus exposed and suffering, nerved their arms and hearts for the contest then not distant."

In connection with the return of the familes to Gonzales, I will insert the following, which was published in the Gonzales *Inquirer*, in February, 1882, and is as follows:

"GONZALES IN 1838 AND 1839."

"EDITOR GONZALES INQUIRER:—Please accept a few reminiscences of 'Old Gonzales,' with a view of introducing other and abler pens to place upon record, before it be too late, similar sketches of 'Life and Times on the Guadalupe Frontier.'

"The spring of 1838, witnessed the return to Gonzales of some of the familes who had built homes here in the first settling of this country, but who, with others of the colonists on the Guadalupe river, had been constrained to a hasty flight in the memorable running scrape of 1836. The Alamo had been garrisoned principally by men and boys from this vicinity, and when they were butchered, their families were left smitten and almost helpless, and the enemy advancing rapidly upon them, their homes were left to the flames while they escaped as best they could.

"The defeat of the Mexicans at San Jacinto did not secure peace to the western settlements; on the contrary, rumors of intended invasions were rife every spring, and Indian depredations were common. Thus the prospect of good times was remote to the surviving families who had buffeted about until they had mostly used up their personal property, but yet owning excellent lands in this region, they resolved to return, re-establish and rebuild their former homes. This spirit and indomitable energy of these people, was worthy of note, and was exemplified while they were moving from place to place, anxiously waiting for some protection and security to be offered their frontier. One excellent matron declared to her associates in distress, ' I had rather return to the ' Warloope' river, drink of its waters aud subsist on catfish and buttermilk, while risking all enemies, rather than settle down any where else.' The return was difficult, the country being waste and desolate for two or three years. There was nothing but wild game to subsist upon. They must bring their corn from the Colorado, or from Washington county, and grind it by hand upon steel mills. Groceries and store supplies could only be obtained at Houston or the Lower Brazos. Having no cattle to spare, they hunted deer, which were plenty; while wild hogs, bears, and occasionally a buffalo, were found. By the last of June of this year, among others who had got back, were Judge McClure, ten miles east of town, occupying one of the most exposed places in the country; Mr. Havens, and the Lockharts, ten miles below on the west side; the DeWitts, and old Simon Bateman, beyond whom the wide extant of land reaching to the San Antonio, was uninhabited; over in the forks, were Mr. Duncan, and the Hodges, with Colonel King, nine miles above, and still more remote, was Colonel J. D. Clements. Nearer town, were the widow Rowe, Frazier, George W. Davis, Almon Cottle, the Berrys, Daniel Davis, John Clark, I. J. Good, and in the inner town, there were Eli Mitchell, Captain M. Caldwell, James Patrick, Esquire, Adam Zumwalt, Ezekiel Williams, E. Bellinger, M. G. Dikes, the Sowells, Nichols, and Darst.

"In June, Mr. ———, while traveling home via. Big Hill and McClure's, was killed by the Indians. He lived near Berry's.

"The Fourth of July, 1838, was observed with some festivities, including the wedding of Captain William A. Mathews and Mrs. Fuqua. The same day brought sorrow into Mr. Bellinger's family, whose son, William, was drowned at the watering place of the town.

"In June of 1838, Major V. Bennett, who was also from Gonzales, was instructed to visit the important points on the frontier, especially San Antonio, and report to military headquarters at Houston, and during the following winter, two companies of the army were brought out, one of which was stationed at Gonzales, Major Bennett furnishing transportation and subsistence for both companies. Among those previously mentioned, two were signers of the declaration of Texas' independence, and there were also a few of the eighteen men who, in 1835, comprised the first company mustered to prevent the Mexicans from removing the cannon from Gonzales.

"In the spring of 1839, Captain Ben McCulloch and H. E. McCulloch, had an efficient company of minute men, and kept their scouts in the field from time to time.   Their encampment was up the Guadalupe, at Walnut Springs.

"The friendly Indians, the Lipans and Tonkaways, frequently encamped at Gonzales, and in one or two instances co-operated with the McCullochs in pursuing other hostiles. On one occasion, the Indians were encamped just below town, on the river, driving a pretty brisk trade in ponies, deer-skins and trinkets, during which time, John McCoy, of McCoy's creek, in the lower part of the county, who owed the red men a grudge, treated one of them pretty freely with whisky, and accepting in return his proposal to ride behind him from town to camp, deliberately scalped the Indian on the road, for which he was blamed by the citizens generally.

"In addition to the citizens already mentioned, there were others of more or less prominence, who may have been earlier or later identified with Gonzales and its surroundings, viz: Wilson and Barney Randall, A. Swift, the Smiths, Kings, Days, V. Henderson, Callahan, John S. Saump, an expert hunter; Baskes and Rhodes, successful bear hunters; Putnam, Kinkennon, William Morrison, Asley Miller, C. Acklin, Clem Hinds, E. Henkins, Nathan Burkitt, Cockrill, Wolfin, Cooksey, Hoskins, George Edwards, A. Gipson, John Archer, Arch Jones, Josh Threadgill, W. B. Hargis, Grubbs, Baker, R. Miller, Joe Martin, Killin, C. C. Colley, Frazier, Poney Hall, and Robert Hall.

"Some of these men were in the humble walks of life, but all counted in times of alarm and distress, for the war with Mexicans and Indians continued to harrass Western Texas long after San Jacinto days. Witness the bold excursions into Mexico under such captains as Jordon, Ross, Switzer and King, in 1839; the burning of Linville, and the battle of Plum Creek, in the summer of 1840: the Santa Fe expedition, in 1841-'42; the Vasquez inroad in the spring of 1842; the battle of the Salado, and the Wall campaign, in the fall of 1842, followed in the winter by the Summerville campaign, including the Mier expedition.

"In all of these, our men participated pretty feely; some fell in actual battle; some endured long and harsh imprisonments; some were permanently disabled by honorable wounds, and a few of them lie in unknown graves in the public burying-ground in Gonzales.

"B."

CHAPTER VIII.

SETTLING GUADALUPE COUNTY— SEGUIN — CALLAHAN'S
MINUTE COMPANY—SHOOTING MEXICAN HORSE THIEVES
—GENERAL ED. BURLESON DEFEATS CORDOVA AT MILL
CREEK—INCIDENTS OF THE BATTLE—THE SCOUTS SUR-
PRISED — MILFORD DAY WOUNDED — PURSUIT OF COR-
DOVA BY THE SETTLERS.

NOT long after the return of the settlers to Gonzales,
Andrew Sowell's father died, and his brother, Lewis,
died a short time before the runaway scrape, as it was
called. The rest of the boys spent a good portion of their
time in the ranging service. Andrew served under Hays,
McCulloch, Mason, Caldwell, Callahan, and others. He
was well acquainted with nearly all the noted characters
in Texas at that time, and on one occasion, swapped hats
with 'Kit Carson,' the famous Santa Fe scout.

Shortly after the death of their father, the Sowell boys
left Gonzales, and moved up and settled on their league
of land on the Guadalupe river, just below where the
flourishing little city of Seguin is now situated ; and when
that place was laid off, bought lots and settled there.

Humphrey Branch was the first settler at this place.
He went there in 1833, and built a house near the spot
where the Andrew Neill house now stands, and called it
the Elm Spring Hill. One morning, while living here, the
family were startled by hearing a noise which resembled
a hurricane approaching, and running out, saw an immense herd of buffalo crossing the prairie north of the
house. At that time there was no brush to obstruct the

view. Branch first settled with his father-in-law, John Sowell, at the mouth of Sowell creek, six miles below.

Among those who settled the place, were the Kings, McCullochs, Sowells, Nichols, Solomon Brill, Milford Day, Callahan, Turners, and others.

Not long after the town was laid off and settlements commenced, the Lipan Indians, who were then friendly to the whites, followed a band of Comanches and had a terrible fight with them, and on their return had a war dance at the Walnut Springs. The white settlers of Seguin were invited to it, and several of them attended. During the dance, the Lipans held the scalps of the slain Comanches in their hands.

On another occasion, the hostile Indians made a raid in the outskirts of the town, while a dance was in progress at the house of Milford Day. They were discovered by John R. King, who was on the lookout, and who fired at them. One of the Indians returned the fire, and they all retreated. The alarm was soon given and the dance came to an abrupt termination. In a few moments William King, Henry King, John R. King, Andrew Sowell, Anderson Smith, Paris Smith and Milford Day, were armed, mounted and after the hostiles. The night was dark, and the scouts. after searching for some time and seeing nothing of the Indians, repaired to the three-mile water hole and remained till morning. As soon as it was light enough they again set out, and struck the Indian trail near the Plum Ridge. The trail led in the direction of where New Braunfels now stands. The men followed rapidly, and came up with the Indians in the prairie, near the Twelve-mile spring. One of them, who carried a rifle, dropped down in the grass, and attempted to fire at William King and Anderson Smith, who were riding close together, but was shot through the head and instantly killed by King before he could do so. The Indians then ran, pursued by the settlers, who tried to fire on them, but could not do so, as their guns had become wet in the night from the drizzling rain. The Indians, however, were in the same predicament; their bow-strings, which were made of sinews, had become wet, and relaxed so that they could not shoot their arrows with any force. In this way the pursuit was kept up until they arrived at the river, the settlers snapping their pieces, and the Indians endeavoring to shoot their arrows. The Indians plunged into the water and soon disappeared on the opposite side. William King, who had reloaded his rifle, and was the only man who had a dry gun, fired and killed another one while in the water.

As the Indians and Mexican horse thieves were bad, the Sowell boys joined Captain Callahan's company of minute men, in 1839. Andrew was almost constantly on the scout.

On one occasion, in company with another man, he left Seguin to take a scout up the San Geronimo, a creek two miles east of town, which ran in a southeast direction through the prairie towards the Guadalupe river. They struck the creek about six miles north of town, at some large springs, and after remaining a few minutes there to refresh themselves with cold draughts of water, crossed the creek and rode out beyond, so they could overlook the prairie to the York's creek divide. The country at that time was clear of brush, and the view unobstructed from the creek to the York's creek hills. It is now covered with a dense growth of mesquite. While standing on an elevation taking a view of the surrounding country, they discovered a lot of carrion crows sailing round in a circle to the east of them, and soon saw that they were slowly moving towards the south.

"What does those buzzards mean, Andy?" said his companion. "I will tell you what I think they mean," said Andrew, after looking at them a short time, "they are following a large body of Indians or men of some kind, to pick up what is left about the camps. I remember when we were following the Indians the time they killed Greser, and his Mexicans, a raven kept ahead of us all the time, following in the wake of the Indians, and would fly up from their camps at our approach. The Indians kill game along the route of their march, which draws the carrion crows; and they will some times follow the trail for days and weeks." "Well, then," said his companion, "if that is the case, let's go back to town and give the alarm; likely they are on their way to attack the place." "No; I am not satisfied yet, I want to see further," said Andrew, "you go back and tell them to be on their guard, and I will see if I can make any further discoveries." And accordingly they separated, Andrew going across to the head of Mill creek, and then turning south towards the Guadalupe river, calculating that in this round to cross the trail of the Indians, if seeing the buzzards had any thing to do with their presence in the country, but saw no signs of Indians for several miles, but when near the place where the Rev. F. Butler's farm is now situated, five mile east of Seguin, he discovered that the prairie was on fire ahead of him, and rode on very cautiously, keeping a sharp lookout, for this some times denoted the presence of Indians. Presently he heard shots fired in the direction of the burning prairie, and riding down into a deep gully, tied his horse and proceeded on foot to reconnoitre. He could hear the cracking of the tall prairie grass as it was being rapidly consumed, mingled with the occasional discharge of firearms. This greatly puzzled him and he kept under cover, with his trusty rifle grasped in his right hand, until he gained the edge of the prairie, but could still see nothing of a human being although he had just heard the report of fire-arms a few minutes before near the spot where he stood. More perplexed than ever, he was just about to turn back to where he had left his horse, when he heard a call on the prairie, and some one answered, and presently two men came together a short distance from where he was concealed in a clump of live oaks. Seeing they were white men, Andrew advanced to where they were, and learned from them that a battle had just been fought there between Burleson's rangers and a motley crowd of Mexicans, runaway negroes and Bilouxie Indians, under General Cordova. The firing which Andrew heard was from loaded guns that had been dropped by Cordova's men in their flight, and were being discharged as the fire burnt over them. The grass was set on fire by paper wads from the shot-guns of Burleson's men.

Cordova was on his way to Mexico from Nacogdoches, and had gathered followers as he went, stealing horses on the way, and committing other depredations. Most of the negroes were runaways from the plantations in Eastern Texas. When they arrived at the Colorado, a runner was sent to Austin to notify Colonel Edward Burleson, (who commanded the rangers), of their presence. On receipt of this intelligence, Burleson lost no time in repairing to the spot where Cordova had crossed the Colorado, and there took the trail with about eighty men. The force of the enemy was said to be about 300. Burleson overtook and fought them near Mill creek, five miles east of Seguin, in the Guadalupe valley. They only stood their ground for a short time, and then fled towards the heavy timbered bottoms of the river, closely pursued by the rangers, who overtook and killed a great many of them, without losing a man and only having three wounded.

During the pursuit, a stout young negro man was shot down by some one of the foremost pursuers, but arose to his feet and was shot down a second time by another man who came galloping by; thinking he had killed him, he went on, but the negro raised up in a sitting posture and received another shot from a ranger who was behind, but seeing that his shot did not kill him, the ranger dismounted, and drawing his bowie knife, gave him some ugly cuts as a finis he thought, and then remounting, dashed on in the chase, but when they returned after the pursuit was over, the negro was still alive, and they concluded not to kill him. A doctor who had accompanied the rangers, dressed his wounds, sewing up the knife cuts. He recovered and was afterwards sold for $800, and the money divided among the men that fought the battle. One old grey-headed negro was captured and taken to Seguin. On the way up there, he said he used to work in a silver mine in the Capota hills with the Mexicans. These hills lie on the south side of the river, about twelve miles southeast from Seguin. The negro was a vicious old rascal, and said he had killed women and children enough to swim in their blood. If such was the case, it would have been better for him to have kept it to himself, for when they arrived at Seguin he was taken out and shot.

Early the next morning, several of the citizens of Seguin visited the battle-ground, that is, the portion of it where the fight first commenced, which was about a mile west of Mill creek, on the high ground between where Mr. Woods and Mr. Handly now reside. It was then an open prairie, but now covered with mesquite. In the deep hollow which runs up and heads near Mr. Handley's fence, they found two dead Mexicans, and further out in the open ground, south of where the Seguin road now runs, were two dead negroes, lying close together; their clothing had been burnt off by the fire which passed over them, and they could see the bullet holes in their bodies. They presented a horrible looking sight. Further up on the rising ground, near some lone mesquite trees, lay the body of a Bilouxie Indian with the head cut off. He had been decapitated by the aforesaid doctor that was with the rangers, and this man of science put the bloody trophy in his saddle-bags and carried it home with him.

It was afterwards learned that Cordova intended to take and burn Seguin as he went through, but the timely arrival of the gallant Burleson somewhat changed the programme, otherwise Captain Callahan would have had the honor of defending Seguin with his twenty-two men, but might have shared the fate of Fannin and Travis, and made a Thermopylae out of Seguin.

Just before daylight, on the morning after the battle, the fugitives came upon James M. Day, Thomas Nichols and David Runnels, three of Caldwell's rangers who had been out on a scout up the country, and were camping out on the river, five miles from town, intending to kill some turkeys next morning and bring in. At the first onset, the scouts sprang to their feet with their rifles, and Day seeing an Indian untying his horse, raised his rifle to shoot him, but received a ball in the hip before he could do so, and fell. His companions, although sorely pressed, seized their wounded companion and bore him off to the river bottom, where they succeeded in keeping their enemies at bay, who, being on the run themselves, did not tarry long, and taking the ranger's horses, continued their flight. Tom Nichols swam the river and carried the news to Seguin. A party was then sent out with a cart and brought in Day, who is still living, but a cripple for life. A force was then raised to pursue Cordova's band towards Mexico, and if possible, to overtake and fight him again, but in this they were disappointed, and they turned back from the pursuit at what is called the Prickly Pear Prairie, near the Nueces river. This prairie has no growth upon it scarcely, except the prickley pear, which is very thick, and is a perfect den for rattlesnakes. Andrew Sowell, who accompanied this expedition, says that from the time they commenced traversing this place until they were clear of it, they were not out of the sound of rattlesnakes, and the men had to pick their way carefully to avoid being bitten, as many of the horses had given out and the men were leading them. The reason why they gave up the pursuit here was on account of the jaded condition of the horses.

Some Mexicans, who were captured in a fight some time afterwards, and were with Cordova on this trip, say that if the Texans had followed them a short distance further, they would have overtaken them, for at the time they turned back, Cordova's band had stopped on the Nueces, and were burying those of their party who had died from rattlesnake bites received in their passage through the pears.

Cordova, who led this party, was afterwards killed at the battle of Salado, when San Antonio was captured by General Wall.

On one occasion, when Andrew was scouting with a squad of rangers near the pear prairie, and were hunting for water, they saw a bunch of mustangs run out from a mott of timber and dash off. Thinking probably they had been watering, they rode down to the place to see, but before arriving there, began to smell a terrible stench and heard they warning notes of a rattlesnake near. They soon found him, and he proved to be an uncommon large one; and being afraid to venture near him with a stick, Andrew shot him in the head with his rifle. He was about nine feet long, and as big around as the thigh of a common sized man. The mustangs had run over him, and he was mad, which caused such a stench to arise from him.

Once, when Andrew was with the rangers, following a band of Indians, west of San Antonio, they came upon their camp, which they had just vacated, leaving nearly all of their camp equipage. As they always kept out spies on the back track, it was very hard to surprise them. The rangers being weary and hungry, concluded to stop at the Indian encampment and eat some of the fat venison which the redskins left in their retreat, before renewing the chase. While engaged in this, they discovered two Indians, the hunters for the band, approaching the camp, who were ignorant of the change which had taken place since they left. The captain told the men to be quiet and let them come as near as they would before they discovered that the camp had changed hands. Their horses were loaded with venison, and they were riding slowly along towards the camp, but before getting within rifle shot they discovered that something was wrong, stopped a few moments, and then threw off their meat and fled. "Catch them, boys, catch-them!" shouted the captain, and several men were soon in their saddles, and in hot pursuit. Andrew, who was riding a good horse, soon came up with one of them, raised his rifle to fire, but his horse, which was going almost at full speed at that moment, jumped a mesquite bush and spoiled his chance, and by the time he could recover himself and rifle, which he came near dropping, the Indian got into the brush, and he lost him; and, although several shots were fired by others, both Indians, owing to the thick brush, made their escape. The rangers returned to the camp and took up the main trail, but did not succeed in overtaking the Indians.

About this time Andrew's brother, John, killed an Indian on the San Geronimo, just above where it empties into the Guadalupe river, about three miles southeast of Seguin. He was returning from Gonzales, and as he neared the creek, discovered two Indians sitting on a rock, which projected out over the water. They seemed to be engaged in eating something. At sight of the red-skins, John reined his horse back under cover and dis-mounted, without being seen by the Indians. He then tied his horse and crept within gunshot of the unsus-pecting savages, and selecting the largest one, as if shooting at a buck, laid his rifle against a sapling, took deliberate aim, and fired. At the crack of the gun, the one at which he aimed, fell over and commenced strug-gling, but soon rolled off into the creek and sunk. The other one bounded up the bank and disappeared in the thickets. John reloaded his rifle quickly, and went back to his horse, keeping a sharp lookout for the other Indian, but seeing nothing of him, mounted his horse, and con-tinued his journey to Seguin.

On one occasion, a band of Indians were running buffalo on the prairie, north of Seguin, and chased one of them into town and shot it with such force with an arrow that the spike came through the hide on the opposite side. The Indians made no halt, but dashed on to the river bottom south of town. The dash was so sudden that before a man could get a gun and come out on the streets, the Indians were gone. The buffalo staggered about a while and then fell where the court house now stands, and was skinned and cut up by the citizens. One old broad-shouldered gentleman, just from the States, had been making his brags, before this occurred, that he was not afraid of men who fought with bows and arrows. "Why," said he, leaning back and expanding his chest, "I would stand and let them shoot at my breast, ten steps, all day, with their splinters." But he changed his tune after inspecting the dead buffalo on the square.

About this time, Mexican horse-thieves, as well as Indians, annoyed the settlers, and Captain James H. Callahan and his rangers, used every exertion to catch them, but were for some time unsuccessful; but finally they were trailed to their hiding place by Milford Day, who was a splendid scout and trailer. Their location was in a large and very dense thicket, cut through by a deep and rugged gulley. This place was about eight miles northeast from Seguin, on York's creek. Callahan, with a portion of his men, penetrated this thicket, and surprised them in their camp. which was near the deep gulley. A fight ensued, which resulted in the defeat of the Mexicans. with a loss of some three or four of their number. Owing to the density of the underbrush, where they fought the Mexicans, those who were not killed very easily made their escape after the defeat.

Next morning Callahan, with some of his men, returned to the thicket to see if they could pick up any stragglers that might still be in the brush. After riding about some time without seeing any signs, and becoming thirsty, he and his party repaired to a spring, to get water, and on coming to it, found a wounded Mexican lying by it. Although wounded in the leg, he got up at the approach of the rangers, and made signs to them that he wanted to surrender. Callahan rode near and asked him if he wanted to go to Seguin. The Mexican replied in Spanish that he did. " Come, then," said the captain, " and get

13

behind me." The Mexican then took a large silk handkerchief, and binding it around his wounded leg, hopped to Callahan's horse to get up, but was instantly shot dead with a pistol by the ranger captain.

In our day and time, this would look cruel and brutal, but those were desperate times, and it was death to all horse thieves when caught; and we, too, must remember that the Texans had suffered terrible things at the hands of the Mexicans. And the Alamo and Goliad was still fresh in their minds, but they never shot Mexican soldiers taken in battle.

Near the spring, where the wounded Mexican was killed, there was a round rocky hill, with a grove of live oaks growing on its top, and there the Mexican was buried; and that place to this day goes by the name of the " Rogues' Grave ;" and the place where they fought, is called the " Rogues' Hollow."

On one occasion, some of Callahan's men captured two Mexican horse thieves, brought them to town, and turned them over to the captain, to make such disposition as he thought proper. The captain being convinced that they were regular horse thieves, condemned them to death without much ceremony, and ordered a portion of his men to follow him with the Mexicans. They did so, and went a short distance west of the town, and halted under some live oak trees. Andrew Sowell and his brother, Asa, at this time, were both members of Callahan's company, and were of this party. In a short time after halting, the captain gave orders for the Mexicans to be shot. They were furnished with picks and shovels and made to dig their own graves. One of them was an old man, and worked away at his grave as composedly as if he was working for wages, taking particular pains to do it good, and seemed perfectly resigned to his fate.

But not so with the younger one, he bewailed his fate in piteous accents, and often quit his work to beg for life, and fearing his captors could not understand all he said, asked if there was one there who could speak the Spanish language, as he wanted to converse with him.   The captain then told young Asa Sowell, who spoke the language fluently, to listen to what he had to say.   The Mexican then quit his work, and in fervent and excited tones, bewailed his situation, and said he did not want to die; that he was too young to die; and that he was not a horse thief, and if ever he had stolen any thing the value of a pin, he did not know it, and begged his interpreter to help him to plead for his life.   But all that he could say did not change Captain Callahan from his purpose.   He was determined to break up these bands of horse thieves, and knew that this was the only way to do it.   There was no place to confine men in those days; the proof against him was too plain, and he must suffer the penalty of a horse thief, and the captain ordered him to resume his work, and with tears streaming from his eyes he complied.

They then drew lots to see who would do the shooting, Andrew Sowell proposing to take his brother's place if he drew to shoot, providing he himself drew a blank. The process was that they should cut up small bits of paper, corresponding with the number of men present, and write the word "shoot" on one-half of them, the balance to be left blank.   They were then placed in a hat, and a handkerchief spread over it, and the drawing commenced.   Both the Sowell boys drew blanks.   There were about eight men, I think, in the party.   The Mexicans were then made to kneel in front of their graves, and handkerchiefs bound over their eyes, the young one all the time proclaiming his innocence.   The old one said nothing.   Those that were to do the shooting, then took their places. At the signal, the guns all fired except one. Calvin Turner's missed fire. Both Mexicans fell over at the discharge. The old man was killed dead, but the young one was breathing freely when they came up to where the Mexicans lay. "Turner," said Callahan, "being as your gun missed fire, you can finish this fellow." The ranger thus addressed, without a word, primed his rifle, and stepping back a few paces, took a quick aim, and fired, the ball striking in the head, and killing him instantly. The brains came out at the bullet hole, and the troubles of the young Mexican was over, in this world, at least. This took place near where the residence of General Jefferson now stands.

CHAPTER IX.

ACK HAYS' FIGHT WITH THE INDIANS ON THE SACO AND
NUECES—INDIAN RAID IN BEXAR COUNTY—JAMES CAMP-
BELL KILLED—TREATY WITH COMANCHES IN SAN AN-
TONIO BREAKS UP IN A FIGHT — SETTING AN INDIAN
HEAD ON FIRE—BATTLE OF PLUM CREEK—INCIDENTS
OF THE BATTLE — JOHN H. MOORE DEFEATS THE IN-
DIANS ON THE COLORADO.

ABOUT the time the incidents narrated in the latter part
of the last chapter took place, Jack Hays, with his rangers,
were scouting in the mountains seventy-five miles west of
San Antonio, and meeting up with a large force of
Comanches on the Saco, a desperate fight ensued between
them. The rangers held their ground, although greatly
outnumbered, and killed a great many of them. The
Indians, confident in their numbers, made the mountains ring with their war-whoops, and made several
desperate charges on Hays and his men. In one of
the charges, where Hays had dismounted and formed
his men under cover, sixteen Indians were killed. The
Indians finally took a strong position among the rocks,
and awaited the movements of Hays, who, knowing his
force was not sufficient to dislodge them, also moved
back to a strong position, where he could better defend
himself and take care of his wounded. He then sent a
runner to Seguin for Callahan to come and help him,
while he, in the meantime, would hold the Indians in
check and watch their movements.

On receipt of this information, the ever-active Callahan

at once set out with a portion of his company, Andrew
Sowell being one of the number, and by rapid traveling
soon joined Hays, being guided by the runner to the
scene of the battle.   In the meantime the Comanches had
left their position and commenced retreating towards the
high and rugged mountains at the head of the Sabinal
river.   The combined force of Hays and Callahan now
pursued them with alacrity, although the Indians still
outnumbered them.   The retreating Comanches were
overtaken in the valley and a running fight commenced,
which lasted until the Indians entered the mountains and
scattered about among the big rocks that were piled up
on every hand.   A large squad of them then let themselves be seen on the rocks near the top of the mountain, out of range of common rifles.   Several shots were
fired but were answered by loud defiant yells from the
Comanches when the balls fell short of the mark.

Ben McCulloch, who afterwards became a noted Confederate general, and was killed at the battle of
Elk Horn, was with Hays on this occasion, and was the
owner of a very long-ranged gun, which he brought to
bear on the Indians ; and, when he fired, they scattered,
and were soon out of sight.   He did this several times
when they appeared in view, and they always moved
when he fired, and it was thought he killed some of them.
It was finally agreed that part of the men from each
company should scale the mountain and attempt to drive
them off, while others should be posted near the base to
cut off their retreat, and also to take care of the horses of
the dismounted men.   Andrew was one of the scaling
party from Callahan's company.   They found the ascent
very difficult, having to pull up from crag to crag, encumbered with their rifles, which were long and heavy, and at
the same time being fired on by the Indians, who had dis-

covered their approach. Occasionally the rangers would return the fire, but without much effect, as the Indians were mostly concealed. At length one of Hays' men was wounded and begged to be carried back down the mountain, as he was shot through, and it was all over with him. They agreed to do so, as it seemed almost impossible to dislodge the Indians under the difficulties which they had to surmount in the ascent, as they could scarcely find a foot hold to stand and shoot.

They assisted their wounded comrade, who breathed heavily, down the mountain, and he said, " Boys, they have knocked the black out of me this time; I am done for." When they rejoined the other party they proceeded to examine the wounded man, and when his coat was removed the ball dropped out at his feet, not having penetrated at all, but probably hitting and glancing from a rock before it struck him, but it made a large black spot in his breast, and, no doubt, felt as though it went through him.

In the meantime, the Indians commenced escaping from the mountain in small parties and could not again be brought to battle, and the rangers, after some further scouting, returned to Seguin.

On one occasion, when Andrew was a member of Jack Hays' company, the Comanches in large force committed fearful depredations upon the settlers west of San Antonio. Hays followed them with forty-two men, and came up with them on the Nueces. Just before sighting them, Hays knew by the signs that the Indians were near, and dismounting, told a Mexican guide who was with him to mount his (Hays') horse, and ride ahead and see if the Indians were near, and if so to make all haste and report to him. The Mexican mounted and set off, and Hays, with the rangers, followed slowly on, and in a short time heard the yelling of Indians and the clatter of horses' feet, and presently saw the Mexican coming back at full speed closely pursued by a band of Comanches, who had secreted themselves in the rear of the main body and came near cutting him off before he discovered them.

Hays ordered the men to advance, and quickly dismounting exchanged horses with the Mexican, and then galloped on in pursuit. The Indians seeing the rangers, ran back to the main body, making the woods ring with their yells, and commenced preparing for battle.

Hays made no halt, but spurred his horse furiously on the Indians, who numbered several hundred, and a short but desperate fight ensued.

The Lipan chief, Flacco, tied a red handkerchief around his head to prevent mistakes during the mixed-up fight, and remained near the person of Captain Hays, following him in several desperate charges among the Comanches. The rangers in the end were the victors, and pursued the flying Comanches some distance, who suffered heavy loss in the fight, while that of Hays was small.

After this fight Andrew continued scouting for some time, Hays' headquarters being at San Antonio. One evening after coming in from a scout the rangers camped on the ditch east of town, near the old Alamo fort. The next morning several of the boys turned their horses loose with drag ropes on, so they could get a chance at the fine mesquite grass that was in abundance around the camp, while the men were getting through with breakfast. They had kept their horses tied up during the night. After breakfast was over, the men who had turned their horses loose set out to gather them up, most of them being out of sight in the mesquite bushes. Andrew and his brother, John, who had also turned their horses loose, set out together, and finding them on the hill-side, near the Seguin and San Antonio road, concluded to play a joke on the boys by charging down the road and shouting "Indians!" just to see a stir in camp, and as they did so, saw the men running here and there grabbing guns, and some coming towards them.

Thinking they had carried the prank far enough, they had stopped their horses and commenced laughing, but hearing the clatter of horses' feet behind them, looked back, and what was their astonishment to find that they were closely pursued by two Indians, and what commenced in fun ended in reality, as they dashed into camp and secured their rifles. The Indians made no halt, but dashed on across a small bridge which spanned the ditch below the ranger camp and shot a Mexican woman in the suburbs of the town. They then wheeled and ran back to make their escape, as the rangers had saddled up and commenced mounting. French Smith ran down to the crossing of the ditch to intercept them, and was in fifteen or twenty steps of them when they crossed, and, leveling his double-barreled shotgun loaded with buckshot, was almost certain of killing both of them, as they rode close together, but unfortunately his gun had got damp through the night, and both barrels misssd fire. The Indians were pursued and fired at by other members of the party, but without effect, and seeing a large body of Indians swarming across the hills, Captain Hays was notified, who came out from town and followed the Indians, but his force was entirely too small to engage them, as the Indians numbered about 500, and he abandoned the pursuit.

In the meantime, the rangers had missed one of their men, James Campbell, and search was made for him in

the mesquite and chaparral bushes east of town, for he
had gone that way in search of his horse, and fears were
entertained that he had been killed by the Comanches.
But for some time their search was in vain, and finally
they came across two little Mexican boys who were
making their way to town as fast as they could run, and
seemed greatly frightened and nearly out of breath.
They said they were hunting for some calves, and seeing
some Indians, hid in the thick chaparral brush, and
while there, the Indians ran a man down the hill and
caught up with him near where they were hid. They
said he has a big, tall man, with long arms, and having
nothing to shoot with, stopped at a pile of rocks, and
fought the Indians with them as long as he could stand
up, but being shot full of arrows, he finally sunk down,
and the Indians went to him and run their lances through
his body. They said he hurt some of the Indians badly
with the rocks. The rangers knew the man was Jim
Campbell, and asked the little Mexicans to guide them
to the place, which they did ; they found Campbell horribly mutilated and scalped, and with a curse on the bloody
fiends, the rangers bore their dead comrade back to camp,
and there lay his rifle and pistol which he thought-
lessly left behind when he started after his horse, and the
report of which would have brought assistance in this his
dire extremity.

Andrew was in San Antonio when a treaty was made
with the Comanches. They had promised that on a
certain day they would come to San Antonio, make a
treaty with the whites, and give up some prisoners which
they had in their possession. They came at the time
appointed but failed to bring the prisoners. The council
was held in a large building, and as the Indians were in
considerable force, a squad of rangers and citizens were

placed around the house to aid the peace commissioners if it should break up in a row, as some had conjectured it would.

The council was long and tedious. The Comanches were very exacting in their demands on the whites, and when asked why they did not bring the captives according to promise, would give no satisfactory answer. Finally the whites told the interpreter to tell them that they would hold them in custody if the captives were not forthcoming. The interpreter did not like to tell them this, and said to the commissioners: " They are going to fight if I tell them this, and they are going to get out of here, and some one will get hurt." However, he was told to make known to them what they had said, and as soon as he did so the Indians drew their weapons and made for the door, yelltng and striking down who ever opposed them, but the armed men outside were prepared for them, and commenced firing as soon as they cleared the house. The Indians made no regular stand to fight, but scattered and attempted to make their escape from the town, but the most of them were killed. One citizen killed two with an ax as they were trying to crawl through the crack of a fence. Several of the whites were killed and wounded.

One Indian, being hard-pressed, ran into a two-story house, and fixed himself in such a position that only one man could approach him at a time, and knowing that it would be death to the first one that entered, for the Indian was well-armed, they concluded that it was no use to give a white man's life for the Indian, and thought best to devise some plan to get him without so much risk, and finally the following means were adopted: Taking a large augur they went up stairs and bored a hole through the floor over his head. The Indian knowing he would be shot if he ran out, remained quiet while the work was going on, and awaited the issue. After the hole was bored through, they could see his black bushy head directly under them. They procured some tar and turpentine and poured it through on his head. saturating it good. The Indian knew that if he changed his position he would expose himself to somebody's rifle, and concluded to stand the tar and turpentine. But he knew not what was coming. Suddenly a lighted match was dropped on his head, and in a few seconds his hair was in a terrible blaze. This was more than he could stand, and with a loud yell, he bolted from his hiding place and ran into the street, but was soon shot down. Andrew says when he ran out his head was blazing like a bonfire, and presented a fearful looking sight.

When not in the ranging service, Andrew spent most of his time in attending stock, farming a little and hunting a great deal. He was ever ready to mount his horse at the first alarm of Indians or Mexicans, and with his long rifle before him, would ride day and night to a rendezvous where the pioneers would be concentrating to oppose the progress of Indians or Mexicans.

In 1840, the Comanche Indians made a raid through Texas with 500 warriors, and burned the little town of Linnville, on the coast, killing a number of the inhabitants, and carrying others into captivity. Runners were sent up the Guadalupe, San Marcos and Colorado, calling on the settlers to concentrate at some point and fight them on their return. Andrew Sowell was among the Guadalupe boys who promptly obeyed the call and set out to the place of rendezvous, which was on Plum creek, in what is now Caldwell county.

The "American Sketch Book" says:

"The Indians passed through what is now Caldwell county, which was not organized until eight years afterward, and reached

Victoria on the 6th of August, and after burning part of the town and committing other depredations, went on to Linnville, a trading point on the Lavacca bay, and reached that place on the 8th. Most of the men of the village were absent, and the savages proceeded to pillage and burn the place. Three families took refuge on a small sail vessel in the harbor. While Major Watts, collector of customs, was trying to reach the vessel, he was shot down and his wife was taken prisoner. From Linnville the Indians hastily withdrew with their valuable booty."

As the news of this raid spread through the settlements, the people rallied under their favorite leaders to intercept them. Plum creek was the place of rendezvous, near where the town of Lockhart is now situated, in Caldwell county.

Mr. Z. N. Morrell, in speaking of this fight, says:

"We made our trip up the Colorado valley as rapidly as we could to Bastrop, notifying everybody as we went. Here Colonel Burleson called a council, and it was agreed that the Indians should be intercepted in their retreat at Goods, on Plum creek, twenty-seven miles below Austin. Colonel Burleson requested me to follow up the express man to Austin and urge the people to come forward promptly to the point designated. Here I rested at night, after a circuitous ride to Austin of about seventy miles. In the morning, rising early, we rode to the point designated, and found Colonel Burleson and his men had been gone about thirty minutes. Riding very rapidly, we came upon the Texas forces some two or three miles (as well as we could remember) southeast of the present locality of Lockhart, and at the forks of Plum creek.

"Here was concentrated the companies of Captain Ben and Henry McCulloch, Clark L. Owen, Edward Burleson, Mathew Caldwell, Thomas W. Ward, W. B. Dewees, Jack Hays, John H. Moore, and others, who were on the ground. General Felix Houston was in command, and preparations were being made for the fight, when I, with the company from Austin, rode up. The Indians had just started their pack-mules and were preparing to follow, when they were attacked by the Texans. The Indians hastily retreated; as they could not carry off their prisoners they shot them. Mrs. Crosby, taken near Victoria, was killed. The fight opened with about 200 Texans, against what we thought to be 500 Indians. The enemy was disposed to keep at a distance and delay the fight in order that the pack mules might be driven ahead with the spoils. During this delay, some of their chiefs performed some daring feats.

"According to a previous understanding, our men watched for the Indians to retreat beyond the timber, before the general charge was made. One of these daring chiefs attracted my attention specially. He was riding a very fine horse, held in by a fine American bit, with a red ribbon eight or ten feet long, tied to the tail of the horse. He was dressed in elegant style from the goods stolen at Linnville, with a high top silk hat, fine pair of boots and leather gloves, an elegant broadcloth coat hind part before, with brass buttons shining brightly right up and down his back. When first he made his appearance, he was carrying a large umbrella stretched. This Indian, and others, would charge towards us and shoot their arrows, then wheel and run away, doing no damage. This was done several times in range of our guns. Soon the discovery was made that he had on a shield, and although our men took good aim, the balls glanced. An old Texan living in Lavacca, asked me to hold his horse, and getting near the place where they wheeled as was safe, waited patiently until they came, and as the Indian checked his horse, the shield flew up, and he fired and brought him down. Several had fallen before, but without checking their demonstrations. Now, although several of them lost their lives in carrying him away, yet they did not cease their efforts until he was carried in the rear.

"Their policy was now discovered, and Colonel Burleson with his command on the right wing, was ordered around the woods, and Captain Caldwell, on the left, with his command, charged into the woods. Immediately they began howling like wolves, and there was a general stampede and a vigorous pursuit. The weather was very dry and the dust so thick that the parties could not see each other but a short distance. Some fourteen or fifteen Indians were killed before the retreat, and a great many more were killed afterwards. Our men followed them some fifteen or eighteen miles.

"Just as the retreat commenced, I heard a scream of a female voice, in a bunch of bushes close by. Approaching the spot, I discovered a lady endeavoring to pull an arrow that was lodged firmly in her breast. This proved to be Mrs. Watts, whose husband was killed at Linnville. Dr. Brown, of Gonzales, was at once summoned to the spot. Near by was discovered a white and negro woman, both dead. They were all shot with arrows when the howl was raised and the retreat commenced. As the doctor was approaching, I succeeded in loosening her hands from the arrow. The dress and flesh on each side of the arrow was cut, and an effort was made to extract it. The poor sufferer seized the doctor's hand, and screamed so violently, that he desisted. A second effort was made with success. My blanket was spread upon the ground, and she rested on this with my saddle for a pillow. She was soon composed and rejoicing at the escape. Death would have been preferable to crossing the mountains with the savages. She had ridden a pack mule all the way from the coast, and when they stopped she was required to read the stolen books for their amusement.

" When we went into the fight, there were present about 200 Texans, but before night we suppose there were near 500. They continued to come in all evening, many of them from a great distance. Men and boys of every variety of character, composed that noisy crowd, that was busily engaged all night long talking of the transactions of the previous eventful days. Here were the Baptist preachers, R. E. B. Baylor, T. W. Cox, and Z. N. Morrell, all in the fight, with doctors, lawyers, merchants and farmers."

Captain Ben McCulloch and Dr. Switzer were the greatest of enemies. During the Plum Creek fight, just as McCulloch was loading his gun, an Indian was seen by Dr. Switzer in the act of killing him. He rushed up and shot the Indian just in the act, but McCulloch never once turned to thank him for the saving of his life ; though in a few moments McCulloch found Dr. Switzer in a like perilous situation, and in like manner the Indian was killed by him. It this way he returned thanks for the kindness, but neither one spoke to the other. W. B. Dewees says that among the spoils taken from these Comanches were found large portions of human flesh, evidently prepared for cooking. And also were found in their bundles, young alligators that they were carrying back with them, some thought as a curiosity, and others thought it was to prove to the rest of the tribe that they had gone down as far as the coast.

Dewees said that one woman, who was taken prisoner by these Indians, told him that two of her children had been taken with her. One of them being very small, hindered her progress. The Indians perceiving this, one of them snatched it from her and dashed its brains out against a tree. The wretched mother kept on her course grieving sadly, yet not daring to utter a word of complaint. Soon her other child, that had been placed on a horse, manifested evident signs of failing strength, and an inability to keep up with the savages. Then the mother's feelings were destined to undergo fresh trials. The cup was filled to the brim, and she was forced to drink the bitter draught; her fortitude was put to another test, and wrought up to the highest pitch. The Indians perceiving the failing strength of the child, fell upon him with their spears, and having deprived him of the last flickering flame of life, cast his mangled corpse aside to be food for the hungry vultures. Who can paint the agonies of that mother's feelings, as she beheld both her little ones destroyed in this brutal manner by the hands of her savage masters? Her own safety required her to witness this horrid spectacle with composure; one word of murmur or complaint from her would have caused them to put her to instant death.

After this fight the Indians were never very bad in this country; though they would occasionally come in and steal horses.

In 1847, old Mr. Montgomery was killed by Indians while out hunting horses.

Andrew Sowell said when they were fixing to go into the fight, General Felix Houston told the men to ram an

xtra ball down their rifles without patching, and if they
ecame thirsty during the fight to hold one in their mouths.

In this fight, Andrew killed an Indian chief. He fired
t him more than a hundred yards off, just as the Indian
vheeled his horse and exposed his back. He fell forward,
ut was caught up by others and borne away.

He says while they were pursuing them after the rout
ommenced, an Indian had his horse killed, and ran on
oot about thirty yards, when suddenly turning around,
hrew up his shield, and came back in a quick run to his
lead horse. Andrew, who was close upon him, fired,
ut heard the ball strike the shield. The Indian then
matched the bridle off his dead horse, and turning, ran
ike a streak with the bridle in his hand; but another
nan dashing up with a loaded rifle, fired and brought
im down. Andrew examined the shield of the dead
ndian, and saw the slick mark on it made by his ball.
The Indian had risked and lost his life for a bridle not
vorth more than two dollars.

While the men were scattered in small squads, pur-
uing the flying Comanches, Andrew, with several others,
aw a band of about fifteen Indians running up a slight
elevation about a quarter of a mile off, and close behind
hem, going under whip, was a man, who, from his horse
nd hat, they took to be Ben McCulloch, and one of
hem shouted, "Look at Ben McCulloch, he is run-
ing a whole gang of them! hurrah for Ben!" and then
hey all yelled, "Hurrah for Ben McCulloch!" as
hey saw the man close upon the heels of the flying Indians,
ut what was their surprise, when they saw him mix in
vith them and go on. It was an Indian riding a horse
he color of Ben's, and wearing a broad-brimmed hat,
vhich he had got at the sacking of Linnville. Andrew
kept with the chase until his horse was run down, and

14

then collecting a crowd of Guadalupe men, set out for their return home. One of the men from Seguin, James Nichols, was shot between the fore and middle finger, while in the act of shooting at an Indian. The ball was cut out at the wrist, and as the wound healed the two fingers grew together up to the first joint. He is still living and draws a pension. Among the noted men that participated in this battle was "Big Foot Wallace." In this battle Captain Mathew Caldwell was fighting Indians on the soil that was afterwards organized into a county and named after him.

In the fall, after this battle with the Indians, Colonel John H. Moore collected about 100 men and followed the trail of the Comanches, which led up the Colorado river, and on the 24th of October, came upon their village, 300 miles above Austin. A terrible slaughter of Indians took place. They fled in every direction, and suffered a more severe defeat than they did at Plum creek. One hundred and twenty-eight were killed and drowned in the river together, and thirty-four captured, besides 500 head of horses. The loss of Colonel Moore was small, and he and his party returned safely to the settlements with their booty. The old veteran Pleasant McAnelly was in this fight, and now resides in Guadalupe county, and so do other worthy veterans. John F. McGuffin, E. V. Dale, Thomas D. James, Pendleton Rector, Gustav Elly, and John A. Wells, also reside in this county. McAnelly says when they drew near to the Indian village, the friendly Indians who were with them, were sent ahead to find them, and when they returned stating that the Comanches were just ahead, Colonel Moore gave orders for a quick, but silent advance, so as to surprise them, but the friendly Indians seeing the white men advancing to the charge, fell back in the rear and set up a terrible

ᵣelling, which alarmed the hostiles, and when the rangers
lashed into the village, they had left it, and were attempt-
ng to cross the river.

CHAPTER X.

" THEY came, impatient for the fight;
    Burning to rush into the slaughter;
    Ready to pour their blood like water,
    For what they deemed the right."

SAN ANTONIO CAPTURED BY GENERAL WALL — GATHER-
ING OF THE SETTLERS—BATTLE OF THE SALADO —IN-
CIDENTS — MASSACRE OF DAWSON'S MEN — THE FUGI-
TIVE FROM THE BATTLE-GROUND—DESPERATE RIDING
—KILLING A MEXICAN LANCER.

ON September, 11, 1842, the Mexicans under General
Adrian Wall, very unexpectedly to the Texans, advanced
and captured San Antonio. The district court was in
session, and the members were taken prisoners. The
news flew down the country, and spread from settlement
to settlement, and, once more the call to arms was
sounded along the border to repel Mexican invasion.
This call was, as ever, promptly obeyed by the brave
pioneers of the Guadalupe, San Marcos, and Colorado
valleys. And once more the gallant Hays, Caldwell and
others, rallied their chosen scouts and rangers around
them. They rendezvoused at Seguin, and all night long
before the start on the following day, men were up busy
making preparations to meet once more the dusky sons
of Mexico on the battle-field. There was a great scarcity
of horses on account of the recent Indian raids, and men
gave large sums for Spanish ponies that would carry
them to San Antonio. All night men were coming in
from the east, and but few slept that night. Rifles were

cleaned, bullets moulded and provisions cooked. Those that had no horses were going here and there trying to make trades, offering land, and anything they possessed for ponies, which could now be bought for $25. Two men fought over a stray horse which happened to be in town until neither one was able to go. Andrew Sowell was sick at this time, and told his brother, Asa, whose horse had been stolen by Indians, that he might have his horse as he was not able to go, but next morning when they were about to start, said he could not stand it, and, rising from his bed, dressed himself, got his rifle and pistols, and was soon on his way to the Salado.

Mathew Caldwell was in command of the force, which amounted to about 200 men. Caldwell advanced to the Salado, and took up a strong position on this creek, about seven miles northeast of San Antonio.

While encamped here, Creed Taylor went down to the creek, a short distance below the camp, for the purpose of washing out his shirt, and not having a change in camp, had to wait for it to dry. While doing so, he ascended a pecan tree, for the purpose of filling his pockets with pecans, but as soon as he arose above the level of the prairie, was fired at from camp, the balls cutting the limbs around him. He hastened down, donned his half dry shirt, and proceeding to camp, demanded an explanation, and was told that some Irish recruits from Goliad, who had just arrived, had taken him for a Mexican spying out the camp, and commenced the fusilade upon him.

Captain Jack Hays then advanced with about fifty men to San Antonio, and drew the Mexicans out. In his (Captain J. C. Hay's) company, H. E. McCulloch was first lieutenant, and C. B. Acklin orderly sergeant. They were chased back from within half a mile of the Alamo, by 400 cavalry, to the Salado. McCulloch covered the retreat with ten picked men, and they had a lively time. The names of the ten men are as follows : William Polk, Green McCoy, Stuart Foley, C. B. Acklin, Cloy Davis, Creed Taylor, Josiah Taylor, Pipkin Taylor, Rufus Taylor, and James Taylor. The Mexicans made a desperate effort to cut Hays off, by passing up on his right flank. McCulloch kept between him and the Mexicans, sending couriers every half mile or so urging him to put for the timber, and finally when the timber was reached, McCulloch had only one man with him, Creed Taylor. These two were targets for the Mexicans for the last half mile, and at from 150 to 200 paces, there must have been from 100 to 200 shots fired at them on the run, but fortunately not a ball struck man or horse; but Creed Taylor was wounded in the battle which followed on the creek. The men in camp had killed some beef cattle and were engaged in cooking and eating when Hays and McCulloch dashed in, closely pursued by the Mexican cavalry. Every man was soon at his post and ready for action. The whole Mexican army then advanced from San Antonio, and crossing the creek, took up a position on the hill-side, east of Caldwell's position. There they planted a battery and opened fire on the Texans, but without effect; for Caldwell's men were protected by the creek bank, behind which they were formed. The only danger they had to guard against was the falling limbs which the cannon shots tore off from the large pecan trees over their heads. Seeing he could not dislodge them with artillery, the Mexican commander ordered a charge. The Texans as yet had not fired a shot. The cannons ceased, bugles sounded, and the rush of tramping feet was heard in the flat, as the Mexicans advanced to the charge. Caldwell gave orders for half the men to reserve their fire, while those in front were to step back after a discharge and reload, while those with loaded rifles were to man the bank. The Mexicans had to advance very close before they could see the Texans; and then firing their escopetes, they fell back before the deadly fire of the rifles. A loud, keen yell went up from the Texans as the Mexicans broke and dashed back in disordered squads out of range, leaving quite a number killed and wounded behind them. They rallied again on the crest of the ridge and formed, and the officers were seen riding to and fro among them. The Texans elated with their success, had no fears of the final issue, although greatly outnumbered. They continued to whoop and yell at the Mexicans, and some resumed their repast of beef, bread and strong coffee, which had been interrupted by the advance of the Mexican army. The Mexican cavalry kept dashing about and prancing around, but kept out of range. Finally they stopped on the hill some distance up the creek. Green McCoy noticing this, came to Andrew Sowell and proposed to him that they would lead their horses up the creek a short distance, tie them so that they would be at hand in case of need, and then slip within rifle shot of the Mexican cavalry, get a good shot each, and then fall back to their horses, and make their escape in case they were pursued. Andrew agreed to this readily, and they left the camp, keeping out of sight of the Mexicans until they went far enough, and then tied their horses to a mesquite tree. They could see part of the cavalry through the bushes, not far off, and bending low, started to slip within range. They had taken but a few steps when they were started by a low, keen whistle near them, and hastily looking around, saw a company of Mexican infantry in fifty paces of them, where they had been concealed in the high grass, and

had just risen up and whistled to them like a hunter
would to a deer, to make it stop until he could shoot it.
They saw the Mexicans were fixing to fire, and sprang
towards their horses, and bent low for a few seconds
and received the first fire. The bark and mesquite beans
fell on their hats which were cut off by the bullets, but
neither one of them was touched, and drawing their
knives, quick as lightning almost, cut their ropes and
mounted the terrified horses, which had begun to rear
and plunge about. They were young, active and good
riders, or else they would never have been able to mount
under the circumstances. They received the second fire
from the Mexicans as they bent low in their saddles and
dashed off. The balls cut the air around them, but still
they were unhurt. Andrew ventured one look behind
as they started, and some of the Mexicans were so near
that he said he could see half-way down the barrels of
the big-mouthed escopetes as the Mexicans presented
them to fire. They dashed into camp just as the Mexicans were again advancing to charge; but as before, they
could not stand the unerring aim of the riflemen, and
were again driven back with great loss. General Cordova, whom Burleson fought at Mill creek, was killed in
the charge. He had taken refuge behind a small mesquite in the retreat, to avoid a discharge, and was killed
when he attempted to leave it. Cordova was a noted
man in Mexico, and on receipt of the news of his death,
the bells were rung in Monterey, and an ode was published to his memory at Saltillo. (Sal-teé-o). The
Texans, as yet, had not lost a man, and had but few
wounded. The Mexicans invariably overshot them,
knocking over more coffee pots, which were in the rear,
than Texans. Calvin Turner received a glancing shot in
the head, and fell; his brother, William, who was near,

vainly endeavoring to force a tight ball down his rifle, dropped it, and ran to him, and assisted him to regain his feet, and he soon recovered. The Mexicans, who had been freely supplied with mescal from San Antonio, and being now pretty much under the influence of it, somewhat lost their terror of the Texas rifles, and once more advanced to the charge, yelling like Indians. They threw away their hats and came down the hill bare-headed, and with their dark skins and black hair, very much resembled a host of savages. They made no halt when fired on, but came on like demons, firing their escopetes in the very faces of Caldwell's men, at not more than fifteen paces, and for a few moments the cracking of rifles and the yells of the combatants were terrific. But drunk or sober, they could not stand such a deadly fire at short range, and again fled out of reach, followed by scattering shots and loud yells.

It seems somewhat surprising that Caldwell's 200 men could defeat such a large force of Mexicans, numbering nearly a thousand men, but their superior marksmanship was one thing; and they were all true and tried men; had all seen service before, some having been with Bowie at Mission Concepcion and the storming of San Antonio; some in the charge at San Jacinto and Plum Creek, and nearly all had fought Indians, and were splendid shots. And here were the gallant Caldwell, Hays, and the McCullochs, whom none could surpass as commanders in such warfare. Santa Anna, while a prisoner, and bit-terly lamenting the destruction of his army, said: "Why, a Texan would think he had made a bad shot if he did not hit a Mexican's eye a hundred yards."

During the retreat, after this charge, one Mexican being considerably behind, some one called out, "Who has a loaded rifle?" Andrew Sowell, who had just loaded, stepped forward and took a careful aim at the retreating Mexican, and fired. At the crack of the gun the Mexican jumped forward, clapped his hands to his back, and after running half bent for a short distance, fell forward on his face. Miles Dikes, who was standing just behind Andrew, watching the effect of the shot, clapped him on the shoulder, and said: "There; that's the way to do it Andrew; you got him."

In this last charge a good many Mexicans were killed and wounded near the bank of the creek, behind which the Texans were posted. French Smith, who was walking about among them, picked up a small wounded Mexican and brought him down the hill into the camp and laid him down. He was a small man, and had on a fancy jacket. He was shot in the breast, and was suffering great pain. He jabbered Mexican all the time, and eyed the long rifles of the Texans, who stood around him, and when some one lit a pipe and commenced smoking, he, with great pain, raised himself to a sitting position, and asked for a shuck and some tobacco, and this being given him, made a cigarette, and calmly sat there and smoked it, with a rifle ball through his body, occasionally making some remark in Spanish, and pointing to the wound in his breast.

Just before the fight commenced, one of Caldwell's scouts, named Jett, was cut off from the camp and killed by a small band of Indians, who were secreted in the brush down the creek.

One man was shot in the stomach, who had that morning eaten a large quantity of fresh beef, and after the doctor had examined him, said it was the most fortunate shots he ever saw. "For," said he, "if it had not been for the beef, the bullet would have killed him, and if it had not been for the bullet, the beef would have killed him."

During the progress of the fight, the Texans noticed that the Mexicans moved their artillery, also the cavalry, and a portion of the infantry, and presently they heard cannon shots in the prairie some distance to the east of them. Boom after boom came ringing across the prairie, and the Texans were satisfied that some brave band of men had encountered the Mexicans in trying to join them. But they dared not move from their position for here was the only place where they could successfully fight Wall's army, with his superior force, flanked by large bodies of cavalry, and supported with artillery, which was between them and the brave men who were at this time selling their lives so dearly. Swift scouts were kept out to watch the movements of the Mexicans, who disappeared from sight after the firing ceased on the prairie, and left Caldwell master of the situation on the creek.

A scout came in and reported that the Mexican army had gone back to San Antonio. A small party was then sent out to see what discoveries they could make in the direction of the firing, which they heard on the prairie east of them. One fugitive, Woods, gained Caldwell's line, and reported that Captain Dawson and his company of fifty-two men from Fayette county, had been surrounded and cut to pieces by the Mexicans. The scouts sent out, returned, and reported that thirty-two of Dawson's men were lying dead on the prairie. Z. N. Morrell, the Baptist preacher who was at the Plum Creek fight, was here, with Caldwell, and knowing that Dawson's men were from his neighborhood, and fearing that his son, whom he had left at home, might have followed the ill-fated Dawson, mounted his horse, and in company with others, set out for the scene of the massacre to examine the slain, and to see if his boy was there. The Rev. Morrell was not at home when he heard of the

Mexican raid, and came with Caldwell, without acquaint-
ing his family of his intentions, as they were some distance off.

Some one told Andrew Sowell that they thought his
father-in-law, old man Billy Turner, was among the
slain. Andrew knowing the vim of the old man when
stirred up, for he had been a soldier under Jackson, and
was one of the dragoons who pursued the great chief
Weatherford after his defeat, when he made his famous
leap off the bluff into the river, and made his escape.

(Massacre of Dawson's Men.)

He saw Sam Houston wounded at the battle of the Horse
Shoe, and was himself wounded at Talladega and Talla-
hasse, and was with Jackson at New Orleans. Although
Andrew could hardly believe it could be the old man, for
he left him at Seguin, he hastily mounted his horse and
set out, and on reaching the battle-ground and viewing
the dead body of the gray-haired old man, it proved to be
Zodack Woods, an old man eighty years of age, from
La Grange.

Z. N. Morrell searched among the dead for his son,

and, greatly to his relief, could not find him, but he looked into the faces of his neighbors whom, a few days before, he had left at their homes in good health, and with a prospect of long life before them, now stark and stiff in the battle-field.

These gallant patriots from the Colorado valley, were ever ready to peril their lives for their country, and there was hardly a battle of any importance fought in Texas, but what their blood stained the soil. And when the fiery Dawson came among them, they seized their rifles, and told him to lead the way, and rushed day and night to their death.

Yoakum says of this affair:

"Just as the fight ceased between Captain Mathew Caldwell's command and the Mexicans, the fearful massacre occurred. Captain Dawson, with fifty-three men from La Grange, in attempting to join Caldwell, was discovered and surrounded by the enemy. Captain Dawson found a grove of mesquite bushes, in which he rallied his men and commenced his defense; but the Mexicans withdrew from the range of the rifles, and poured in upon his unprotected company, a shower of grape-shot. Dawson sent out a white flag but it was fired on. Thirty-two of his men were killed, two or three escaped, and fifteen were taken prisoners. Among those that escaped was Woods, who, in the act of delivering up his arms, received a cut from a sword. He seized a lance in the hands of one of the enemy, killed the lancer, mounted his horse, and reached the position of Caldwell, in safety."

CHAPTER XI.

INCIDENTS OF THE DAWSON MASSACRE—CAPTURE OF THE PUTNAM CHILDREN BY INDIANS — THE UNSUCCESSFUL PURSUIT—DEATH OF AN OLD VETERAN — CONCLUSION.

THE people of Seguin watched anxiously for messengers from the scene of action, after the departure of the 200 brave boys under the gallant Caldwell.

Only six years had elapsed since nearly that many had perished in the Alamo with the gallant Travis, and they had left as light-hearted and confident as those under Caldwell. And once more the wives and mothers of the Guadalupe valley had to watch and wait with aching hearts for news, every minute expecting the messenger of death to dash in upon them, bringing the sad news of defeat and slaughter like that which befell Travis and Fannin. And they thought their fears were realized when Aulcy Miller rode into town bareheaded and his horse covered with foam, a fugitive from Dawson's battle-ground, and bringing the news that Dawson's men were nearly all killed, and that he, himself, and one other, alone made their escape by hard and desperate riding. He knew nothing of the fate of Caldwell's men. They heard heavy firing in the direction of the creek, and were pushing rapidly to their assistance, when they were surrounded by the whole Mexican army and cut to pieces. Asa Sowell, father of the writer, gave Miller a fine Mexican hat.

The following is taken from the American Sketch Book:

" We are indebted to Major B. P. Dunn for the the names of

those that were killed from Fayette county with Captain Dawson, on the 18th of September, 1842. They are as follows: Captain Dawson, First Lieutenant Dickerson, Zodack Woods, David Berry, John Slack, John Cummins, ———— Church, Harvey Hall, Robert Barckley, Wesley Scallorn, Eliam Scallorn, Asa Jones, Robert Eastland, Frank Brookfield, George Hill, John W. Penelton, J. B. Alexander, Edmond Timble, Charles Field, Thomas Simms, ———— Butler, John Dancer, and a colored man belonging to the Mavericks. He had been sent out by Mrs. Maverick to communicate with his master, who had been captured while attending court at San Antonio, a few days before, by the Mexicans. His family were living on the Colorado, near Ed. Manton's. They had sent this trusty man out, hoping that he might be able to learn something of Maverick. Poor fellow! faithful to his trust to the last, he died with his brave leader, his face to the enemy at the breech of his gun.

"Zodack Woods, eighty years old, had ridden in a gallop for several miles, keeping up with his company, before reaching the scene of action, eager to relieve Caldwell, bounding on over the prairie to find, too late, that they had mistaken the enemy for our forces. The old man fell while loading his gun."

The bones of these brave men now rest on Monument Hill, opposite La Grange. We quote what the publisher of the American Sketch Book says in describing a trip to this place:

"While on the bluff, what strange feelings of awe I had while standing at the tomb of that band of heroes (the remains of Captain Dawson's company, and the decimated prisoners), who, when the first tocsin of war sounded, left their homes and loved ones, and, after deeds worthy of the ancient Romans, immolated themselves upon the altar of Freedom. It was with regret I stood by the pile of stone where ' memory o'er their tomb no trophies raise,' to tell the stranger their glorious record of how they lived, dared and died. Certainly, the day is not far distant when Fayette county will erect a handsome monument to the memory of her brave sons."

General Wall did not halt long in San Antonio, but set out the next day after the battle, and soon put the Rio

Grande between him and the infuriated Texans. The Mexican loss in the battle was 120 men killed and wounded. Caldwell entered San Antonio next day with his men. There was a Mexican woman in San Antonio at that time, who had once lived on the Guadalupe, near Seguin, and was acquainted with nearly all the settlers. When General Wall paraded his men on the plaza, just before starting to attack Caldwell on the Salado, she walked out where he was inspecting his troops, and asked him where he was going with all this fine array of soldiers: " Going out," said he, " to kill those Texans on the Sala-do." " You had better be very careful," said the woman, " I know those men from the Guadalupe ; they are very brave men, and shoot well." When Wall came back, she again accosted him with, " Well, General, did you kill all of those Texans ? " " Well, yes ; " said he, " that is, I killed all those out on the prairie, but those on the creek howled like wolves, and fought like devils. I did not kill quite all of them." This Mexican woman was a friend of the Texans, and was glad to see them when they came into town, going about among them, and calling a great many of them by name. When she saw the Baptist preacher, Z. N. Morrell, she said: " Oh, Mr. Morrell ; I stood here on the sidewalk and looked at the prisoners as they marched them up the street, and your son was with them ; he had his coat off, and was all bloody." What sad news was this to an affectionate father, his son, a mere boy, wounded and being carried a prisoner to Mexico, away from home, and loved ones, to languish as a captive in a foreign land, in dark and dreary dungeons, and, perchance, in the end, to be led out and shot as others had been before him.

Among those who stood by the gallant Caldwell at the Salado, were the following : Captain Jack Hays, Daniel

B. Frior, James H. Callahan, James Bird, Ewing Cam-
meron, Lieutenant Henry McCulloch, Sergeant C. B.
Acklin, C. C. Colley, John Henry Brown, Jesse Zumawlt,
Clem C. Hines, Eli Hankins, Joe Powers, Solomon Sim-
mons, Rev. Karl, Cattle Perry, Stokes, Judge Hemphill,
Henry Bridger, Isaac Zumawlt, John H. Livergood,
George Walton, Wilcox, John W. Smith, Ezekiel Smith,
Solomon Brill, Archer Gibson, Creed Taylor, Josiah
Taylor, Pipkin Taylor, Rufus Taylor, James Taylor,
Green McCoy, James Clark, Miles Dikes, Calvin Tur-
ner, Hardin Turner, William Turner, French Smith, Z.
N. Morrell, A. J. Sowell, William King, John King,
Milford Day, and many other gallant men whose names
I could not learn.

After the battle, Lieutenant McCulloch was left in
charge of the wounded, some ten or twelve in number,
and as he had no wagons, was sorely perplexed as to the
means for transporting the wounded men from the battle-ground, and while trying to devise some plan, Solomon Brill came along with a cart and team which he had
captured, and which contained several pairs of blankets,
and in this rude structure the lieutenant succeeded in
carrying off the wounded men.

The prisoners taken at Dawson's massacre were carried
to Mexico and confined in the dungeon of Perote, and it
was two years before the Rev. Morrell saw his son again.

As the Mexicans were once more driven from Texas
soil, the men dispersed and returned to their homes.
Andrew Sowell, after this, spent part of his time in the
ranging service, under Captain Henry McCulloch, and
was stationed for some time in Hamilton's valley, on the
Colorado, about sixty miles above Austin, but was in no
important engagement with the Indians. After this, he
moved to San Marcos, a small place just starting at the

15

head of the river of the same name.   He was living here when the Indians captured the Putnam children, while they were gathering pecans, below the town.   Andrew and several others, trailed the Indians until they crossed the Guadalupe, at the mouth of the Comal, where the German city of New Braunfels is now situated, but here they lost the trail, as it entered a rough mountainous country, and they were obliged to abandon the pursuit.

The children were two girls, and a boy, James.   The latter was purchased by traders and sent back about eight years afterwards.   The oldest girl in the meantime had become the wife of a chief, and would not come back. The other sister returned when she was a middle–aged woman, to Gonzales.   James says the Indians carried him all over Texas, Arizona and California, and often when he was left with the squaws on some high mountain, he had seen them fighting with the immigrants and Santa Fe traders on the plains below.   When James first came back, he would neither sit in a chair, sleep on a bed, or eat with a knife and fork, and it was impossible to slip up on him.

In 1852, Andrew, in company with several other families, moved and settled in a beautiful valley on the Blanco river.   They carried some stock with them, and, indeed, it was a country that flowed with milk and honey; for it was while living here that he found twenty-seven bee trees in one day.   Besides that, the country abounded in deer, turkey, bear, and antelope, and the streams were full of fish.   This place still goes by the name of Sowell valley.   From here, he moved back to his old place below Seguin, where he still owned some land, and commenced farming, but becoming dissatisfied, he sold out, and moved to Nash's creek, twelve miles east of Seguin.   At the breaking out of the war between the

North and South, he joined the Confederate army, but was in no important battles. When the war closed he returned home, and turned his attention to stock-raising and farming. He belonged to the Veteran Association, and drew a pension. When the Veterans met at Waco, in 1882, he somewhat surprised some of the good people of Waco by telling them the last time he was there before this, a tribe of Indians lived there, and they called it the Waco village, after the name of the tribe. And also at Houston, when the Veterans met there, he made some of them stare by telling them that he helped to nail the boards on the first house that was ever built in Houston. He died in 1883, honored and respected by all who knew him. His wife survived him only a few days.

It is strange, but nevertheless true, that nearly all the old Texans lived hard at times and died poor. They fought the battles, subdued the wilderness, and paved the way for others to come in and make fortunes, which thousands have done, since the hardy pioneers first pitched their cabins on the banks of the Guadalupe, Colorado, San Marcos and Brazos. And now, in winding up this brief sketch of life and times on the Texas frontier, I will say to my readers, that I trust they will not think it boasting or egotism in me to have penned a few lines in memory of an old Texan, for he justly deserves all I have said of him, and, had it been any one else, not a relative, I would have as cheerfully done the same, had I been as well acquainted with the incidents as I was in this case. They will all soon be gone, and their deeds and actions will be things of the past. Therefore, let us keep their memory green. We hear of the death of some one of these heroes every few days. Colonel Jack Hays died last year, 1883, at his home near Piedmont, California. When we mention the counties of Bowie, Crockett,

Travis, Bonham, Hays, McCulloch, Burleson, Kimble, Caldwell, Lamar, Burnet, Fannin, Milam, Dewitt, and Karnes, including a host of others, it is like calling the roll of the old Veterans.

In a recent visit to Gonzales, I called on the old Texan David Darst, and spent a pleasant hour conversing about early days. He gave me several items concerning the run-away scrape, as it was called, at Gonzales, after the fall of the Alamo. I left town in company with Mr. Jack Hodge, another old Texan. When we arrived at the outskirts of the town, he pointed out to me a tall post oak tree which must have had the marks of 500 rifle balls on it, where, in early days, Henry and Ben McCulloch, Wilson and Barney Randall, Pony Hall, and others, used to engage in rifle practice.

In conclusion, I will insert the following taken from the Galveston *News:*

"Texas has an individual history exclusively its own. The archives of its old autonomy contain a heritage of honor and renown in which we, of the rest of the United States, have no part. Our lineage of 1776 inheriting its own hard-won laurels, can most graciously accord to the white-haired survivors of the struggle for Texas independence, all the honors which belong to that successful achievement. Nobly has Texas perpetuated the fame of her heroes by ingrafting their names upon one-half of its 227 counties. Recognizing them as our kith and kin, we cannot but feel as we walk among them, as if we had somehow been moved back three-quarters of a century to our forefathers; as if our good ancestors of '76 had stepped forward, and up into the halo of the present time. Let old Texas rest on her laurels. Let the mantle of peace and charity fall indulgently over the old Texan. Both are of the past."

CAMPAIGN OF THE

TEXAS RANGERS TO THE WICHITA MOUNTAINS,

IN 1871.

CHAPTER I.

"Come all you Texas Rangers,
    Where ever you may be,
And I will tell you of some troubles
    That happened unto me.

"My name is nothing extra,
    So that I will not tell;
But here's to all the Rangers,
    I am sure I wish them well.

"At the age of sixteen
    I joined that jolly band,
And marched from San Antonio
    Out to the Rio Grande.

"Our captain, he informed us,
    Perhaps he thought it right,
Before you reach the station,
    Said he, you will have to fight.

"I saw the smoke ascending,*
    It seemed to reach the sky,
And the first thought that struck me,
    Is this my time to die?

"I thought of my mother,
    Who, in tears, to me did say,
To you they are all strangers,
    With me you had better stay.

"I told her she was childish;
    The best she did not know.
My mind was bent on roving,
    And I was bound to go.

* Indian camp fires.

" I saw the Indians coming,
   I heard them give the yell.
My feelings at that moment,
   No tongue can ever tell!

" Oh! then the bugle sounded,
   Our captain gave command:
'To arms! to arms!' he shouted,
   And by your horses stand.

" I saw the Indians coming,
   The arrows round me hailed,
And for a moment, boys,
   My courage almost failed.

" I saw the glittering lances
   The painted warriors bore,
And we fought them full two hours
   Before the strife was o'er.

" Five of the noblest Rangers
   I ever saw the West,
Were buried by their comrades,
   I hope they are at rest."

In 1870-'71, the Indians were very numerous and hostile on the Texas frontier, and a call was made by the Governor for several companies of volunteers to go on a campaign against them. There was an immense scope of country to protect, stretching from the Rio Grande to Red river. The Indians were more numerous in the northwestern part of the State, and committed many depredations under the notorious leaders, Big Tree, Satanta, Sittanke, and others.

In writing this sketch, my aim is to give as near as I can an account of the true condition of the Texas border at that time, especially in the northwest, and to relate such incidents of Indian warfare, as I think would be interesting, which I learned from old settlers in that region. It was during the administration of Governor

E. J. Davis, that these companies of which I speak were raised for frontier protection. Being anxious to see some of the great State of Texas, besides the vicinity where I was raised, Seguin, Guadalupe County, I enlisted in Captain David Baker's company, and at once set out for the rangers' camp on the Salado, seven miles northeast of San Antonio, near the old battle ground. There were about sixty men in camp when we arrived, waiting to be mustered into the service. They were mostly young, unmarried men, and anxious to be off and view the red man in his native wilds.

We were mustered into the State service on the 5th day of November, 1870, and were pronounced by our mustering officer, to be one of the finest looking and best mounted companies which had been sent out. Our destination, as soon as mustered in, was the Wichita mountains, the hunting ground and camping ground of the Kiowa and Comanche Indians. The captain immediately started a detail to Austin for the purpose of procuring wagons, mules, carbines, ammunition, etc., which we needed for the trip. Our company was made up from the counties of Guadalupe, Gonzales, Caldwell, and Bexar. Our officers were D. P. Baker, captain; Asa Hill, lieutenant; William Thorn, orderly sergeant; E. H. Cobb, first duty sergeant; Joel R. Payne, second sergeant; William Murphy, Charles Robinson, Charles Figurs, and Dan Woodruff, corporals; Dr. Fred. Gillespie, physician and surgeon. John Fitzgerald was bugler.

We numbered fifty-two men, rank and file. We had to furnish our own horses, clothing, six-shooters, etc. The State furnished us carbines, cartridges, provisions, etc., and we were to get fifty dollars per month.

The detail under Sergeant Payne returned from Austin on the 18th, with six wild mules, two large wagon horses and two wagons, one of them very small. And this was the outfit for a company of Texas rangers, to traverse nearly five hundred miles of frontier country, most of it an uninhabited wilderness, over mountains, and across rivers; but the boys were in good spirits, and anxious to commence the march, and every man received a new Winchester carbine and plenty of cartridges, and everything being in readiness on the 19th, we broke camp and the long march commenced. The first day we went about ten miles, and encamped in a live oak grove. Our little mules were very contrary through the day, which somewhat retarded our progress. During the night it commenced raining and was very disagreeable, but that was only a foretaste of what was in store for us.

On the morning of the 20th, it took nearly all hands to hitch up our team, but finally we got everything ready for a start, the driver mounted, and the wagons started, the lead mules in a gallop, and the balance trying to hold back, followed by the company in fine spirits, and on prancing horses. Our team, however, soon calmed down and went tolerably well. It blew up a norther in the evening, and shortly after we camped in the timber for the night. About sundown, Captain Baker arrived from San Antonio, having remained behind to attend to some business. It was very cold during the night, but we had plenty of wood, and the boys amused themselves singing, telling yarns, playing the violin, etc., until late in the night. Next morning we called our stopping place Camp Baker, and once more we turned our faces to the northwest. It continued cold during the day, and was very disagreeable, as we had to face it.

There has been a great deal said about Texas and the rangers, and I will here give a description of the

Texas rangers, as they were at that time. In the first place he wants a good horse, strong saddle, double-girted, a good carbine, pistol, and plenty of ammunition. He generally wears rough clothing, either buckskin or strong, durable cloth, and generally a broad-brimmed hat, on the Mexican style, thick overshirt, top boots and spurs, and a jacket or short coat, so that he can use himself with ease in the saddle.

A genuine Texas ranger will endure cold, hunger and fatigue, almost without a murmur, and will stand by a friend and comrade in the hour of danger, and divide anything he has got, from a blanket to his last crumb of tobacco. This description will also suit the Texas "cow boy," who has abroad got a very bad reputation; but he is not so bad, after all. He generally settles down into a quiet, sober citizen.

When the Marquis of Lorne was with a hunting party on the Staked Plains, in 1882, he took refuge at a camp of cow boys during a violent storm, and says he was treated with the greatest civility and hospitality. They were a fine looking set of men, he said, and moved about with that air of dignity, which stamps a man as being the sovereign of the soil. He left them with his mind considerably changed in regard to them, for, heretofore, he did not wish to encounter them, but necessity compelled him and his hunting party to go to their camp.

It was the cow boys and rangers of Texas, that stood by Hood, Terry, McCulloch and Lee, in the hour of their greatest need, and bore the blood-stained banner of the South over a hundred battle fields during the late war.

Of course our Indians fights will appear rather insignificant compared to great battle fields, for instance, Wellington at Waterloo, Lee at the Wilderness, or Napoleon on the Alps, "where cannon roared above the clouds, and cavalry charged on fields of ice," but never-theless, there is sometimes more danger in an Indian fight where there are not more than two or three dozen men engaged, than where thousands fight; for when the ranger and red man meet in battle, quarter is neither asked nor given. I will here relate an incident which occurred before the war, when McCulloch, Ford, and Van Dorn, were on the Texas frontier with their rangers. They were stationed at old Fort Belknap, on the Brazos.

The report came to camp that a large body of Indians were some distance below them committing depredations. A scout of fifteen men, under a sergeant, were sent to ascertain the whereabouts of the hostiles and their num-ber; but the unfortunate sergeant was led into a trap and himself and most of his men were killed. They had pursued five Indians for some distance, and saw that they were being led in between two deep gullies, and suspecting an ambush, the sergeant gave orders to wheel and take the back track, but too late. The Indians rose up, swarmed in behind them and cut off their retreat. The sergeant and his men fought desperately, but only two succeeded in cutting their way through and getting clear of the Indians. One of them, looking back, saw his brother, a boy, of only seventeen years, fighting desperately among the Indians. For an instant he hesitated; he had got clear, and it was almost certain death to go back; but he thought of the last words of his mother when they left home: " Jimmy take good care of Dick, now, and don't you come back without him." He saw that his brother's horse was killed; saw him club his gun and beat a warrior from his horse, and make a frantic effort to secure the bridle, but failed; the horse wheeled and galloped off. This was enough for James, and he determined to rescue his brother or die with him, and setting his teeth hard, madly spurred his horse among the Indians, shouting to his brother as he did so, to spring up behind him as he wheeled his horse.

In less time it takes to write it, his brother did so, and they were speeding away, lying low on the horse, with the bullets and arrows flying thick around them. The horse was wounded in three places, but they were untouched, and made good their escape to the fort, preceeded only a short time by the other man, who made his escape.

The gallant sergeant and twelve of his men were scalped by the savages. The Indians were pursued by the whole force of the rangers, and overtaken at the Flat Top mountain, and suffered a total defeat, with loss of a great many of their warriors.

CHAPTER II.

COLD WEATHER — A VICIOUS MULE — GAME — SCOUTING
CAMP ON THE COLORADO—A BEAUTIFUL LAKE IN THE
WILDERNESS — KILLING A SPANISH COUGAR — CAMP
COLORADO—SWISHER'S MEN—PECAN BAYOU—ROPING
A WILD INDIAN—CAMPING AT THE SPRINGS—INDIAN
ALARM.

IT remained cold during the day, after we left Camp
Baker. The wind lulled about night, and we had a
heavy frost. Nothing of interest occured at the camp, only
one of those devilish little mules came near breaking one
of Charley Brown's ribs, as he was trying to hopple him
out for the night.

Next morning, after we had saddled up, and were
waiting for the wagons to move, one of the boys left his
horse and went to fill up his canteen, and while he was
gone, his horse became frightened at something and
dashed off through the hills, carrying off the carbine,
wallet, etc., of the ranger. Instantly, a dozen men started
off in pursuit, and after a lively chase of about two miles,
succeeded in capturing him, with everything intact,
greatly to the satisfaction of the dismounted ranger.
Everything being again in order, we resumed our march.
In the course of a few days, we passed through the little
German towns of Fredericksburg and Boerne. The
latter place is beautifully situated near the head waters
of the Cibolo river and has a thrifty and enterprising
settlement around it. Shortly after passing Boerne we
came to a place called Camp Hays, it derived its name

from Captain Jack Hays, who often camped here with his men, while he was guarding the Texas frontier. At this place we found plenty of wood and water and spent a very agreeable night.

The next morning we had a little carbine practice in order to get our horses used to firing; one man only was dismounted during this fusilade. Our boys did well, firing rapidly and riding splendidly.

We will now skip over the monotonous details of camps and only mention such things as would likely interest the reader. On our route we passed through Fort Mason. This place is situated on high ground, is healthy, and is a good farming and stock country. Gen. Robert E. Lee was at one time stationed at this place, before the war, when he was on duty in Texas, as a United States officer.

About eighteen miles from Fort Mason we crossed the San Saba river, a clear, beautiful stream. Near the crossing lives an old Texan, William Turner, who came to this county some time before the war, for the purpose of raising stock. He has been very successful, and now has plenty. He was one of the first settlers in this part of the country and was troubled a great deal by Indians. We crossed the river and camped about one mile from his house, in a prairie dog town, the first we had seen since starting. I got permission from the captain to go back and spend the night with Mr. Turner, for he was a relative of mine. I was on guard duty that night, but my friend and comrade Bud Seglar, volunteered to stand in my place, and in company with Dan Woodruff I set out for the ranch. I was very much disappointed in not finding the old man at home. He was out on a hog hunt and was camping out up the river, in the mountains. We received a hearty welcome from

the members of the family and had a good time. Mr.
Turner is an old veteran; he was with Caldwell at the
battle of Salado.

Well, back to camp next morning, and off again.
Now the traveling becomes delightful; we begin to strike
the game—deer, turkey and antelope. We had a lively
chase to-day after a herd of antelope. They ran in
such a dense mass it was no trouble to kill them with the
carbine, while running at full speed. That night we
feasted on antelope steak. I will state here that Doctor
Gillespie killed the first deer on the trip; it was a small
one, not more than half-grown, and he killed it at a
distance of three hundred yards with a Winchester
carbine.

We began now to have strict watch at night, for we
were in the Indian country. Scouts were sent out during the day to look for Indian trails. Through this part
of the country was the route they traveled over when
they made a raid on the settlers down the Colorado or
San Saba.

One of the scouts under Private Jackson came in and
reported that they came suddenly upon three Indians, as
they rode around the foot of a mountain. The Indians
were about four hundred yards off, on the prairie; they
were leading two horses by lariats. At sight of the
rangers they left the lead horses and fled, going in the
direction of some timber, about a mile off. The boys
pursued them, firing every now and then as they ran,
but they could not hit an Indian, and as they were well
mounted, could not come up with them. As they were
nearing the thickets, a ball from a carbine struck one of
the horses rode by the Indians, and he fell, throwing his
rider. The boys thought sure they had him, but he
jumped to his feet and ran like a jack rabbit, his long

black hair waving in the wind, and made his escape
despite the balls which were sent after him.   The boys
took the back track and secured the two horses and
brought them to camp, leaving the Indian's wounded horse
on the prairie.

Plenty of game was now killed every day.   The night
we camped on the Colorado there were a great many
deer brought into camp, in fact more than we could eat
for supper and breakfast.   Doctor Gillespie, sitting by a
blazing camp fire watching the boys eat their supper,
with abundance of fat venison and turkey on every side,
with the lurid glare of the camp fires in the tree tops, and
trusty scouts guarding the camp while we feasted, could
contain himself no longer, but rubbing his hands in glee,
exclaimed, "Boys, this is ranging; regular, genuine,
Texas ranging.   Won't we whoop things up, though,
when we get to the Wichitas?"

The next morning, after we left our camp on the Colorado, I went with a scout that was detailed to make a
detour from the main route for several miles, and then
travel parallel with the route taken by the company,
until time to close up at night.   We traveled up the left
bank of the river for some distance before we could find
a crossing.   The Colorado at this place is enclosed with
high bluffs and is very narrow and swift.   We finally
found a place where it looked fordable and plunged in ;
the bed of the river was thickly strewn with large rocks,
and some of the boys came near being thrown into the
water, on account of the plunging of the horses in crossing these boulders, but we made it across without accident, and after going up through a deep cut in the bank,
came on to a level flat several hundred yards wide.   We
then ascended a mountain and had a magnificent view
of the surrounding country ; Santa Anna's peak was visi-

16

ble, although about thirty miles off.   Our regular trailer, Swift, was with us to-day, and Sergeant Joel R. Payne, commanded the scout.

We could find no trail of Indians, although we closely examined the country and rode hard most of the day, finally we turned to the right to intercept the command before night if we could, but we had miscalculated the distance we had traveled west before the turn.   We rode hard until nearly night, but could still see nothing of the company.   To-day I killed the first prairie dog that I got; it was very fat and heavy.   Some say they are good to eat, but as I did not feel very hungry at the time I postponed eating any of it.   I afterwards saw a ranger broil and eat a large slice of one, and he said it had a very good flavor.

Towards sundown we rode through a belt of timber and came out on the edge of a steep bluff and saw one of the most beautiful sights I ever beheld in nature.   The valley stretched for miles below and above us and bordered with a winding stream.   About half way between the bluff and the creek was a beautiful lake, its surface dotted here and there with wild ducks and geese; it looked wild and lonely, yet beautiful, in the rays of the setting sun.   We had some difficulty in finding a passage down this high table land, but finally succeeded and entered the valley.   After crossing the level flat and riding down the creek some distance, we struck the Fort Griffin trail and found our wagon tracks.   We immediately turned towards the North, and followed the trail of our company, but we soon came to a recent camp, which plainly told us that the boys had stopped there for dinner   The sun was now down and we knew not how far the company was ahead.   We knew they traveled slowly on account of the rough country, and we had some

hopes of overtaking them before the night was far
advanced. There had been wagons passing through
before, carrying supplies to the forts, but the trail was now
almost obliterated and made it tedious for loaded wagons
to travel. We crossed the creek, rode through the bottom, and reached the open glades before dark. About
dusk we discovered four beautiful animals playing in an
open glade to our right. They were about the size of
half-grown dogs and thickly spotted. We at once opened
fire on them and gave chase. Billy Sorrell killed one,
and the balance made their escape. The trailer, Swift,
behind when we commenced firing, dashed up at full
speed, thinking we were fighting Indians. As soon as
he saw what it was he reined up his horse, taking no
interest in the sport, at the same time remarking, he
believed us boys would shoot at anything. He was an old
scout, and nothing less than a brush with Indians in the
way of sport had any interest with him. It was astonishing to those who had no experience in woodcraft to
see with what ease he could trail Indians, when there
was hardly any perceptible sign. As a general thing,
our boys were inexperienced in Indian warfare. We
had one old California gold digger with us, and on several occasions he found signs of gold and silver, but none
of the precious metal. One of the places was near Fort
Mason. As soon as Billy had secured his game
to his saddle, we set out at a brisk trot. It was
now dark and we had some difficulty in following the
trail, and finally lost it altogether; but we knew our
course lay towards the North, and we kept on for several
hours in that direction, and had about concluded to camp
for the night when, on ascending a small hill, discovered
the camp fires of our men burning in the distance, and
shortly afterward we were halted by our guard, who

being satisfied that we were not Comanches, let us pass, and we were soon in the midst of the camp. The captain came around and interviewed us, and said he had concluded to stop the company there the next day and send out another scout to look for us if we failed to come in during the night.

The animal which Billy Sorrell killed, was pronounced by those who seemed to know, to be a Spanish cougar.

The next morning we could plainly see Santa Anna's peak, although about twelve miles away. It stood out in bold relief in the prairie and we passed near the base of it during the day. Some of the boys ascended this noted landmark and reported that it had once been a rendezvous and council ground for Indians, from the signs which they discovered on its crest, which was smooth and level, by the tramp of many feet. After crossing Jim Ned creek, we came to Camp Colorado. Here we found a company of rangers commanded by Captain Swisher. The captain was absent, but we found his lieutenant to be a gentlemanly fellow, who gave us such information as we wanted and furnished us some flour, which we much needed. He said there were plenty of Indians on the frontier, and predicted lively times for us when we arrived at our station, which would be in the Cross Timbers, near Red River. Some of Swisher's scouts, while out one day, came upon a solitary Indian, and immediately gave chase. The Indian made for the nearest brush, which was not far off. One of the rangers, who was splendidly mounted, dashed ahead of the other boys and ran directly between them and the Indian and thereby prevented them from firing, and he was making no attempt to kill the Indian himself. The savage, in the meantime, was nearing the brush. The ranger was bent on taking this one alive. He quickly, and dexterously adjusted his rope, and making a quick run on the flying Indian threw the loop over his head, and, wheeling his horse, quickly jerked the hostile to the ground, his horse dashed on into the thicket, and was not followed. The Indian made no resistance, but regarded the rangers with a frightened look, as they gathered around him. The captive was carried to the fort, with the rope still around his neck. Swisher's men were active and did considerable hard scouting. On one occasion they struck a fresh trail of Indians, and by hard riding came up with them about sundown. The Indians had stopped, and were playing some kind of a game on horse back, in an open prairie near a mountain, little thinking that a band of Texas rangers were on their track. The rangers charged and the Indians fled toward the mountains, leaving their horses, when they struck rough ground, and succeeded in getting into a cave before the rangers came up. They fired several shots in after them and then moved back, and camped, thinking they would get them in the morning, for by this time it was nearly dark. But the night being dark and stormy, the Indians made their escape. By daylight the rangers were again at the cave, but found the red men gone. When they fired into the cave, the evening before, they either killed or badly wounded some of them, from the amount of blood found inside. But if one was killed, the others carried him off, as they always do, if they have a chance. Fifteen miles out from Camp Colorado, we crossed Pecan Bayou. This is beautiful place : the pecan trees stand very thick ; the soil looks as rich as it does in the Guadalupe valley, and will some day be thickly settled with thrifty farmers, if it is not already at this date, (1883). It has been twelve years only since I was there, but immigration and settlements have made rapid strides in the North and Northwest since that time. Twelve years ago, in 1870 and 1871, nearly all the country from Fort Mason to Red River was a howling wilderness. I will skip over the dry details of camp life and the different camps we made until we get near Fort Griffin. Suffice it to say that the weather at times was fearfully cold; for it was now in December, and sometimes wood was scarce. Indians prowled around us and the coyotes and the big lobos (wolves) made the nights hideous, with their ceaseless howlings. The ranger on guard, during these bitter cold nights, 300 or 400 yards from his companions, keeping the lonely vigils with such music around him, thinks of home, of father, mother, brothers and sisters; the cheerful fire, and a warm bed, and he will ask himself this question: "Why did I forsake all these comforts, and start on this long winter campaign, to suffer all this and, perhaps, be finally scalped, and left on the prairie, the last object my eyes resting on being the painted face of a Comanche warrior. The love of adventure, characteristic of all Americans, and especially Texans, is the cause. Just as we went into camp one evening, in a thick wood, we saw a body of mounted men through the timber, some distance off, and one of them was dressed in red. Knowing the peculiar taste of Indians for this color, we at once put him down for a big chief, and the balance for warriors, out on a raid. Our camp was alarmed in a second; every man jumped for his carbine, and the cry of Indians! Indians! was heard through the camp. Officers gave command; horses were closely corralled, and everything put in trim for a fight. In the meantime the other party had discovered us and halted. The red coat was moving about through the timber, and we imagined the "Big chief" giving command to his braves. We presented a rather formadable appearance ourselves—fifty-two men, well posted among trees, each with a Winchester carbine, a six-shooter, a bowie knife and a belt full of cartridges. The other party having satisfied themselves. advanced into open view, and we saw that they were white men. It proved to be a government hay contractor, named Ship. His contract having been completed, he was furnished with an escort to San Antonio, by the Colonel commanding the post at Fort Griffin. He wore a red-blanket coat. They had also taken us for Indians, until Ship scouted around a bit, and saw we were white. The soldiers had placed themselves in readiness for action. They were aiming for this place themselves to camp, on account of the convenience of wood and water. The timber also afforded some protection from the cold wind, which was blowing from the North. It was also a stopping place at times for raiding bands of Indians; for there was but little water in this part of the country.

CHAPTER III.

WE were distant now about sixty miles from Fort
Griffin, and our supplies of flour, bacon and coffee were
running short, and some of the men were out of tobacco.
Our only chance to get supplies was Fort Griffin, and if
the weather continued bad, we would make but slow
progress. We traveled the next day, but the weather
was so bitter cold we stopped before night, and went
into camp. The weather had changed to a driving sleet
from the North, and the ground was frozen hard, and
we were in an unprotected situation, between some low
hills, in a prairie country, and our only chance for wood
was some scattering scrub mesquites, and they green at
that. But this was the best we could do; for ahead of
us the bleak, timberless prairie stretched for miles away
towards Hubbard's creek. The boys went to work with
a will, and soon cut and dragged into camp a good supply of the dwarf mesquites, and made some tolerable
good fires. We had only two tents—one a very small
one for the use of the captain, lieutenant and the doctor, the other one was for the sick, so that if a man got
into that tent he must go on the sick list. We had
plenty of blankets and good overcoats, and, when not
on guard duty, faired tolerably well. As the sailor says,

it was my trick at the wheel to-night, or in other words, I had to stand guard three hours in the sleet, while it peppered down like shot all the time. Our trailer, Swift, was sick, but, as yet, had not been placed on the sick list, and it was his night to stand guard in the regular turn. He was unequal to the task on such a night as this; but, rather than be put on the sick list, he offered any man five dollars to go on duty in his place. Several of the boys offered to take his place for nothing, but the Captain hearing of it, immediately ordered him to be placed on the sick list and go into the tent. Dr. Gillespie examined him and pronounced it pneumonia. Swift suffered very much during the night, and his moanings were piteous. I came on the second watch, and taking my gun, followed the sergeant of the guard to my post, on a bleak, cold hill-side, some distance from the camp. He bade me good night and hastened back. As I listened to his receding footsteps, over the frozen ground, I felt lonely indeed. It seemed as if all the coyotes and wolves that roamed these vast solitudes had collected, and taken their position on the hills around our camp, to serenade us with dismal howls and yelps. I could distinguish the different species, as they put in their notes from time to time. The keen, quick, yelp of the coyote, the smallest size, and the prolonged howl of the yellow wolf, with the coarse voice of the lobo, as bass, to this cold, midnight serenade. It was anything but pleasant, in a place like that. Several times they passed in close pistol shot of me, but it was against orders to shoot wolves while on duty at night. Most of the boys were asleep and the crack of a carbine would bring every man to his feet, and we wanted no false alarms on such a night as this. Minutes seemed almost like hours, as I kept the watch this fearful night. I had to keep continuously tramping with my feet, to keep from freezing. I thought it must be nearly day, and that the officer of the guard had gone to sleep, or forgotten me, but I was mistaken. The faithful fellow was at his post, and often looked at his watch when the time drew near to relieve a guard, for fear he would make him stand a few minutes over his time. At length I saw dark objects approaching the spot where I stood. My gun was up in an instant: "Halt! Who comes there?" "Sergeant of the guard, third relief." "All right, sir; you are welcome about this time of night. You are the man I have been looking for," and I stepped away, leaving one of my companions to shiver in my place. In a few moments, I was by the guard-fire, warming my almost frozen feet, and after getting thoroughly warm, hunted up my bed-fellow; pulled off my boots and got under four or five blankets and over-coats, on the south side of my companion, and soon fell asleep, but it did not seem to me that I had been asleep more than five minutes, but likely it had been an hour or more. when I was aroused by the report of a carbine, and the loud command of the lieutenant, to "Fall in, men, quick! Indians!" Blankets and overcoats were thrown about promiscuously; guns were snatched up; and about thirty-five men followed the officer in their sock feet, over the frozen ground, west of the camp, towards post No. 2, where the shot was heard, but No. 2 had only shot a wolf, and laughed at us, as we rushed up bootless and hatless, with presented carbines. Well, you may know whether we were mad or not. I think some of the boys felt like giving post No. 2 a Christmas salute. He was, however, put on double duty, and we went back to re-adjust our cover, and try to get a few minutes of needed repose. It was well enough for us to keep ever on the alert in this part of the country, for the Indians were numerous and daring. A few days before, they had been fighting the cow boys on Hubbard's Creek, ahead of us. The next morning, it was still fearfully cold, and Captain Baker concluded to remain where we were another night, as we could not better our condition by moving. Swift was worse, in spite of all the Doctor could do for him, and we spent another day and night in this uncomfortable place, on the bald prairie. By the second morning, wood had become scarce, provisions were running low, and we were put on half rations of bread. Tobacco was very scarce. Orderly Sergeant Billy Thorn, had one sack of smoking tobacco, which he freely divided with those that smoked. Our trailer was no better, and fears were entertained that he would not recover. Alas, too soon to be verified! But the weather was still so cold, that it was almost impossible to cross the prairie, and we concluded to remain another day and night, and then start, at all hazards, whether the weather moderated or not. Without wood; our provisions nearly exhausted; with no chance of getting any, unless we could eat coyotes, we were in a sad fix. Coyotes by the million. This is the place the wolf hunters, which we read about in "Texas Siftings," should have come. On the third morning, we made preparations for a start, when it was discovered that John Fitzgerald's mare was gone. She had gotten loose and had wandered off. Search was made, and she was found some distance from the camp, dead, with her ears cut off, which proved that the Indians were prowling near us, cold as it was, and not being strong enough to attack us, had done this in defiance and in the spirit of bravado. It was likely they were well mounted and did not need this one. Well,

John had to mount the baggage wagon, and we started, making poor Swift as comfortable as possible, under the circumstances. We bid farewell to "Camp Freezeout," as we named this place, without casting one lingering look of regret behind. We suffered very much in crossing the prairie, for it was still very cold. That night we camped in a low flat, where we found some wood and plenty of water and grass. The weather had moderated somewhat, and we would have fared very well, had we only been supplied with plenty of provisions. We had been on half rations for several days, and now we were out of bread entirely, and had killed no game for several days, and fat bacon was hard to eat without bread. Tobacco was a trouble, too, and those who had any, doled it out very sparingly. During the night Swift became delirious, and we took it turn about by the couch of our sick comrade, and spent a very uncomfortable night. By this time we had begun to suffer with hunger, and being without tobacco, and seeing the sad condition of Swift, we did not feel disposed to be gay. Almost for the first time since we started, the camp was silent, except the munching of the horses, the tramp of the camp sentinels, and the moaning of poor Swift. We made an early start next morning, intending to reach Fort Griffin if possible that day, as there was no chance to get provisions short of that post. The game had left the prairies, and sought shelter on the hills, to avoid the cold wave, that, for several days, had been sweeping across those lonely prairies. We made a short halt at noon, without removing our saddles, and only remained long enough to make some coffee. We had nothing to eat. We then resumed our march, and at sundown, came in sight of the fort, which was about three miles off. A cheer went up from the boys at the welcome sight. As there was some wood and water near at hand the company was ordered into camp, and a detail started to the fort with sacks, to bring out bread for the company. The men by this time were suffering acute pangs of hunger, and it seemed a long time to wait. But they went to work, preparing the camp for the night, securing our horses, placing guards, etc. After this was done, we gathered around the camp fires, and waited as patiently as we could the return of the boys from the fort. As I was on second relief that night, I was placed on guard just before the boys returned with the bread and had to stand about three hours before I would be relieved. I saw the boys return; saw them hurrying to and fro around the fires, making coffee and eating. This increased my hunger, but I had more than two hours to stand yet, on the prairie, far out from camp, in the cold, cutting, north wind. But my mind was soon diverted from thoughts of feasting, to that of duty, as I heard footsteps hastily approaching the spot where I stood, at the same time, I could see the outlines of a man. I instantly brought my carbine to a level and commanded a "Halt! Who comes there?" "Friend," and indeed it was. It was Billy Sorrell, and in his hand he carried a loaf of light bread. "Say, old pard, don't you begin to feel kinder lank," was his cheery greeting, as he came up. Amid the confusion of the feast, at the camp, he thought of his friend and messmate. Dear boy, how I loved him! He was only sixteen years of age, with a face like a girl's; with rosy cheeks; black, sparkling eyes, and raven locks. Only a few months after that, he was shot down by my side, in a wild fight, on the prairie, with Comanche and Kiowa Indians. For hours our little band fought against fearful odds around his body, and at night, when the bloody fight was over, I held him on his horse, for miles across the prairie, to a place of safety. After telling me he would have some hot coffee for me when I was relieved, Billy returned to camp and left me to enjoy my bread, the first that had passed my lips for several days. Our sick comrade was unable to eat, and barely conscious of what was transpiring around him. Early next morning, we were off for the fort, and was very anxious to get there, as the captain had informed us that we would go into camp on the river beyond. where there was plenty of wood, and and there we would wait a few days, for the weather to moderate, and rest ourselves and horses, for we had now traveled nearly 400 miles, in bad weather nearly the whole time. As we passed through the fort, near the parade ground, we saw a United States soldier chained to a post, exposed to the sleet and the cutting north wind. We learned that he was there under death sentence, for killing an officer. He was a fine looking young man, and held his head erect, walking with a proud step around the post to which he was chained. They say he was from Kentucky, and of good and wealthy family, and had moved in the highest circles. He enlisted in the army, while on a spree, and his command was sent to Texas. We further learned that he was insulted by an officer, to whom he replied in hot words, and received a blow in the face with the flat part of a sabre, and in the heat of passion, drew his pistol and shot the officer dead. We learned afterwards that he died chained to the post where we saw him.

Fort Griffin is situated on the Clear Fork of the Brazos, on a hill, overlooking the river and valley towards the North. It is a beautiful place, and commands a fine view of the surrounding country. At the time of which I write it consisted only of the soldiers' barracks, head-

RANGERS AND PIONEERS OF TEXAS.

quarters of the officers, a bakery, sutler's store. etc.
There were about six hundred soldiers there at the time,
commanded by Col. Wood. The Tonkaway tribe of
Indians also had their village there. It was situated at
the foot of the hill, between the fort and the river. They
were employed by the United States Government to act
as scouts and trailers, against the Comanches. For this
the Comanches hated them, with all their revengeful,
savage nature. and sought every opportunity to kill them.
The Tonkaways were a weak tribe and not able to cope
with them in the open field alone, but were more than a
match for the Comanches in a fair fight, man to man.
Through treachery, the Comanches came near exter-
minating them years ago, near old Fort Cobb. The
circumstance was this: The Comanches (which means
snake in the grass), proposed to make a treaty with the
Tonks, to live with them like brothers, and to kill buffalo
in the same hunting grounds. For this purpose they
were all to meet at Fort Cobb. The Tonks agreed to
this very readily, as they were debarred from hunting in
the best hunting grounds' on account of the hostility of
the Comanches, and their superior numbers. Accordingly the whole tribe, about five hundred in number,
packed up and set out for the place designated; but as
might have been expected, they were ambushed on a
little creek, about nine miles from the fort, by a largely
superior force of Comanches, and a desperate battle
ensued, and in the end the Tonks were utterly defeated,
leaving 400 of their number dead on the ground. Among
the slain was their old chief, Placadore. The young
chief, Casteel, succeeded in making his escape with the
remainder, and was head chief of the tribe when we
were there. " Big Nose Johnson " was the war chief
of the tribe, and was a powerfully-made man, standing

nearly seven feet in his moccasins, with broad shoulders and deep chest. He was a terror to the Comanches, and a match for half a dozen common warriors. He wore a hunting shirt of buckskin, heavily fringed, with broad belt around the waist. He would scalp his enemies slain in battle, and tuck the reeking trophies under his belt. On one occasion he went with the soldiers after the Comanches, and surprised them in their camp, and defeated them, although in considerable force, and outnumbering the soldiers and a few Tonks, which Johnson had with him. On this occasion he was fearful to behold; running from place to place, shouting his war cry, and overcoming all opposition, killing and scalping his enemies, as he came to them; sometimes tearing the scalp off before they were dead, and came out of the fight with seven scalps dangling at his belt. He was often wounded, and they said his broad breast bore many scars.

CHAPTER IV.

CASTEEL THE TONKAWAY CHIEF—MARCHING THROUGH
THE SNOW — SUFFERING OF THE SICK — DEATH OF
SWIFT, THE TRAILER—A SHOT FROM THE THICKET—
CROSSING THE BRAZOS—OLD FORT BELKNAP—STAGE
CAPTURED BY INDIANS—JACKSBOROUGH.

WHEN we arrived at the fort, the captain gave us permission to remain in the place some time, to look around
and purchase such articles as we needed, and for some
time the sutler had a lively trade in tobacco, and some
in whiskey, although it cost four dollars per quart. A
portion of the company soon moved across the river,
with the wagons, and went into camp.

We had an opportunity before we left, to interview
Casteel, the Tonkaway chief. He was a low, heavy-
set man, painted and dressed in the Indian garb, except
that he wore a black hat, decorated with a plume. He
could speak some English, and readily answered any
questions which we asked him. He told us his name,
and said he was fifty-seven years of age. When we asked
him where the Comanches were, he pointed to the northwest. He wore a strap, fastened to the scalp-lock, which
reached the ground, and was decorated with silver ornaments, from the size of a five-cent piece to the size of
a dollar. They were fastened to the strap about six
inches apart, commencing with the largest and tapering
down. When we asked him where he obtained the silver,
he pointed to the northwest. Noticing Billy Sorrell, who
was standing by him, with his carbine in his hand, he

patted him on the head, and said: "Too leetle warrior;" then, making a flourish around Billy's head, as if using a scalping knife, said: "Comanche scalp him." Billy laughed and said, "I reckon not." He little knew how near the words of the old chief would come of being realized. After telling us he hoped we would "kill heap Comanches," he drew his blanket around him and walked away.

During the day I was taken sick, with something like a chill, and in company with the captain and Dr. Gillespie, rode to the camp. I took two drinks of brandy from the captain's flask, but still felt a chilly sensation, which I could not shake off; and, during the night, the doctor said I had symptoms of pneumonia. I was not put on the sick list that night, but laid down in the open air, with Sergeant E. H. Cobb. During the night, it commenced sleeting very hard, and I suffered very much. Swift was raving all night, and it required several men to control him. By morning, my top blanket was frozen stiff, and I could hardly breathe, and had considerable fever. Some of the boys informed the lieutenant of my condition, and he came down to where I was, with the frozen blanket pulled over my face, to ward off the driving sleet, which was still falling fast. The lieutenant stooped down, and uncovering my face, looked at me a few moments, and I heard him remark: "My God, this is terrible!" and immediately gave orders for me to be removed to the tent. Room was made for me beside my sick comrade, and there I lay that day and next night almost unconscious. Dr. Gillespie was a good physician, but we could not have the comforts that we needed. As the weather had not moderated, the captain concluded to send the sick back to Fort Griffin, and continue the march to our post, which was still distant about 150 miles. He was anxious to get there and go into permanent camp, until winter was over. Besides there was not much grass where we were, for our horses, and it was out of the question to get grain. I had a perfect horror of returning to Griffin, and going into the hospital, and asked some of the boys to induce the captain to let me go on with the company. Lee Lewis said I should go if I wanted to, or there would be a row in camp. The captain objected to it at first, as he thought it was for my good. In a few moments the tent was full of men, telling the captain that they would take better care of me than any one else, and that I should not suffer from cold, as they would give up their blankets to me, and arrange everything comfortable for me in the covered wagon. I felt very grateful to the boys for their zeal in my behalf, and waited anxiously for the captain's reply. I felt as if it would be the last of me if I went into the hospital among strangers, but the captain consented to this arrangement, and I felt greatly relieved. He said, however, that Swift must go to Griffin, as he was then delirious, and in an almost dying condition. Poor fellow! he never knew when they carried him off; that was the last time we ever saw him. He died in the hospital at Griffin, and was buried by the soldiers, with military honors, firing a salute over his grave.

Everything being in readiness for a start, I was carried to the wagon, and well wrapped up. My horse was saddled and turned loose behind the wagon, which he followed; with my carbine, belt and pistol hanging to the pommel of the saddle. Through the day it commenced snowing, and most of the boys dismounted and traveled on foot. At night, we camped in the timber, where the boys had good fires, and fared tolerably well. My fever had somewhat abated, but I had no appetite to eat, and was very restless. The doctor continued to give me medicine. On the third day, after leaving Griffin, we camped in a thick wood; the ground was covered with snow and frozen hard. It had now been nearly a week since I had taken sick, and eaten nothing, but still I had no appetite. As I lay in the wagon, listening to the roaring fires, which the boys had built near the wagons, I had a desire to get out and lie by them. It seemed that it would help me to lie with my feet to the fire. I called Ed. Cobb, and made known my wish. He asked the doctor's advice, and with his permission, I was taken out, and placed on a good, soft bed of blankets, with my feet to the fire, and in a few minutes felt better, and began to feel like eating something. From that on, I recovered rapidly. The next morning, about two hours after we had resumed our march, as we were passing through a thick brushy country, a shot was fired to the left, in a dense thicket. We heard the whiz of the ball, which passed close to George Jackson's head. Search was instantly made for the hidden foe, but he could not be found. He either kept well hid, or else beat a hasty retreat. Men were deployed to the right and left, while we were passing through this country of dense undergrowth, to prevent an ambush. During the day, we passed over the ground where the stage from Fort Richardson had recently been captured, and overturned by the Indians, near Salt Creek. They ripped open the mail bags and scattered the letters and papers about over the prairie, and took the stage horses with them. The driver made his escape by leaping from the stage and running into the brush. When we passed the place, some of the newspapers were still blowing about on the prairie. Most of the letters had been picked up and carried to Fort Griffin.

Shortly after, the stage was again attacked near the same place. It contained no one but the driver, and was followed by a mounted sergeant, from Fort Griffin. But the soldier was equal to the occasion, telling the driver to whip the horses into a fast run and stay in the road. He followed behind, and kept up a running fight with the Indians, for several miles. He succeeded in killing one, and keeping the others off, until they gave up the chase and left, and the stage arrived safely at Fort Richardson, *a little ahead of time.*

The country through here, was said to be the most dangerous on the route, and was about half way between the two forts. It was near this place, that a large government train was captured and burned, after we passed through, and which I will give an account of in its regular order.

While we were crossing the Brazos, the sun shone out for the first time in about two or three weeks. It was greeted by a loud cheer from the boys. They had suffered much on this trip; enduring cold, hunger and fatigue. Lying on the fozen ground at night, without shelter; at times, on half rations, and at others, with nothing at all. Standing guard on the desolate, ice-covered prairie, with constant Indian alarms, at midnight hours: waiting on sick comrades, etc. All without a murmer; ever ready to rush to the front when danger threatened. This long, severe, cold spell had made several of our boys sick. Dave Smith had pneumonia, and Thompson had his ears and heels frost bit. But our hopes of fair weather, was not of long duration. It was snowing again before we reached Jacksborough, (or Fort Richardson). Shortly after we crossed the river, we passed by old Fort Belknap. This place was a station for rangers and soldiers before the war, but was not now occupied by troops of any kind. Shortly after we passed here, eighteen colored troops were sent to this post, under command of Brit Johnson, a negro sergeant, but theirs was a sad fate, the place was besieged by Indians in the dead of winter, and the entire command killed, scalped and horribly mangled. There was none left to tell the tale, of how they fought, or how they died. The body of Johnson was found two hundred yards from the fort; whether he was carried there, or was attempting to make his escape none could tell.

On the 19th of December, we arrived at Jacksborough. It was very cold and snowing again. We made a short halt, and the captain gave orders for the company to move on to the timber, which was about three miles distant, and encamp for the night, were we could get wood, and have some protection from the blast, for the snow was coming in eddying whirls across the prairie. I was still weak, but could sit up and see what was going on. I think the boys got something stronger than water while in town, from the way they raced and yelled from there to the timber. I think, that evening, they would have fought the whole Comanche nation, with Big Tree and a hundred of his Kiowas thrown in. That night we had good fires, plenty to eat, and some fisticuffs.

Jacksborough is situated on Lost creek, in Jack county, It has a beautiful location, and is very healthy, except when the red man, like yellow jack in the East, pays them a visit. It was a military post at the time of which I write. The soldiers' quarters being on the east side of the creek, and was called Fort Richardson. Jack county has a bloody record, being constantly overrun by Indians, ever since the first settlements were made. About forty miles west of Jacksborough is Lost Valley. This place has been the scene of many deadly encounters, between the white and red man, and, in fact, this part of Jack county was seldom ever clear of Indians. Lost Valley is a wild, desolate looking place; hid away among the mountains, rocks and brush; and was the rendezvous of war parties, in their frequent raids through these sparsely settled counties. When pursued, they would often retreat to this place, and make a bold stand; sometimes ambush and defeat their pursuers. On one occasion a large body of them, were hotly pursued, by a company of United States soldiers, and a small company of rangers. It seems, that the Indians, after entering the valley, were re-enforced, and selecting a favorable place, awaited in ambush, the approach of the whites. On arriving at the place, the troops hastily entered the valley, without using as much caution as they should have done, and penetrated the ambush, before they were aware of the presence of the Indians, who then, showed themselves on every side, and with loud yells, commenced pouring in deadly volleys of bullets and arrows. The captain commanding the regulars, was a brave man, and cooly gave his orders, amid the dire confusion of yelling savages and falling men, he formed his troop in the open ground, in close line, and fired regular volleys into the bushes and rocks, where the Indians were mostly concealed. The ranger captain, seeing Indians rising up in the rear, and firing, knew that their command was surrounded, and made his way to the captain in command of the regulars, and urged him to turn his men back and charge through the Indians in the rear, and get out of the valley, before it was too late, as the enemy were concentrating at that point, but the officer refused, in the same spirit that General Braddock replied to Washington, at Monongahela, when the British troops were being cut to pieces by a concealed foe: "What!"

said he, " a beardless youth teach a British General?"
But in the end, the brave, though misguided Braddock,
was slain, and his army utterly routed.   The youthful
Washington covered the retreat with his Indian fighters,
from Virginia : and had the body of the British general
buried in the road, and caused the army and the baggage wagons to pass over the grave, to prevent the
Indians from finding and mutilating the body.   And so
it was in this case ; the United States officer refused to
receive instructions from a ranger captain, who knew
nothing about military tactics.   The captain of the
rangers then determined to force his way back, if possible, with his men.   It was a fearful undertaking, for the
Indians had collected in strong force, near the pass, but
it was the last chance, and with an answering yell to the
savages, they charged, firing rapidly as they advanced.
The Indians tried in vain to block their way, but being
well mounted, the rangers rode down every obstacle,
giving and receiving death shots in their passage ; but
finally, got clear, leaving twelve of their gallant comrades dead on the ground.   Of the troops they left behind
them, none escaped.   When the rangers carried the
news to the fort, and re-enforcements were sent back,
they found the most of them lying in the open glade,
where they first formed : the brave captain with them ; a
victim to the mistaken idea of fighting Indians, in the
brush, with military discipline enforced.

Captain Baker and Lieutenant Hill remained in Jacksborough until morning, and then came to camp, telling
us we would remain where we were until next morning,
as the weather was still very bad.   We were well pleased,
and went about making ourselves as comfortable as possible under the circumstances.

CHAPTER V.

ON the morning, of the 20th of December, we again
commenced our march, having been one month on the
road, but unfortunately for us, we were unable to procure provisions at the fort, and had to depend mostly on
game, which we found quite abundant, the balance of
the way; for we had reached the "Cross Timbers,"
which abounds in game; such as deer, turkey, and antelope. Arriving at Big Sandy Creek, near the old Government saw mills, which had at one time been in operation, but was now abandoned, we went into camp,
intending to spend the balance of the winter there; but
our provisions had become exhausted, and game scarce
in our immediate neighborhood. Our Christmas dinner
consisted of parched corn and salt; and to add to our
straightened circumstances, it commenced snowing again,
and it was almost impossible to hunt. Our nearest point
where provisions could be had, was some flour mills,
below Decatur, in Wise county, and it required several
days to reach them with wagons, and in going to that
point, east of us, one would have to cross the prairie,
and it was fearfully cold, and the ground covered with

snow; but supplies must be had, and the captain called for volunteers, to make the trip with the wagons. Bud Seglar and Dave Smith came forward, and said they would go, and it was decided to make the start on the following morning. The lieutenant also said he would go, and take Harvey, the colored blacksmith along, to help. It was also a dangerous route, on account of Indians, as they generally came out this way. after raiding the settlers in the "Cross Timbers." Next morning we bid the boys farewell, and they were off through a blinding snow storm. We employed our time, while they were absent, in building a corral, for our horses to stay in at night. We had a hard time of it, and were often hungry, and having nothing to eat. we killed some wild ducks, and occasionally a deer or turkey. One evening, while Jim Schuler was out hunting, above our camp, near the creek. he stopped under a large tree, to listen for turkeys to fly up to roost, (for it was getting late), and heard a noise in the tree, over his head, and on looking up, discovered a large panther, with its eyes fastened on him, and in the act of springing down upon him. He instantly threw up his gun and fired. The ball striking the animal in the shoulder, brought him down; but the ferocious beast, maddened by the pain, made a desperate effort to reach him, and it took a second shot from the carbine to lay him out. The next morning, another one was killed, just opposite our camp, across the creek. One of our boys, John Fitzgerald, was an inveterate hunter; the weather seldom ever getting too cold for him to try his luck in the woods, in search of game. He would walk for hours, over frozen ground, through pathless woods. across mountains and deep cañons, and would only come to camp, when fatigue, hunger, and exhaustion compelled him to. On

one occasion, when we had nothing to eat, and all the
hunters had failed, John shouldered his gun and set out
one moring, remarking, that he would have game before
night, if there was any in the country.   The ground was
covered with snow, and it was very laborious traveling.
Miles were traversed through the lonely, snow-covered
forest; and it was getting late in the afternoon before
he sighted game, which proved to be a large buck, within
close rifle shot.   A quick report rang out, and John was
soon standing over the fallen deer, almost exhausted
with cold and fatigue.   After a short rest, he set out for
camp, where he arrived before night, in an almost helpless condition.   Being unable to return, some of the
boys, mounted on good horses, followed his track back
through the snow, to where he had killed his game,
which they secured and brought to camp after night.
One deer did not last long in a company of fifty men,
and, bad as the weather was, we were compelled to hunt
the greater portion of our time, to secure something to
eat, until the return of the wagons, sometimes with very
good success and sometimes with none.   But things took
a sudden turn in our camp, when one evening the wagons
came in, loaded with flour, meal, bacon, etc.   The men
had suffered very much on the trip, especially when
returning across the prairies, being obliged to face the
cold wind, which was blowing from the north.   At one
time, Lieutenant Hill was so near frozen, he could not
speak.   Things now put on a more cheerful aspect, and
the men were anxious for winter to break so that they
could commence scouting.   While encamped here, some
of our men came near losing their lives at the hands of
their comrades, each party supposing the other, Indians.
The circumstance was this: Two hunting parties had
gone out on foot, neither party knowing which way the

others were hunting. They sighted one another about twilight, in the thick woods, near Big Sandy creek, and, supposing each other to be Indians, every man on both sides sprang to cover, and the firing commenced. But fortunately, no one was hurt, and they soon recognized each other as friends, instead of enemies, by their voices; but there were some narrow escapes. One ball struck a tree, behind which John Fitzgerald was standing. Dan Woodruff dropped down behind a log, just as a ball knocked dirt and leaves over it. Sergeant Payne, in making a quick movement, accidently stepped into a sink-hole, and sank down about seven feet, in the black-berry vines, and was making frantic efforts to extricate himself, while the firing was going on. Although, in a good position to stand fire, the gallant sergeant was more afraid of snakes than Indians, but was unable to get out until assisted by his comrades. After laughing over the adventure, the boys returned to camp, and found it in a state of alarm—the firing had been heard from the camp, although some distance away, and a scout was just ready to start when the boys arrived.

As soon as the weather was favorable, we commenced scouting, but at first, without any success, not finding an Indian track in the whole surrounding country. But one night they interviewed our corral, and made an attempt to capture our horses. Jim Townsend was on guard that night, at the corral, and the wind blowing cold from the north, he sat down on the south side of the enclosure, and kept very still, with his face turned from the wind. The gate was fastened and everything quiet. I think Jim must have dozed a little. Anyway, he said he was aroused by a movement among the horses; and, raising up to see what was the matter, discovered an Indian, inside the corral, attempting to drive out the horses at the gate, which he had opened. The horses were very much frightened, and were running about the pen. The savage evidently thought there was no guard with the animals. The heart of the ranger beat quickly; now was the time for him to kill an Indian; and, slowly raising his carbine, covered the red skin, who was not more than ten paces off, and pulled the trigger, but his gun missed fire. The Indian heard the click of the hammer, as it went down, and knew what it meant; with a loud "ugh," and several quick bounds, he cleared the corral, and disappeared in the forest. His trail was followed some distance next morning, but was finally lost. We supposed there were more of them near by, to take charge of the horses, provided this daring warrior succeeded in driving them out. Some of the boys in camp, heard the commotion at the corral, and the alarm was soon raised and the camp aroused. Jim said it was the first time his gun had ever missed fire. On an average you will not find more than one cartridge in a hundred that will fail.

About the middle of January, the weather was clear, and considerably warmer. The most of the snow having melted away, we scoured the country far and near, in search of the hostiles. We learned, from settlers below, that the Indians were giving trouble north of us, near the line, on Red river, which separates Texas from the Indian Territory. For the information of those who are not aware of the fact, I will state here, that all that scope of country, lying between Texas and Kansas, and called the Indian Territory, is not the abode of the wild Indians, but it was set aside by the United States Government, for such of the Indian tribes as were friendly. Among them, are the Choctaws, Chickasaws, Cherokees, Caddoes, and others. These Indians are considerably advanced in civilization, and some of them have fine farms. The wild Indians, also, raid upon them, as well as upon the Texans, across the river. The Fort Sill reservation is in this Territory, and some portions of the wild tribes have been induced to come in; but they are very treacherous, and give a great deal of trouble; leaving nearly every light moon to invade Texas.

It was impossible for us to keep the Indians from coming into the settlements; for they were constantly doing so, in spite of all we could do to prevent them. There was such a large scope of country for the rangers to protect, that we could not watch all points at once. Capt. Cox, of the rangers, was on the Brazos, and Captain Sansom had come up after us, and was stationed at Fort Griffin. He was senior captain of the three companies, his own, and those of Cox and Baker. Cox had already engaged the Indians on the Brazos, killing eight of their number, and having three of his men wounded. These men were wounded by Indians after they were shot down; the boys invariably running to one when he fell, and if not dead, the Indian would fight to the last. It was a running fight, the Indians firing as they ran. It was understood, between the rangers and settlers, that whenever the Indians made a raid, a messenger was to be sent, post haste, to the ranger camp, with the news. One great drawback to the settlers, following and chastising a marauding band, was their isolated condition. Sometimes the nearest neighbor being ten or twelve miles distant; and as the Indians generally raided in bands, from ten to three hundred in number, it would take some time, and a great deal of rapid riding to collect men enough to make a successful fight, if the raiding band was large. And often, the brave and hardy pioneers, would follow them, with an insufficient force, and suffer defeat, and sometimes massacre, then homes would become desolate along the border.

While in camp, on Big Sandy, news was brought to us of a fearful massacre, of women and children, on a small creek, about thirty miles north of our camp, near the line of Montague and Wise counties. We lost no time in getting off, with eighteen men, well mounted and armed, to the scene of the slaughter; and by rapid riding, arrived at the place before night; which was at Keenon's ranch; but we soon discovered that it would be impossible for us to follow the trail, as it had been snowing since the Indians were there. As we rode up, we saw seven new-made graves, on the north side of the cabin, under some trees, the settlers from down the country, had buried the dead. There were only two ranches west of them; Col. Bean's and O. T. Brown's. Bean was absent at the time. His ranch was about two miles from Keenon's. The Keenon house consisted of only one room, about twelve by fourteen feet, made out of logs. There was a small field south of the cabin, at the foot of the hill, near the creek. On the northwest side, about two hundred yards from the house, was a small lake of water, at the foot of some hills; on the east, was a crib of corn. Keenon himself, was not at home, when the Indians made the attack on his ranch, and massacred the helpless inmates. We dismounted, entered the yard, and walked to the door and looked in. It was a horrible sight. The door was torn from its hinges, and lay in the yard, covered with blood; blood on the door steps; blood everywhere met our sight. The inside of the cabin was like a butcher pen. Quilts and pillows, were scattered about over the floor, stiff with clotted blood. The dress, which Mrs. Keenon wore, was hanging across the girder, which extended from one wall to the other. It had been hung there by some of the party who buried the victims. The dead were as follows: Mrs. Keenon and two of her children, and the widow Paschal, who was living with the Keenon family, and her three children. We obtained the particulars of the attack from one of the Keenon children; a boy, about eight years old, who made his escape on that fearful night. He said it was about 10 o'clock at night; the ground was covered with snow; and it was very cold. The inmates had all gone to bed, except Mrs. Keenon, who was sitting up by the fire, smoking. On the north side of the cabin, was a small window, with a shutter, which fastened on the inside, with a wooden pin, entering a hole in one of the logs. The door was in the south side. Everything was still and quiet, on that cold, winter night. The children were all asleep, probably dreaming sweet dreams, which seldom visit the couch of any except innocent childhood, when suddenly, crash, came the end of a rail, through the frail shutter; bursting it wide open, and the hideous, painted face of an Indian looked in, and began to crawl through, into the cabin. One brave man, or resolute woman, armed with an axe or hatchet, could have held them at bay; but poor Mrs. Keenon was timid, and instantly sank on her knees, and began to pray and beg for her life. As fast as one Indian got through another followed, until nine hideous wretches stood inside. By this time, the balance of the inmates were aroused. The children began screaming, and the work of death commenced. Pen cannot describe the scene; the cold and lonely night, far out in the western wilds; the painted faces of the Indians, lit up by the wood fire; the frantic, and heart-rending cries, of the women and children; the sickening blows of the tomahawks, etc., make one shudder to think of it. Who can blame a Texas ranger for placing his six-shooter to the head of a wounded savage, and pulling the trigger, as they often do in battle, when they are the victors?

It was during the confusion that the little boy made his escape, through the window, by which the Indians had entered. He received a severe cut in the hip, with a knife, as he went through, but succeeded in getting clear of the house, and was able to run off and hide himself until the Indians left. Crouched in some bushes near the corn crib, and bleeding profusely, he waited and listened, until all was still. The work was done; the fiends had reveled in blood. This boy displayed a presence of mind that was truly astonishing, for one of his tender years, before he made his escape from the house. He noticed the number of Indians that entered, and when they came out to take their departure, counted them, to see if they ware all leaving. The Indians had left their horses at the lake, and came to the house on foot, and as the ground was covered with snow, he could plainly see each form, standing out in bold relief, against the white back ground. He then left his place of conceal- ment, and watched them until they mounted their horses, and disappeared over the snow-clad hills, towards the west, and being satisfied that they would not return, came back to the house and entered. What a sight for a boy of his age to behold. His mother lay near the hearth, with three arrows in her breast, tomahawked, and scalped. Some of the children were killed in bed, others lay on the floor in pools of blood; one of his sis- ters was crouched in a corner, with her throat cut. There was at least a quart of blood in that corner when we were there. The widow Paschal was lying on the door

18

shutter, in the yard. She had three broken arrows in her breast. She had broken them off in attempting to pull them out; she was also scalped. The youngest child, about eighteen months old, was taken by the legs and its head dashed against the wall of the house, and then thrown out through the window, on the frozen ground, where they thought it would undoubtedly perish, if not already dead. But the boy brought his little sister back in the house, and laid her down before the fire and she recovered. While in the house, attending to his sister, he heard a noise in the yard, and on going to the door, saw Mrs. Paschal sitting up on the door shutter, upon which she had been lying. She looked horrible— covered with blood, and her scalp taken off. But the brave boy went to her, and she asked him for a drink of water, and there being none at the house, he got a gourd and went to the lake and brought the water. Mrs. Paschal drank it and then immediately expired. On looking around in the house, while we were there, I saw the old lady's pipe lying on the hearth, about half smoked out, where she dropped it, on that fatal night. We also saw a bent arrow spike in one of the logs, just above the bed. It had been shot at some of the children that were on the bed, and missed. The shaft had been removed. The next evening, after the massacre, a set- tler passed the house, and was hailed by the boy, who soon told his tale of woe. The man took a hasty view of the victims, and then galloped of to give the alarm. The next day, the dead were buried, and the news car- ried to the rangers' camp, and when we arrived the ranch was deserted, the children having been taken away and cared for, until their father arrived, who was off somewhere with a wagon, and had one of his children with him; which circumstance saved its life, no doubt.

As we could accomplish nothing, the trail now being covered by a fresh fall of snow, after about an hour's stay, we mounted and set out for camp, vowing vengeance, if we should ever meet the red man face to face.

Some time after our first visit to the Keenon place, a small party of us returned after a load of corn. Keenon had returned, and was preparing to move away from the frontier. Our captain hearing of it, had purchased his corn crop, which amounted to about three hundred bushels. I was detailed on this trip as one of the guards, and saw the little girl, who was thrown out of the window, and so nearly killed by the Indians. She was very lively, and when we asked her where the Indians hit her, would tuck down her head, so that we could see the back of it; which still looked discolored and bruised. The boy looked pale and thin, his wound was not yet healed.

CHAPTER VI.

INDIAN RAID—THE YOUNG COURIER—RANGERS IN PUR-
SUIT OF THE INDIANS—BEAN'S RANCH—SERGEANT E.
H. COBB AND HIS SCOUTS—VANCE AND FRUMAN'S FIGHT
WITH THE INDIANS—DEFEAT OF THE SETTLERS—OUR
NEW TRILER, WILLIAM MARLETT.

A short time after the Keenon massacree, the Indians
made a raid northeast of us, about twenty miles distant,
and succeeded in carrying off some horses, but without
killing any one. A boy, twelve years old, was sent with
all speed to our camp, to notify us of the fact, so that
we could cut across and intercept them. It is surprising,
how these frontier boys of tender age, will undertake
such perilous trips alone, fraught with danger on every
side, and with what judgment and coolness, they will
accomplish them. This boy, arrived at our camp on a
panting steed, and hurridly gave the captain the information, telling us, at the same time, about how far the
Indians would pass north of our camp, and after resting
his horse a short time, this gallant boy of the border,
again set out to traverse the pathless woods, back to
the settlements, it seemed, without one thought of fear
or danger.

In a few minutes, after receiving the news of the raid,
sixteen of our boys were in the saddle, and ready to
start. The plan was to gallop straight towards the
north, until they intercepted the trail of the retreating
Indians, and, following it as rapidly as possible, endeavor
to come up with them before night, and if not, camp on

the trail, and follow it as long as there was any chance to overtake them. Having to camp on an Indian trail, is a great drawback to a successful pursuit, as the Indians often travel all night, if they know they are pursued, in order to put as many miles between them and their pursuers, before daylight, as possible. Indians can travel at night, but rangers can not trail them, hence, the rapid movements of rangers and settlers, when after them; the idea is to overtake them before the sun goes down, if possible.

We had enlisted another trailer, in place of Swift, who died at Griffin, his name was William Marlett. He was raised on the frontier; was a splendid shot, good horseman, and an excellent trailer. Under his guidance the boys set out rapidly towards the north, through a sandy black jack and post oak country, and a trail could easily be seen when crossed, provided the Indians had passed, which the boys judged they would do, by the time they could arrive on a line with the course the Indians were traveling, and in this were correct, for about six miles out from camp, the trail was intercepted, coming from the east, and going west. The Indians had just passed, and were evidently traveling in a great hurry, thinking they were pursued. The rangers had no trouble in following the trail at a rapid gait. The snow had about all melted off and the sand was very wet. Some of the boys could hardly suppress a whoop, so anxious were they to sight the foe, and they had not long to wait, for the Indians were sighted before sundown. They had halted at a pond of water, and were watering the stock. There seemed to be about twenty Indians, and they had about eighteen head of horses, besides the ones they rode. The pond was in an opening, with dense thickets on the west, and open post oaks on the east, north and south, so it was impossible for the rangers to advance on them without being discovered. They wanted to cut them off from the thickets, if possible, but in attempting to make a flank movement, they were discovered. The Indians gave the alarm cry and began to scatter. The boys raised a yell and charged, but the distance was too great; the Indians disappearing in the brush, before the boys came in range. They penetrated the thickets at different points, but without success. The red men had vanished, like a vision of the night, and nothing was left for the rangers to do but gather up the horses and return to camp, where they arrived without further incident. The next day, the horses were corraled, and a man sent to the settlements, to notify the citizens of the capture, so that they could come and get their property, which they did in a short time.

Captain Baker now deemed it necessary to divide the company, so that we could take a wider range in scouting, and more effectually protect the settlements, north of us, in Montague county, which was constantly overrun by Indians, from the Wichita mountains. Accordingly, eighteen men, under the command of Sergeant E. H. Cobb, was ordered to Bean's ranch, about twenty-five miles north of our camp on Big Sandy, and being furnished with one small wagon, to convey our blankets, provisions, etc., we set out about the middle of January. We had a very fatiguing and laborious trip; the recent melting of the snow had left the ground very soft, and our wagon was constantly bogging down, in the low flats, which we were compelled to cross, but the boys put their shoulders to the wheel, and managed to keep moving, although it was slow and tedious work, and in fact, we had to abandon part of the road, and take a

straight course for Bean's ranch, thus avoiding the
sloughs and marshes of the low bottoms, of a creek we
had to cross, before reaching our destination. We
were not familiar with the country, and supposed we
could cross the creek most anywhere, but we found out
our mistake when we came to it, for it was deep, with
straight banks, and impossible to cross the wagon.
Men were sent below and above, but could find no crossing near, and in order to get to the nearest crossing,
would have to travel down the boggy flats, which to
avoid, had brought us into this difficulty. There were
but two points to be settled: either go through the bogs,
miles out of the way, or build a bridge. It was only a
short distance from where we reached the creek to the
ranch. We finally decided to build a bridge and cross
where we were. To compare great things to small ones,
it reminded me of Napoleon, at Lodi, when some of
the French commanders thought it advisable to fall
back. Napolen straightening himself up in his saddle,
and pointing with his sabre towards the Lodi bridge,
which was strongly defended by the Austrians, said:
"That it is the way to Rome, Milan and Italy;" and in
this case, across this deep creek, was the way to Bean's
ranch. We did not feel disposed to turn back, and
being provided with some tools, in case of an emergency,
we set to work, to try and construct a bridge, of some
description, that we could cross a loaded wagon on.
We first felled two large elm trees, and cut them off,
about twenty feet long, which required hard labor; for
the ground was boggy. We succeeded in getting them
to the place, where we intended crossing, and shoved
them into the water. Some of the boys then stripped,
and carried the ends across, and placed them on the
opposite bank. We then had the creek spanned, by two

stout logs. The width of the stream was not more than fifteen feet.   The logs were placed about eight feet apart.   We then cut poles nine feet long, and laid them cross ways on the logs.   We then bored holes with a large auger, through each end of every pole, and corresponding holes in the logs, and then pinned them down with strong, wooden pins.   It took us till nearly night to complete the job, but we succeeded in getting everything across before dark and then camped.   We reached Bean's ranch early next day.   Col. Bean was absent, but we moved into the enclosure and took possession.   We found large cribs, full of good corn, and the sergeant issued out corn for our horses, carefully keeping account of every barrel that was used.   Late one evening, after we had been there about a week, we saw a large, fine-looking man, mounted on a large horse, and carrying an immense, double-barrelled shot gun, open the gate, and ride up to our camp.   He saluted us very pleasantly, as he came up, and said: " You have taken possession have you."   We told him it seemed so from the looks of things.   He laughed and said: " Rangers are you not?"   We told him we were. " Well." said he, " My name is Bean ; this ranch belongs to me, but that is all right: I am glad to find you here. We have needed some help in this country for a long time.   Make yourselves perfectly at ease, and use anything on my ranch that you need."   By this time, Sergeant Cobb had walked up, and we told Colonel Bean, that there was our commander, Sergeant E. H. Cobb. He shook Cobb warmly by the hand, and told him, he was glad to make his acquaintance.   The Sergeant then pulled out his account book, and showed the colonel the amount of corn we had used, up to that time, and the captain of our company was responsible for the amount, whatever it was.   Bean said he could get three dollars a bushel for his corn, at the forts, but he would let us have it for one dollar per bushel, and we could have as much of it as we wanted.

Colonel Bean's farm was surrounded by small lakes and marshes, and the soil was very rich.   He spent a part of his time in the east, and would come up to his ranch in planting time, and stay there until his corn crop was laid by ; then take a trip back, and come again at gathering time.   He made splendid corn, which always commanded a good price.   It was generally bought by the Government, to feed cavalry horses with. Colonel Bean had a great many adventurers with the Indians, and they soon learned to dread him.   He seldom ever failed to kill some, when he came in contact with them.   He would fearlessly charge, without counting numbers, and fire heavy loads of buckshot, from his enormous shot-gun. and seldom failed to put them to flight, with the loss of some of their number.   I do not think Bean had any family at that time.   He was a fine type of the frontiersman ; almost a giant in size, brave and generous.   The colonel only stayed one night at his ranch, as he merely come up to see how things were getting along, and was glad, he said, to leave it in such good hands.   He feared that if the Indians found out he was gone, they would come down and burn up his corn.

We did not remain long at Bean's station, as our services were needed further up the country, near the line of Texas and Indian Territory.   Our horses were now in good condition, and we soon received orders from Captain Baker, to move up near Red river. and go into camp, in the lower edge of the Cross Timbers, and then scout between Bean's station and Red river.   While the balance of the company, on Big Sandy, would scout north to Bean's and then circle west towards Jacksborough.

This year, (1871), was a year of Indian raids, murders, plunder, etc., by the Kiowa and Comanche tribes of Indians. Regular troops, rangers, and citizens were almost constantly engaged, either in pursuing or fighting them. All along the border, from the Rio Grande (Big river) to Red river, a distance of 600 miles, the war whoop was heard, and the scalping knife reeked with the blood of the pioneers. The men of Kelso, Swisher, Cox, Sansom, and Baker and others were almost constantly in the saddle. They killed numbers of the Indians, besides recovering a large amount of stolen property—principally horses and mules, which they returned to the owners; besides they opened the way for settlements, in the finest country in the United States. The Cross Timbers, in which we were now stationed, extended from Red River to the Brazos, a distance of more than a hundred miles. The timber is chiefly post oak. but having a mixture of various other kinds. The soil is rich, and tolerably well watered, and when we were there, abundant in game. This belt of timber, is about twenty miles wide, with beautiful prairies on the east, where roamed the buffalo, deer, and antelope. On the west, it is somewhat mountainous, but interspersed with beautiful valleys and prairies, until you reach the great plains, which stretch away towards Arizona and Santa Fe—the hunting ground and home of the Apaches, Navahoes, Arapahoes, and various other tribes of hostile Indians, who depredate mostly on the settlers of New Mexico.

Our camp was beautifully located, in the edge of the timber, overlooking the vast prairies on the east. Red river was about twenty miles north of us. Fort Sill, in the Indian Territory, was about forty miles. Here, at this fort, was the reservation; where all of the hostile Indians, who could be induced to come in, were under the eye of the military. They drew rations, blankets, ammunition, etc. Every effort was made to civilize them, but with only partial success. The Comanches and Kiowas that came in, were very hard to manage, and it was impossible to keep them all the time, inside the reservation. Small bands would slip out, keep up the river, through the Wichita mountains for some distance, and then cross over into Texas, and commence depredating; running off stock, killing settlers, and carrying off women and children into captivity; and if they were ever recovered, large ransoms had to be paid.

It was on one of these forays, that a large band of Comanches carried of the children of Vance and Freeman, two settlers living in Wise county. I think it was in 1868 : A number of men were hastily collected, who pursued them, led by the almost frantic fathers of the captives. The trail was easily followed, and they came up with them in the hills, near the Cross Timbers. The Indians outnumbered the whites, about four to one, and were well posted, and awaiting the white men, when the latter came upon them. The brave, and gallant Freeman, instantly ordered a charge, without counting the odds, which were against them, in point of numbers, and locality of battle ground. The men fought well, and sustained the unequal fight for some time. Vance and Freeman were furious, at the sight of their captured children, surrounded by scores of painted savages, and repeatedly charged among them, until both were almost exhausted, with wounds and loss of blood, and would have fallen a prey, to their rash, but commendable bravery, if it had not been for their friends and neighbors, who stood by them, in this, their hour of greatest need. Numbers of the Indians were slain by the unerring rifles and revolvers of the settlers, but being overpowered, on every side, and some of their comrades killed and wounded, they began to give way, fighting as they went, and carrying their wounded men with them. The Indians did not pursue them far, and the white men halted, for a few minutes rest, and to give aid to their wounded companions, who were suffering very much, from deep arrow wounds. Vance had fainted and fallen from his horse. The Indians yelled triumphantly, at the defeat of the whites, and even brought the captives to view, on a hill, to tantalize them. Suddenly Freeman wheeled his horse, and galloped back towards the Indians, yelling and brandishing his revolver. William Marlett, being mounted on a good horse, followed, thinking he could overtake and fetch him back, before he ran into the Indians, but he could not; and drawing his revolver, dashed on, determined to save the frantic man, or perish at his side. The Indians were closing around Freeman, when young Marlet dashed up, firing with deadly precision at the nearest ones, causing them to fall back, leaving three of their number dead on the ground. Marlett then drew his other pistol, and holding it in his right hand, seized Freeman's bridle with the left, and started back, followed by the yelling Comanches. Freeman made no resistance, as he had received another wound and was in a fainting condition. The balance of the men were not idle, although dreading another close encounter, with the savages, they came back, firing at the Indians as they galloped up, and succeed in keeping them off, until Freeman was carried away. The Indians did not follow, and they slowly returned to the settlements, with heavy hearts. They had done all that men could do, but had failed. The captives and the dead bodies of some of their comrades, were in the hands of the savages. How could they go home to expectant wives and mothers, with this sad tale of defeat, instead of bringing back the captive children, to almost agonized mothers ? · They returned with their wounded and almost dying husbands; pierced with sharp arrows, pale and haggard, with hope gone. And the news had to be carried to some; that their husbands or sons, had fallen by the side of Freeman, in the desperate fight.

Such is a true sketch, of the horrors of the Texas border, at the time of which I write. Vance and Freeman both recovered, after many days of anguish and suffering. Freeman spent twelve months, after his recovery, in searching for his children. He joined all expeditions to the Indian country, and sometimes penetrated the wilds alone. Hanging on the trails and around the camps of the hostile savages, in the vain hope of seeing and rescuing his children, but all was of no avail, and finally gave it up, and returned home, never expecting to see his loved ones again on earth, but such was not to be the case. Some traders found them, high up on the Canadian river, and bought them from the Indians, and also the children of Vance, and returned them to their parents. The three children of Freeman cost him $900.

·William Marlett, the young man who displayed such courage, in the Vance and Freeman fight, was the trailer we enlisted in place of Swift. He was a handsome young man, and the best shot in the company. Several of the parties, who participated in this desperate fight, still lived in Wise county, when we were on

that part of the frontier.   As I kept no account of these
things at the time, I cannot give dates and places as well
as I would like to, and after a lapse of twelve years,
have to trust to memory, and can only give the main
incidents of pioneer battles, as they were told to me by
settlers.   In the next chapter, I will give an account of
the killing of Red Cap, a Comanche chief, in a fight at
Ball's ranch.

CHAPTER VII.

BALL'S RANCH—RED CAP, THE COMANCHE CHIEF—FIGHT AT BALL'S RANCH, AND DEATH OF RED CAP—HAND TO HAND ENCOUNTER WITH THE GREAT CHIEF—DEATH OF BAILEY—THE FALSE ALARM IN THE SETTLEMENT— SHIRA'S RANCH.

IN 1871, there lived near the western boundary, of Wise county, a ranchman, named Ball; the incident which I will now relate, occurred about two years after he settled in that part of the country, which I believe was in 1867. The Indians were very troublesome, and the old man being one of the outside settlers, was constantly harrassed by hostile bands. He was compelled to keep his horses locked up at night, and on one occasion, they killed two good horses through the cracks of the stable, out of spite, because they could not get at them; but the old man was a true-grit frontiersman, and toughed it out. He had a beautiful place; good land; plenty of cattle and hogs, and made a good living. Mr. Ball was a kind and hospitable gentleman; often had Baker's scouts rested and feasted beneath his roof. But the blow fell heavily one day, when a raiding band carried off one of his boys, a lad about twelve years old. The boy was only a short distance from the house, when he was surrounded and captured, before his father's eyes, and him powerless to render any assistance. He knew, from the waving red plume, in the chief's head dress, that it was the notorious "Red Cap," the terror of the Northwest. Mr. Ball had several neighbors, and after the Indians left, mounted his horse and gave the alarm. Clark, Bailey, Shira, and others responded to the call, and, mounting good horses, were soon on the trail of the now retreating Indians, who had taken a northwest course, in the direction of the Wichita mountains. There was not enough men, in those sparsely settled counties, to successfully fight Red Cap and his band. All that they could do was to follow them, and see that they had left the country, in order to quiet the fears of the people. For twelve long months nothing was heard of the captive boy, by his parents, and they had about given him up as lost, when one day, he suddenly walked into his father's yard, greatly to the joy of the family. He was considerably sunburned, and his hair had grown long, so they hardly recognized him at first sight. He had a sad experience to relate, of hardships that had befallen him since his capture. He said the Indians traveled rapidly at first, expecting pursuit, but after crossing Red River, traveled slowly, and took a northwest course, over a rough, mountainous country, and across beautiful prairies, killing game by the way, in abundance, until they reached a large Indian village, at the head of the Canadian river, where they spent the winter. He belonged to the chief, Red Cap, who treated him kindly, but the other Indians abused him very much, especially when the chief was absent, which was often the case. He seemed restless, and longed to be on the warpath, either against the whites, or other Indians, hostile to his tribe. It was while he was on one of these raids, that some white traders entered the Indian camp. They offered to buy the white boy, and the Indians readily consented; gladly exchanging him for such articles as suited their fancy, among the goods of the traders. When the chief returned, the traders and the boy were far on their way towards the settlements. The chief was furious when he found out what they had done, and raved like a madman; threatening vengeance on those who had sold the boy, and finally determined to make up an expedition to Texas, for the purpose of recapturing him. Early in the fall, he set out, with two hundred and eighty warriors; and one evening about 3 o'clock, arrived at Ball's ranch. So rapid and secret had been their movements, after they had crossed the

(The Fight at Ball's Ranch.)

Texas line, they had not been discovered, until they arrived at the ranch. Bailey, the son-in-law of old man Ball, and the boy the Indians came in search of, were in the field, about three hundred yards from the house, on the east side, pulling corn; when Red Cap made his appearance, at the head of his blood-thirsty band. They came in behind some hills, south of the house, and were not discovered, until they were very close. A considerable number of the Indians, headed by their chief, had

19

crossed the fence, and were advancing towards them, before being discovered by Bailey and the lad. Bailey was a brave man, and took in the situation at a glance. He saw that they were nearly cut off from the house, and told the boy to run, climb the fence, as quick as possible, and make his escape, and he would fight the Indians. The lad had a mortal terror of again being captured by the Indians, and started off on a quick run, towards the house. Bailey drew his pistol, and followed him, firing at the nearest Indians, who were now close upon him. The Indians returned the fire, yelling furiously. The firing and yelling was the first intimation the inmates of the house had of what was transpiring in the field.

It happened that two of the neighbors, Clark and Shira, were at the house, conversing with Mr. Ball, when the first shot was fired; they immediately ran out into the yard, and were almost struck dumb with amazement, to see the whole valley and field literally swarming with Indians. They saw Bailey fighting in their midst, and the boy running towards the fence, pursued by the dreaded chief. Red Cap, who they at once recognized by his plume; and they saw too, that it was almost out of their power to render any assistance, against such fearful odds. But these three men were true and tried, and seizing their rifles advanced towards the Indians, coming as near as they dared. in the face of such a horde of yelling demons, and opened fire on them with effect. Bailey, after firing all his shots but one, retreated towards the fence, nearest the house; but saw the chief seize his little brother-in-law, while attempting to scale the fence. and drag him back towards the other Indians. Bailey was wounded, but would likely have made his escape, if he had kept on and left the boy to his fate, but he turned and charged the chief; aiming his pistol at Red Cap's head as he came up, who was then compelled to let go his captive and defend himself, against this fearless and dangerous foe. He quickly placed an arrow and drew it to the head, discharging it full in Bailey's breast, as he came up, only a few paces intervening between them. But at the same time, there was the flash of a pistol, and the chief fell dead in his tracks, shot through the brain. Bailey was determined that his last shot should find a victim, and at the same time rid the border of a terrible scourge. That shot, was indeed his last; his empty weapon dropped from his relaxing hand; he staggered forward a few steps and fell, near the body of the chief. The boy, finding himself again free, once more, turned and fled; closely pursued by the Indians, but succeeded in reaching the spot where his father and the other men were loading and firing upon his pursuers. The Indians closed around the body of Bailey, and took off his scalp; while others removed the dead chief from the field. The party near the house continued to fire on them, which they returned, but without effect. The wife of Bailey was standing in the yard, watching him. When she saw him fall, being a delicate woman, it was more than she could bear, and fell fainting, where she stood, and was carried into the house. The Indians took up their dead and hastily left. It is not known how many were killed. None but the chief was found; they stopped and buried him, in the head of a ravine, about half a mile from Ball's ranch. His arms, ammunition, blanket, etc., were buried with him, and his horse turned loose at the grave. The Indians believed that he will have need of all these things, when he arrives at the happy hunting ground. But after they left, the white men found him;

dug him up, and divided out his accoutrements among themselves.

One day, while stopping at Ball's ranch, I saw the blanket and pipe, of Red Cap. His blood was still upon the blanket; it being red, the blood spots were black. His pipe was of stone, and would weigh nearly two pounds. I also saw the spike, which was cut out of Bailey's breast; it was about three inches long, keen and sharp. In attempting to extract an arrow, the spike generally pulls out. It is wrapped with fine sinew, and when it becomes saturated with blood, relaxes, and the spike is easily drawn from the arrow. This is one reason why the arrow is so dangerous.

Bailey was brought to the house, and temporarily laid on the floor, until a place could be prepared to lay out his body; his wife still being unconscious, and when she revived, the first sight which greeted her, was the mutilated body of her husband. She again swooned, and for a long time, life itself seemed extinct, but she finally recovered. It seems that this would be enough to drive the stoutest hearts from the Texas frontier, but these brave men still remained at their homes, determined to fight it out to the bitter end. In passing through this settlement, we sometimes stopped at the ranch of old man Shira, who lived two or three miles north of Mr. Ball. We always found him and his excellent wife, kind and hospitable; never charging us a cent for a night's lodging, but always telling us to call again, when passing that way, and if this should ever meet his eye, he will remember the man he made the buckskin jacket for. It is seldom we rangers slept under a roof, and only then when some of us were on detached service, down in the settlements, buying horses. Some of our men were constantly losing horses, either dying or getting killed.

We sometimes had to go a considerable distance into the settlements, before we could find good horses for sale. To give a correct idea of the rapid movements, of the settlers of this remote frontier, in case of an Indian alarm, I will relate an incident, which occurred in the Ball settlement, while on that part of the frontier. George McPhail and I, were returning to camp, from a trip below; where we had been to see about buying a few saddle horses, and intended staying over night in the Ball settlement, as it would take us all of the next day to reach camp, and preferred spending a night with the ranchmen to sleeping out. We took a straight course for the settlement, as there were but few roads in that country; and towards night, after having ridden hard all day, began to think it was time to sight a ranch, if we were on the right course, and for this purpose, left our horses, and ascended a hill, in order to take a survey of the country; and we were right, in our conjectures, for there was a ranch, straight ahead, not more than half a mile off. After waiting a few minutes, we went back, and mounting, soon came to a field fence, and went round it towards the house. I forget this man's name; but think it was Davis. Anyway, as we rode up, the man of the house was in the yard, near the fence, with his gun, watching us very closely. McPhail and myself were both sunburned; wore long, black hair, and might easily be taken for Indians, at a distance, especially on the frontier, where every man is on the lookout. The settler soon became satisfied, and came out from the fence towards us, and in answer to our salutation of "Good evening, sir;" said: "How are you. Was that you fellows on the hill yonder, a few minutes ago?" We told him it was, and asked what of it. "Why, the great geminy," said he, "the whole country is alarmed

by this time, or will be shortly. I spied you, as soon as
you topped the hill, yonder, and thought certain it was
Indians, spying out the ranch, and started my boy, like
thunder and blazes, on a good horse, to give the alarm.
Some will begin to drop in directly, to learn the particulars; but get down and come in, and rest yourselves, and
stay all night. I see from your looks and shooting-irons
that you are rangers, and they are always welcome."
We thanked him, and said we would get some water;
but if it was not too far, we would go on to old man
Shira's. When we entered the house, we saw a double
barreled shotgun, six-shooter, and loose buckshot and
caps lying on the bed, ready for instant use. Noticing
my observations, he said: "See, boys, I was fixed for
'em. I calculated, if it was Indians, and they attacked the
ranch, to open the ball with the old rifle, and then dodge
in and give them buckshot, thick and fast." His wife
and children, were in the back room, but came out when
we entered. The small children looking a little wild at
us, with a tendency to hide behind their mother. We
drank some water, and about that time heard a "hello,"
at the fence. We went out, and saw a man on a panting horse, with a long rifle before him. It was Clark;
he had met the young courier on the road, and hastened
up. The mistake was soon explained to him, and he
turned and galloped off, to notify others that it was a
false alarm. Bidding the settler good bye, we mounted,
and rode on to Shira's. About dark, a man passed us
to the left; tearing at a fearful rate through the woods;
going in the direction of Ball's ranch. The alarm was
not yet checked. When we arrived at Shira's we greatly
relieved him; for he too, had been notified, that Indians
were in the settlement. We expressed our regrets that
we had caused the country to be alarmed; but he said

that was nothing, that they were used to it, and were only too glad that it was not so, but this would help to keep them in practice. We had a good supper and a good night's rest, after our long ride, and the next day made it to camp. On arrival, we learned of an Indian raid near Victoria Peak, and the boys were preparing to make a scout in that direction.

CHAPTER VIII.

THE CAMP IN THE CROSS TIMBERS—SERGEANT COBB
CHASED BY INDIANS—INDIAN RAID ON CLEAR CREEK—
ATTACK ON RIDDLE'S RANCH—THE RANGERS NOTI-
FIED—STRIKING THE TRAIL—THE LONG CHASE—FIRST
SIGHT OF THE INDIANS—PREPARING FOR ACTION.

WINTER had now broke, and we could scout to better advantage. The Indians were very active, and gave
considerable trouble all along the frontier. They generally did their mischief, during the light moons, so they
could see how to travel at night, to a greater advantage.
During the dark moons, were the only times the settlers
could consider themselves and stock safe; when that was
passed, horses were kept close, and every man was on
the alert, until the return of dark nights again. After
one of their raids, if the Indians succeeded in putting
one night's travel between them and the settlers, who
were pursuing, they generally got off safe, with their
booty; unless some daring spirit, like John H. Moore,
raised a sufficient force to follow them to their homes,
in the mountains; then the west was lit up by the burning wigwams of the Comanches.

While here, at this camp, in the edge of the Cross
Timbers, Sergeant Cobb, returning from Red River
Station, was chased by Indians, at Lookout mountain.
It was nearly sunset, when he encountered them, and as
they were between him and camp, the gallant sergeant
was compelled to turn, and run the other way. The
Indians were left behind in the race, and soon gave it

up. The sergeant then made a detour, so as not to come in contact with them again, and arrived in camp about midnight. He gave orders for sixteen men to be in readiness an hour before daylight, on the following morning to go in pursuit. The men were all aroused, and the names called off, of those who were to go. At the appointed time, next morning, sixteen well mounted men were on their way to Lookout mountain; where we arrived about an hour after sunrise, by rapid riding, and soon struck the trail, where they pursued Sergeant Cobb, and followed it easily, until we came to where they gave up the chase, but from that point, we could never strike it again. Our regular trailer, Marlett, was with the other portion of the company, on Big Sandy, which was about thirty or forty miles south of us. We had a citizen with us, from Montague, who was familiar with Indian ruses and strategems, and said the Indians had *covered* their trail, knowing that they would be followed, after they failed to get the white man. They did this, by incasing their horses feet in pieces of buffalo skin, with the woolly side out, which left no impression on the ground, that could be followed. We therefore gave up the chase, and returned to camp. We kept out scouts, but the savages were very cunning, and avoided a collision with the rangers. They had located our camp and generally gave it wide birth, when going down the country on raids. Of course they feared the settlers as much as they did the rangers, but they knew that it would take some time for the farmers to collect force enough to cope with them; while the rangers were ready at a moment's notice, to mount and be off. Another advantage which we had was our improved fire arms, while the citizen still had to use the muzzle loaders. Our boys while in camp, passed off the time in reading, writing, carbine practice, trading horses, etc. One of our men accidentally killed his horse with a carbine. One day, while Henry Lewis and George McPhail were running and firing, at a large turkey gobbler, in a small prairie, Lewis shot McPhail's horse through the head. McPhail ran in ahead of Lewis, just as he was in the act of shooting; the ball struck low enough to miss the brain and the horse recovered.

It was now February, and as the saying is, our men were almost spoiling for a fight. It seemed as if we could not bring the Indians to a stand, and the boys were afraid the campaign would end, before they could have a chance to match their prowess with that of the red man, but such was not to be the case, for a portion of this camp, at least. On the 6th of February, a band of Kiowas and Comanches, crossed Panther creek, below our camp, and at daylight, on the 7th, attacked Riddle's ranch, on Clear creek, ten miles from our camp. Riddle forted up, and kept them at bay, but they carried off some of his saddle horses, and shot one with an arrow, it being hard to manage. Riddle watched them, until they crossed the creek, and disappeared on the other side. He then came out and gave the alarm to his nearest neighbors. George Henson immediately mounting a fine, black race horse, set out for the ranger camp. We saw him on the prairie some time before he arrived, and knew from his speed that he brought important news. As soon as he dashed up, he hallooed out: "Indians, boys, Indians!" then there was mounting in hot haste. Sergeant Cobb gave quick orders, for those who had the best horses to saddle up. The balance would be left for camp guard. Two of our men, who had good horses, John Garner and Frank Sorrell, were out turkey hunting. All of them were very anxious to go. John Fitzgerald, not being well mounted, offered five dollars to any one, who would let him have their place, but could not get his offer taken. G. W. H. Breaker, having to remain in camp, loaned Citizen Henson his Winchester. In a short time, eleven of the rangers were in the saddle, ready to start, I being one of the number. Henson, on his fiery, black steed, rode by the sergeant, in the lead, to guide us by the nearest route to the ranch. As we went at a brisk gallop, Henson gave the particulars of the attack. Riddle thought there was about twenty Indians, and some of them not mounted, the last he saw of them. We then had strong hopes of overtaking them, before night, if they remained together, and provided the Indians who were afoot did not succeed in getting mounted, and this was not likely, before we could overtake them; it being twenty-five or thirty miles to the settlement on Hickory creek, the direction the Indians seemed to be going, when last seen by Riddle, and no loose horses could be found on the prairie, along the route they had taken. In a short time we arrived at the ranch, and struck the trail. The horse, shot by the Indians, was still bleeding; the arrow had been extracted, having stuck between the ribs. The Indians crossed the creek below the ranch, and ascended a steep bluff on the south side; the water still being muddy, where they crossed. We were joined here by John Harvell, another settler; this increased our number to thirteen. The trail led through some thickets, until we got clear of the creek, and then a beautiful rolling prairie, stretched off for miles, towards the south, the direction the trail was leading, it being easily followed, a shower of rain, that morning, wet the tall grass, causing it to remain in a leaning position, when struck down by the hoofs of the horses. we could see which way the trail led two hundred yards ahead, and for some time we followed it at a gallop.

Every thing was in our favor, so far, and occasionally seeing a moccasin track, told us the foot Indians were still with them. We now had every hope of overtaking them; and traveling over a rolling country, kept us in constant expectation of sighting them, when we reached the crest of the next swell, just ahead. But mile after mile was put behind us, and still no Indians were visible.

(Rangers Pursuing the Indians.)

Thus far we had traveled so rapidly, some of our horses began to show signs of fatigue, and we had to slacken our speed. but Kelly's horse, finally broke down, and he was compelled to stop and take the back track. We had galloped our horses almost incessantly for twenty miles. The sergeant told Kelly to take his time for it, on his return, and if any Indians run on to him, to do the best he could, but he thought there was no danger back that way, and now being reduced to twelve men, we again continued the pursuit. We regreted to part with our comrade, for he was a brave boy, and we had none to spare. The absence of one Winchester, and forty rounds of ammunition we knew would be missed in a close fight.

Shortly after Kelly left us, we came upon the carcass of a stray yearling, which the Indians had killed and partly eaten. This was also in our favor, for they must have delayed some time at this. It was near a small branch that ran through the prairie, and the moccasin tracks were thick in the mud, where they had been getting water. After leaving this place, the Indians resorted to one of their old dodges, to evade and delay pursuit; that is, by scattering; and here for sometime, we were sorely perplexed and bothered. It was now passed noon and time was precious to us. They would scatter off across the prairie, for some distance, and then all get together again. and then, again scatter; but as they were traveling nearly a south course, we kept men ahead on the best horses, when the trail was scattered, to find it again, where they came together, and they would notify us of the fact by signals. We would then gallop up to them; thus saving considerable time. We passed one horse the Indians had left, he seemed completely worn out, and stood panting on the trail, never moving out of his tracks, as we galloped passed him. It is likely they had rode him the night before, or else he had been carrying a double burden. The Indians thinking they had now baffled pursuit quit scattering, and traveled together in a body, and we followed with renewed energy, although some of our horses were failing. The sergeant's horse and the black race horse, still kept the lead, and seemed fresh. After a while, we came to where the grass had been burned off recently, and near a lone hackberry tree, discovered something, which made the boys scan the prairie a little uneasily. This was another Indian trail, leading in from the west, and much larger than the one we had been following. Here they had consolidated, and led off together from this place; evidently number-ing between forty and fifty; and only twelve of us, and most of our horses badly jaded. We were now nearly thirty miles from our camp. Sergeant Cobb carefully examined the trail, and pronounced them four to one of us. We then dismounted, to let our horses blow a little, and held a short council. The sergeant said he would leave it to the men whether we continued the pursuit or not. He was willing to go on himself, if the men were, but would not influence any one to go against his will. He was satisfied, he said, that the Indians were not far ahead, and that we could easily overtake them before night; but if we were going to turn back, this was the place to do it; for if we once came on the Indians, we would have to fight. For they seeing our small number, would pursue us, whether we wanted to fight *them* or not; and, in the present condition of our horses, would undoubtedly overtake us; and if we fought them at all, it must be to win; if some turned back, all must turn back. He would leave that for the men to decide. After the talk of the sergeant, the men soon settled the question. They all agreed that it would never do to go back to camp, without seeing the Indians, after get-ting this near to them; that they would take their chances, let come what might, and continue their pursuit. The sergeant smiled, with a merry twinkle in his blue eyes, and vaulting into the saddle, put spurs to his horse, and dashed off on the trail, followed by the balance of the boys. It was now about three o'clock in the evening, and in the next hour, we traveled six miles. The trail was plain, as the Indians stayed together, and double its former size. Some of our horses were failing fast, and the boys became considerably scattered; the best horses being in the lead. The sergeant and the two citizens, Harvell and Henson, were about a quarter of a mile ahead: they being mounted on the best horses. George Howell and myself brought up the extreme rear. Howell's horse was somewhat windbroken, and blowed fearfully. I was riding a large, good looking horse, but he was failing fast, and was thinking my part of the chase would soon have to terminate, when I saw Sergeant Cobb, and those with him, suddenly rein up their horses, on the crest of the ridge ahead of us, and after looking a few moments, turned and waved his hand towards us. Said I, George, there they are; we are in for it now. We urged our horses into a weary gallop. One by one, the boys stopped, around our commander, as they rode up and looked towards the southeast. The sergeant looked at me and smiled, as I came up, stretching my neck to see; and said: "Here they are Jack, now we will have it." When I first came up, I thought the sergeant was going to give up the chase, and was fooling the boys, as I could see nothing; but I was looking beyond them. The Indians were in the low ground, between the two swells of prairie, and about six hundred yards off. They had discovered us, and were moving about, and all looking towards us. We could distinctly hear their yelling at that distance, on the prairie. It seemed that about half of them were afoot, and as near as we could count at that distance, numbered forty-one. Our squad looked rather slim, in comparison. Our men looked serious, but you could still see fight in their eyes. We noticed one Indian leave the balance, and gallop to elevated ground, so that he could see beyond us, to ascertain whether that was all our force, and being convinced of this fact, returned, and I suppose communicated the same to the balance of the band; for they instantly set up a terrible yelling, and some advanced towards us, shaking their shields. They were a picturesque looking set, with long, black hair, gaudy trappings, feathers, etc. Sergeant Cobb gave the boys a short talk; telling them if there was any one present, that felt as if he could not face the music, to turn and ride back, as he would force no man into a fight against his will. But as none responded to this invitation, we began to prepare for action.

CHAPTER IX.

A MESSENGER SENT FOR AID—THE KEEP HOUSE—DR.
JAY AND FAMILY—COMMENCEMENT OF THE FIGHT—
THE RANGERS HOLD THEIR GROUND AND KEEP THE
INDIANS AT BAY—INCIDENTS OF THE FIGHT—YOUNG
SORRELLS WOUNDED—DESPERATE CHARGE OF THE
INDIANS—OSKA HORSEBACK, THE COMANCHE CHIEF,
KILLED.

THE boys all dismounted, and tightened the girths of
their saddles, examined pistols, etc. The sergeant then
issued some extra cartridges, which he had brought in his
saddle pockets, in case of emergency, and it is well that
he did, for we needed them that day, before the sun
went down. Sergeant Cobb said, rather than risk the
lives of his men against such odds, that if he thought he
could get any re-enforcements of citizens, that he would
hold the Indians in check, or follow them, until a sufficient force could collect, to warrant a close fight, and
asked Harvell how far it was to the nearest settlement.
He said there were settlers on Clear creek, the timbers
of which could be seen in the distance. He pointed out
the Keep ranch, two miles off on the prairie, nearly east
of us. A stock man, named Keep, built this house for
his hands to live in, that attended his stock, but it was
now occupied by Doctor Jay, and his family, lately from
Illinois, and he thought we might get three men there.
It was then agreed that Harvell should go and alarm the
settlers; and we would fight the Indians, or hold them
in check, the best we could, until help arrived. There

were two things greatly against us: the jaded condition of our horses, and the declining sun. We were
neither in a condition to pursue or retreat. We told
Harvell that if the Indians pursued him, we would charge
them. He started off at full speed towards the Keep
ranch, and had to run a little nearer the Indians than we
then were. They watched him closely, but did not
offer to pursue him. At the same time, we moved nearer
the Indians, some of the boys shouting at them. The
sergeant gave orders not to fire at long range, as it
would only be useless waste of cartridges, and we needed
all we had. Harvell was soon a mere speck on the
prairie, and the sun was only about two hours and a
half high, and we had but little hopes of getting help
before night. The country was so sparsely settled, it
would take some time, to go from place to place. While
we were watching them, and revolving these things in
our minds, the chief galloped out from the band, and
came straight towards us, without checking up, till not
more than three hundred yards intervened, between us.
He then suddenly checked his horse, and turning him
half around, sat, and looked at us for a few moments.
He then commenced running his horse around in a circle, flourishing his shield, and yelling; but as soon as a
carbine was raised, dropped almost out of sight, on the
opposite side of his horse, and galloped back. He was a
large Indian, and had a Mexican serape thrown over his
shoulders. His leggins were of yellow buckskin, heavily
fringed. We saw something glitter on his breast,
like gold or silver. He also had an eagle plume in his
cap. This chief was named Sittanke, a prominent man
among the Kiowas, and nephew of the notorious Sittanke,
one of the war chiefs of the nation. After the return of
the chief, the Indians cut many capers, especially those

that were mounted: coming towards us at times, in full
gallop, as if they were going to charge us; and several
times we put ourselves in position to receive them; but
just before they got in range, would wheel off through
the prairie, rattling their shields and yelling. Finding
they were not going to charge, we changed our position,
and moved to the left. This brought us near to them.
We were close enough now to have a good view of them,
and discovered that there were two bands, each commanded by its own chief. We afterwards learned that
it was young Oska Horseback, who led the Comanches.
He made several dashes towards us, and was the best
rider I ever saw. He was a slim, trim-made Indian,
about twenty-two years old. He was mounted on a
beautiful blood-bay horse, with black mane and tail, and
star in the face. This chief rode no saddle, but had a red
blanket strapped around his horse. He could dismount
and mount again, with his horse in a gallop; displaying
an agility that was surprising. He could drop down on
the opposite side of his horse, as quick as a flash, and
expose nothing but his hand and foot, his horse going at
full speed. He wore red leggins, and fine beaded moccasins. He also wore a beautiful beaded ornament on
his breast, which entirely covered it. He had his scalp-
lock platted, and a prairie chicken's head tied to the end
of it, which hung down to the middle of his back. The
chicken's head was painted a deep red.

Hickory creek headed in this prairie, near where we
were, but resembled a ditch or washed-out road, more
than a creek. Sergeant Cobb told the boys if we could
take a position on this creek, it would be a protection for
us and our horses. The Indians had formed in range of
it, and we could there sustain a regular siege, until
re-enforcements could arrive. Although the men were

willing to fight, our leader hesitated to charge close upon the Indians, knowing there was enough of them to immediately surround and crush our small band in a few minutes. The time was, when these odds would not have seemed so great; when Indians fought almost exclusively with bow and lance. But these were a picked band of warriors, well armed; most of them having revolvers and short carbines, besides the bow and lance. Taking all these things into consideration, we moved further to the left, and bore in towards the ditch. The Indians watching our maneuvers, until they ascertained what our intentions were, and then quickly moved off, out of range of cover, which we were seeking, and formed in a rainbow line, on the side of the ridge, about five hundred yards off, in open ground, without bush or tree near them. Indians dread a concealed foe, and unless they can take cover themselves, prefer open ground, when they intend to fight; seldom following one man into a thicket, if they know he is armed. We halted on the brink of the ditch, and surveyed this motley crowd. The Comanches were on the right, the Kiowas on the left. The latter, were tall, fine-looking Indians. The Comanches were low, heavy-set, broad-shouldered fellows. Some of them were naked to the waist, except the quiver, on the back, and the strap across the breast. As they stood in line, there was a footman between every two horsemen. They all carried shields on the left arm, made of thick, buffalo hide; with dressed deerskin stretched tightly over them; painted in the center with black, red, or green spots. They stood quiet, and almost motionless, with every painted face turned towards us. They looked quite imposing, owing to the scattered line, which extended about three hundred yards, on the side of the ridge.

Some of the boys raised the sights on their carbines, to commence firing at long range, but the sergeant opposed it, telling the boys they would only waste their cartridges at that distance, and we had none to throw away. It is true, our guns would hold up that far, but then an Indian, with a shield, is hard to hit, even at short range, and at that distance, it would be almost impossible to hit him. The men then commenced yelling, and daring the Indians, to see if they could draw them upon us. George Henson hung his hat on the pommel of his saddle, and tying a red silk handkerchief around his head rode up the ditch, yelling and waving his carbine; calling them cowards and dogs. The chief then rode slowly down his line, and seemed to be saying something to the Indians. He then turned, and galloped back to his position, on the left of the line, which was nearest to us. "Boys," said Sergeant Cobb, suddenly looking around, "what do you say to a charge?" "All right, Ed.," came from the rangers, "you lead the way, and we will follow."

Ed. Cobb had seen service in the Confederate army, but had never fought Indians. He was a Virginian by birth, and belonged to Stonewall Jackson's division, during the late war. He was at the battle of the Wilderness, where legions of brave soldiers went down, amidst smoke, and carnage, with the roar of cannon, and the noise of tramping thousands in their ears. It was here the men of Texas, cow boys and rangers, followed Hood, and interposed themselves like a shield, between the shattered ranks of Lee, and the advancing hosts under Hooker.

Ed. gave the boys a short talk, telling them they must stay together, and if need be, die together, and if routed, never leave a comrade as long as there was any chance to save him. If he was unfortunate enough to get wounded, or have his horse killed; and as our horses were nearly broke down, we could make a better fight than a run. I will admit that I felt weak about the knees, and something like a chill would creep up my back every time I cast my eyes towards that black line, stretched across the ridge. I thought of the old folks at home, nearly five hundred miles away, and how my mother begged me not to go, with tears in her eyes. That mother, who, when she heard that my Christmas dinner, consisted of parched corn and salt, sat down and wept: saying, she wished on that day, she had eaten no dinner, since her boy had none. As such thoughts as these passed through my mind, as wicked as I was, I asked God to shield me in the battle, that I might once more behold that dear mother.

With the exception of the sergeant and William Caruthers, who had also been a Confederate soldier, none of our boys had ever been in battle. Billy Sorrells was the youngest, being only sixteen years of age, but he was true-grit, and waved his hat at the painted warriors, as we advanced to the charge. Having crossed the Rubicon, (ditch), the die was cast. No turning back now. We were about to play a desperate game; eleven ranger boys, against forty-one picked warriors, from the Wichita mountains. Well we knew their savage nature, if we were overwhelmed; no surrender; no prisoners taken in this kind of warfare. Sergeant Cobb telling the boys to handle their guns lively, we galloped straight towards the centre of the Indians, without checking, until within eighty yards of them. I shall never forget my feelings at this moment, it seemed as if we had rushed to our destruction. The hideous faces of the Indians, with almost every spot of war-paint visible ; their shields and gaudy trappings, and all, combined, was enough to try the nerves of old soldiers, but the quick command of our leader, to "dismount, they are going to fire," drove all such thoughts away, and I only had time to think of the present, and what was expected of every man. For I knew that every man must do his duty, or we were lost. And like Henry V, to his troops, at Agincourt, every man must fight to-day, as if on his sole arm hung victory. The men were not long in obeying the command, and received the fire of the Indians as they went to the ground. As was anticipated, the balls whistled over our heads, and not a man was hit. Some few balls struck the ground under our horses. We instantly returned the fire, and the Indians charged, making the prairie ring with their war-whoops. Sergeant Cobb told the boys to scatter; we were too close together; stretch our line to fifty yards, and have only one man in a place, to be shot at, and to shun their fire as best we could; drop low in the grass, or shoot from beneath our horses. The Indians evidently were not aware that we were armed with repeating rifles, and it seemed, were trying to run in on us, before we could reload; as they generally did the settlers. But we gave them two more rounds, in quick succession. Some of our balls cracking loudly, on their dry buffalo hide shields, and they fell back in some confusion. One horse having been killed, and evidently, some of them Indians, wounded, from their actions. One of them went off into the prairie, and remained alone, some distance from the fight. But they soon raised another whoop, and came again, running towards us in zigzag manner, like a fence worm. Our boys were good shots, but an Indian is hard to hit; protecting himself with a a shield in front spoils the aim even of the best marksmen.

Our boys handled their guns lively, and there was almost a continuous crack of carbines, during these charges, but we done but little damage. There were no two Indians together, and them darting here and there which also caused their own shots to be ineffectual. Those on horseback swooped around us, and fired from beneath the necks of their horses. Some of the boys had narrow escapes during this round, having holes shot through their clothing. In this charge we killed another

(The Battle.)

horse and one Indian. He fell within about sixty yards of us, and made several attempts to get away, but could not and finally lay still, upon the prairie, nearly hid by the rank grass. After this charge, the Indians drew back some distance, and held a consultation. The chiefs riding among them and gesticulating, and pointing towards us. One of the Indians, who was not mounted, stopped and continued to fire at us at long range. He had the longest gun, I think, that I ever saw. He would drop down on one knee and take aim. His balls would make some of the boys dodge, but no one was hit. When a carbine was pointed at him he would drop down and throw up his shield. Several of the boys tried their hand at him, but he was too quick for them at that distance. The Indians having come to some understanding, concerning their next move, again advanced, yelling as before, and firing at long range. Although greatly outnumbering us they seemed to fear a close fight. They saw that we all had revolvers, which as yet, had not been drawn. Some of them again dashed around to the right and left, and we had to keep turning to fire. While doing this I came near being killed, by one of my comrades, James Ewers; we both turned about the same time, and changed our position to fire at an Indian, who was running on a horse near us. In fact, I was nearer the Indian than Jim, and almost between the two. He stepped to where I was, and was in the act of firing, when I turned to fire; this movement brought my face almost in contact with the muzzle of his gun; as he fired, I came near going to the ground, and my face was badly powder burned. He and I were on the extreme left. The Indian was not hit. About this time, two daring young bucks mounted a mule, belonging to their party, and made a run together. The mule running almost as fast as a horse. This unusual sight, drew the fire of several carbines, at the same time, and the mule fell, shot through. The Indians were thrown to the ground, but quickly sprang to their feet, and ran back; neither being hit, though fired at several times. The Indians did not wait long after this charge, but came again with redoubled yells; every one seemed to be making all the noise possible. "Stand firm, now, boys," said the sergeant; "I believe they are coming to us this time. Hold your fire

until they come close, and if it comes hand to hand, draw
your pistols, if not use the carbines." Suddenly there
rose up out of the grass, about sixty yards to our right,
one of the most hideous objects I ever beheld. It was
an Indian; with buffalo head, mop, and horns on his
head and shoulders; having pieces of dry hides fastened
about him. He made a fearful, snorting noise, and rat-
tled his dry hides, as he rose up. Judson Wilhoit was
the nearest man to him, and as some of the boys hol-
loaed: " Look out Jud! There is the devil on your
side." He fired, striking the buffalo head, which
cracked loudly. The Indian advanced a few steps, still
making a terrible noise, and received another shot from
Wilhoit, then seeing he could not scare our horses, beat
a hasty retreat, mixing up with the other Indians, who
were running towards us, and discharging arrows. Only
one of our horses became frightened at the Indians
during the fight. This was a little singular, as the sight,
or even the smell of an Indian, generally puts them in
terror, until they become accustomed to Indians, and even
then, you can always tell when they are about, by the
snorting of the horses. I suppose, the jaded condition
of our horses had something to do with it. Some pricked
up their ears, and showed signs of uneasiness, when the
Indians first commenced yelling. Henson's race horse
reared and plunged nearly all the time, and came near
getting away, when we were dismounted. As yet, our
men had escaped well, only a few scratches. Dan
Edwards had six holes shot through his coat, which was
rolled up and tied to his saddle. The fight had lasted
for some time, and the manner in which the Indians
scurried around, on their horses, with only one foot visible, drew our fire, without doing any damage, except
now and then, killing a horse. We were wasting car-

tridges to no purpose, and were apt to be picked off, one at a time, or have our own horses killed. We could avoid their shots tolerably well, by lying low in the grass, when fired upon, but it is strange they did not hit our horses more frequent. Sergeant Cobb now decided to change our position, and told the boys when the Indians drew back, after a charge, to mount quick and make for a little knoll, about three or four hundred yards, to our rear, and then dismount again, where we could have better protection for ourselves and horses; as it seemed, the Indians were determined to wear us out, and cause us to exhaust our ammunition, and then swoop down, and make a finish of us, with lance and tomahawk. In vain, we had scanned the prairie, in the direction of Clear creek, in the hope of seeing the settlers coming to our assistance, but all in vain. We could see for miles away, and none were in sight. So, acting on the suggestion of the sergeant, we mounted, and made the attempt to reach the new position, but this move almost proved fatal to our little band. Some of the horses, not as badly used up as others, dashed off rapidly, while others would hardly go at all; causing us to become scattered at the start. My horse seemed perfectly stiff, and moved as though hoppled, and one of my comrades, Gus. Hasroot, was in the same fix, only a little worse. His horse refused to move when he mounted, although he gave him the spur, and struck him several times with his gun. The Indians, thinking we were terror-sticken, and were going to give up the fight, charged us with triumphant yells, and the mounted ones were soon around us. Gus got his horse started, just as a powerful Indian was close upon him, coming at full speed with leveled lance. I was in advance of Gus, about thirty yards, and commenced firing at the Indians

who were close upon him, and at the same time, shouting for the boys to hold up. Two Indians ran close to
me, but passed. I fired at them, without effect; then
turned in my saddle, to look at Gus, and help him, if I
could, but at that instant, he killed the Indian, who was
trying to lance him. He was so near when Gus fired, as
to be enveloped in the smoke from the carbine. The
horse wheeled suddenly at the discharge of the gun, and
the Indian fell to the ground. breaking his lance, as he
did so. All this occurred in less time than it takes to
write it. As soon as the boys saw our situation, they
turned their horses, while on the gallop, and came back,
firing at the Indians around us, and for a few minutes
the bullets came from both ways. The two Indians
that passed us, wheeled off in the prairie, and were not
hit. By this time, the Indians who were not mounted
came up, and a close and desperate fight ensued. They
seemed determined to rout us this time. The rangers
fought on horseback; wounds were given and received,
at the distance of thirty paces; Billy Sorrells was struck
in the left side, by an army pistol ball, and William Caruthers received a glancing shot in the breast, from a
Spencer carbine. Young Horseback rallied the Comanches around him, and made a close charge on the left,
and was killed by Sergeant Cobb, and others, who fired
on him at the same time, killing his horse also; at the
same time the sergeant's horse was badly shot and he
had to dismount. Billy Sorrells was near me when shot;
I heard the ball strike him, and turned to see who was
hit: he was leaning over to one side, but soon dismounted and continued to fire from behind his horse.
As soon as I could, I went to him, and saw that he was
badly wounded. During this contest, I came in contact with a young warrior, carrying a blood-red shield.

Seeing him in the act of firing at me, I dodged at the flash, and in turn, fired at him, but he caught my ball on his shield. He was a devilish-looking fellow, and looked me straight in the eye, while we were exchanging shots. The third round, I struck the top of his shield, and think, the ball glanced, and struck him in the shoulder, for he suddenly wheeled his horse and galloped away, without raising his shield. The Indians were repulsed and ran, carrying their shields on their backs, to receive our fire as they went off. The Comanche chief lay near us, with one leg under his dead horse. Both had been killed instantly. The horse was shot behind the shoulder, and the Indian about an inch below the right eye. The Indians were not whipped yet. Again they advanced within range, and commenced firing, and we again dismounted and commenced dodging bullets and arrows. Billy Sorrells was bleeding freely, and lay down. His color had changed to an almost ghostly whiteness, and we thought he was dying. This encouraged the Indians, and they yelled defiantly; shooting blood-red arrows at us, in revenge for the dead chief; which meant war to the knife. One of our men coolly sat his horse, about ten or fifteen steps from where we were dismounted, while this firing was going on, moving his carbine with the running Indians, trying to get a good sight. The Indians were running in circles, and we perceived that they were getting nearer all the time. Some of the boys advised Cleveland to get down and shelter himself behind his horse, as some of them would hit him presently. He said he guessed not, and again raised his gun to fire. About this time a large Kiowa ran up on his horse, about seventy yards off, and shot an arrow at Cleveland, cutting the brim of his hat. He concluded then to dismount, and just as he got down, another arrow grazed his horse's nose. Larkin Cleveland was a brave boy, and all through this fearful ordeal, which we passed, I think his heart beat with regular pulsations. He knew not what fear was, and laughed when other men dodged from a bullet.

CHAPTER X.

THE LAST CHARGE—DEATH OF SITTANKE, THE KIOWA CHIEF — INDIANS LEAVING THE BATTLE GROUND — RESCUING THE BODY OF THE FALLEN CHIEF—WOUNDED RANGERS—CAPTURE OF THE CHIEF'S HORSE—START FOR THE KEEP RANCH.

THE sun was now nearly down, and the Kiowa chief· rallied his warriors, for a last and final charge, which was intended to crush us out of existence. Again we scanned the prairie, for the welcome sight of re-enforcements, but none were visible. Oh, if we only had twenty-five of our brave boys, who were lying idly in camp, on Big Sandy; little dreaming what a fearful strait their comrades were in; only forty miles east of them, on Paradise prairie, as it was sometimes called, how quick we would be masters of the situation. But these hopes were vain, and we determined to hold the ground as long as possible, or at least, until night, but if then, there was no change in affairs, we were going to get out of there. Our force was too small to risk a night attack, on the open praire; for the Indians would be certain to fire the grass on us. If we did attempt to leave the battle ground, without routing the Indians, we were going to keep together, and move off slowly and fight as we went. We congratulated ourselves on our lucky escape, so far, amid such a hail of bullets and arrows, which we had passed through in the last hour and a half. The chief formed his warriors, after riding among them, and stirring them up for a final charge.

Our sergeant made some change in his little force; the men were moved up a little, and formed in front of Billy Sorrells, he being about the centre, and asked me to ride around and stop on the extreme right, about ten steps from the left-hand man, James Ewers. The Kiowa chief, placed himself on the left of his band, who were thinly scattered over the ground. The mounted ones being mostly on the right and left. The chief's bridle was richly ornamented with silver, which glittered in the rays of the declining sun, as he wheeled his horse and bore down upon us. Our boys dismounted to receive this charge, and were encouraged by the cheering words of our gallant sergeant, who was on foot, a little in advance of us, and seemed as if he wanted to bear the brunt of the fight. The chief came almost at full speed, firing rapidly with a revolver. The yelling of the Indians, almost drowning the reports of the firearms. He seemed determined this time to ride us down, but that mad charge was his last. He received a ball in the breast at the distance of twenty paces, and fell forward, on the wethers of his horse, dropping his shield and revolver, but hung to his horse, until he passed our line, and was soon kicked loose, a short distance in our rear. He was confined to his saddle by leather straps, across the thighs; that was the reason he was so long falling, and if his weight had not turned the saddle, his horse would likely have carried him off. Our fire was so rapid, the Indians no longer tried to face us, after the death of the chief, but turned back, protecting themselves with their shields, until out of range; several were wounded, and one killed, besides the chief, in this last charge.

The boys all mounted their horses, except the wounded, when the Indians turned their backs; and made the

RANGERS AND PIONEERS OF TEXAS.

prairie ring with a regular Texas yell, and some spurred their horses after the routed savages. Sergeant Cobb, being dismounted, told the boys to surround the chief's horse, and secure him, which they did, after a short chase. While this was being done, Larkin Cleveland proposed to me, that we dismount and secure the scalp and rigging, of the fallen chief, as a trophy. Accordingly we rode to the spot, where the dead chief lay on his back, with his painted face upturned. Larkin dismounted, and drew his bowie knife; when our attention was directed to the Indians, who halted a short distance off, on the prairie, when the boys quit pursuing, and were yelling at a fearful rate, and about a dozen of them mounted, were bearing down on us, at a sweeping gallop. As our men were somewhat scattered, in catching the chief's horse, and seeing the Indians making directly for us, Larkin mounted, and we galloped back, to where the balance of our squad was, just as Sergeant Cobb was mounting the Indian's horse; having transferred the saddle from his wounded horse, to that of the chief's. We were now, about one hundred and fifty yards from the body of the chief. As soon as the Indians came up, some of them dismounted, and commenced lifting the body of their chief to the back of a horse, and we charged them. Two men remained with our wounded companion. The Indians fired on us as we came up, but they soon ran, and succeeded in carrying the dead chief with them. He was tied cross-ways on the horse, with a lariat, and the horse turned loose, pursued by two Indians, on good horses, who whipped him at every jump, and they soon mixed in with the main body, and all commenced moving rapidly away, across the prairie, towards the blue hills in the west. Seeing they were about whipped, the rangers yelled and charged, hoping to make them leave the body of the Kiowa chief, but a portion of them held back, and returned our fire, at the same time, uttering defiant yells, in which they were joined by all the band, who swarmed back, and seemed determined that we should not secure the body of the chief. One Indian dismounted in front of us, in order to draw our fire, and attention to him, and to detain us as long as he could, and risk his own scalp to save that of Sittanke, who was nephew of the famous chief of that name, that was afterwards killed in Jack county, by United States soldiers. In vain, our best marksmen, tried to bring down this brave warrior. He danced, yelled, leaped into the air, sprang from side to side, and only mounted and ran off, when we were close upon him. He received one shot, which almost brought him from his horse, after he started; but he recovered himself, and soon mixed in with the balance, who were now on a dead run; those on foot taking the lead. Those who were carrying off the chief, had disappeared across the ridge. We kept up a scattering fire, for some distance further; which was occasionally returned by the Indians, with arrows. We passed over part of the ground occupied by them, during the first part of the fight, and saw several dead horses, and Indians, with shields, bows, caps, blankets, quivers, lances. etc., scattered about. During the fight, I saw a cap shot from an Indian's head. It was made out of the skin of a wild cat; dressed with the hair on; the legs were stuffed, and made in such a manner, that they stuck up straight, when on the Indians head, and resembled horns. One of these legs was cut smooth off, by a bullet. So close was our fire, that one lance ornament had three holes shot through it, and a small bell shot off, which was attached to it. In the last charge, George Howell had a hole shot through his coat. Of the eleven men, who were in the fight, seven of them had the mark of balls or arrows on their person.

In their retreat, the Indians ran with their shields on their backs, and when returning our fire, would wheel half around, and then go again.

As our ammunition was nearly exhausted, and seeing we could accomplish nothing more, the sergeant ordered a return, to where we left young Sorrell. The sun was

(The Last Charge.)

now about down, and we were glad enough to escape so well thus far, and call it even; although we claimed the victory, as we had driven them from the battle ground. After examining the wound of Billy, which was an ugly one near the hip bone, on the left side, and emptying the blood out of his boot, we placed him on his horse, with a man on each side, to support him, and then started for the Keep ranch. Gus Hasroot and myself supported the wounded boy. He was very weak, and leaned heavily on my shoulder, as we slowly moved off. The

Indians halted about half a mile off, and presently began yelling, and advancing towards us ; as if loth to give up the fight. They came so near, that Sergeant Cobb ordered a halt, and placed the men in position, to receive them, if they charged ; and told the boys if they did, to wait until they came close, and then to use the Winchesters. These first until the cartridges were all expended and reserve the revolvers for a hand-to-hand fight, if it came to that. Billy Sorrell was taken from his horse and laid down on the soft grass ; he expressed no fear of the Indians, and lay still, with his white face turned towards the blue canopy of heaven, now fast assuming a red tinge from the rays of the setting sun. But the Indians had no idea of again facing those leveled tubes at short range ; they scattered about over the ground where we fought, looking for their dead and picking up wounded who had crawled off in the grass during the fight. Seeing this we again mounted and moved off towards the ranch, and a swell in the prairie soon hid them from our view.

Ed. Cobb presented a picture as he rode along on the chief's horse, a large iron grey, and had on one of the finest bridles I nearly ever saw ; it fairly glittered with silver ornaments ; the horse was bloody from his withers to his feet, where the Indian bled while he was hanging over, before he came to the ground. The sergeant had blood on his breast, hands and gun, and looked as if he had been wounded, but had not received a scratch, and it is a wonder how he escaped, for I saw many shots fired at him, and every now and then would see him tuck his head quick as a flash, which showed they were not very wide of the mark ; he got the blood on him in handling bloody horses, and helping to lift Billy Sorrell. Before we arrived at the ranch we met Harvell, with only one man with him, a regular Indian fighter, named Ferguson. They had ridden hard, but were too late for the fight. Ferguson was sadly disappointed; he was well armed, and mounted on a splendid horse; he was elated with our success, and rode round the sergeant, examining the blood-stained charger of the Kiowa chief.

He said we had made the best fight that was ever made in that section of country with Indians. When he learned that they were still on the ground he tried to prevail on our leader to go back and engage them again, but the sergeant told him the men were almost worn out with the long chase and nearly two hours' fight; besides, their ammunition was well-nigh exhausted, and pointed to our wounded companion, who was leaning wearily on the shoulder of a comrade, and needed attention bad; his wound was still bleeding, and we feared he would bleed to death if it was not stopped. "Well," said Ferguson, "I am bound to have a look at them, anyway, and if you will send your wounded man on to the ranch and wait with the most of your men to help me, in case I need it, I will gallop to the top of the ridge and see what they are doing." Ed. consented, and told two of us to go on with Billy, and himself, and the balance of the men would wait. It was nearly dark when we arrived at the gate in front of the Keep house. Seeing a woman standing on the gallery, I dismounted and went to where she was. She looked white and scared, with five children clinging to her dress. I politely accosted her, and in a few words told her who we were, and that we craved shelter for a wounded companion.

"Oh, yes;" she said, "by all means; bring him in quick, and I will go and prepare a comfortable place for him."

When we came in with Billy she had struck a light,

and pointed to a soft bed with snowy-white sheets and pillows and told us to lay him there. I told her to spread a blanket over the bed, as he was very bloody. "Oh, no;" she said, "lay him there; there is nothing too good for a wounded ranger to lie on. You have saved myself and little children. I knew that you were fighting Indians on the prairie, and oh, the untold agony which I have suffered in the last three hours. Poor boy! poor boy!" she exclaimed, and tears started to her eyes as Billy groaned when we laid him down. In pulling off his boot some blood ran out on the floor, and as Mrs. Jay was a timid woman and unused to blood and frontier life, had to leave the room to keep from fainting. In a short time the other boys arrived and brought their horses inside the inclosure.

Sergeant Cobb came into the room where Billy was, and examined his wound, expressing the opinion to us that he would not live through the night, as there was no medical aid near, but hoped for the best. Billy had fainted from loss of blood, and lay like a dead man. In the meantime Mrs. Jay had again entered the room, and after looking a few seconds at the bloody sergeant, who, with candle in hand, had turned to salute her as she entered, asked him if he wished a place to lie down, thinking he was literally shot all to pieces, but he smiled and told her he was not hurt at all.

Ferguson said when he went back, the Indians were considerably scattered about over the prairie, but yelled defiance at him when he appeared on the ridge. When he came back he said, "There are scads of them back there, boys, but woe to their hides if they stay there until morning. The settlers will rendezvous at the Keep ranch to-night and act in concert with the rangers to-morrow." "Oh, you will have a big crowd before morning, captain; the news has gone like wildfire down the country, to-night, that the prairie above the Keep ranch is black with Indians, and a small squad of Texas rangers are fighting them and calling on the settlers for help. Oh, they will come; the nearest ones, down on Clear creek, where Harvell went, will stay at home, the most of them fearing to leave their families, but they have sent runners further on, and by morning there will be enough men here to 'corrall' the whole bunch on the prairie and take the topknot off the last painted devil of them. I think the chief you killed this evening was Kickemburg; it looks like his horse. We have fought him down in this part of the country before."

At this time we did not know the name of the chief which we had killed.

CHAPTER XI.

INCIDENTS AT THE KEEP RANCH, AFTER THE BATTLE.

ALL night long, Ed. Cobb, myself, and some others remained by the bedside of Billy, thinking that each hour, as they slowly dragged along, would be his last. "Water, water!" was his cry; "give me water!" Fever had set in and he became at times delirious, and often called the name of his mother, and then, again, he would fight the battle over. "Look out, sergeant;" he would say; "they will hit you."

The nearest surgeon was at Bolivar, thirty miles east of us, and as the settlers began to arrive one of them volunteered to go after him, as none of our men were acquainted with the road to that place. Our own physician was at camp, about fifty miles away in a west direction. Our men built a fire in the yard, for the night was chilly, and some lay down to rest, while others stood guard at various points around the premises. The wind was blowing from the west, and we could occasionally hear the faint yells of the still defiant Indians.

Men continued to arrive at intervals through the night. They were informed by the runners that the Indians were near the Keep ranch, and all made for this point. From where I sat by the side of my wounded comrade, every now and then I could hear the challenge of the sentry at the gate, and in answer, the hearty response of "Friends;" and then the swinging of the gate and the entrance of one, two or three at a time. Late in the night a noted Indian fighter arrived from Denton county—old John

Chisholm, the man who drove the first herd of cattle up the Chisholm trail to Kansas, and which takes its name from him. I had walked out of doors and was at the guard-fire when he arrived, and had a good look at the brave old pioneer as he came up to warm his hands.

He was tolerably small and well made and seemed to be about fifty years of age, and wore short grizzly beard. He asked us all about the fight, the number of Indians, and what tribe. He was very particular in asking us the exact locality of the place where we fought, and after gaining all the information he could, told us he would go out there on a little scout. We tried to turn him from his purpose, but to no avail. He mounted and rode off alone on the prairie towards the battle ground, saying he would give a good account of himself, and in about an hour and half returned, but said he could not make any discoveries on account of a thick fog which arose after he left us. He could not see the Indians, but smelt them very strong.

Most of the men remained up all night, conversing about our fight and other fights which had occurred on this part of the frontier, and laying plans for the morrow. Some favored the idea of moving on the enemy that night, but were overruled by the majority, as it would cost the lives of good men, which could be avoided. The Indians would have all the advantage and ambush the whites as they came up. Before morning there were about thirty men standing around the fires in the yard, all anxious for morning to come.

Mrs. Jay was a noble woman, and remained up all night, and "Oh," she said, "how different are the Texas rangers from what I always heard they were. I supposed they were cruel and fierce, neither respecting God nor man, age nor sex." And indeed this is the impression which has gone out into the world respecting the rangers and cowboys of Texas; but there on that bed lies as gallant a ranger as ever gave back an answering shout to the red man on the plains, with scarcely a perceptible down on his upper lip, and cheeks as fair as her own beautiful daughter; and look at that broad-shouldered fellow standing in the light of the guard fire with the ragged hole shot through the breast of his coat. With his long mustachios and rough ranger garb he looks like a veritable mountain robber, but he has a tender heart and would weep bitter tears over a dying comrade, or stand at the threshold of this lady's door and fight for her and her children as long as his strong hand was able to grasp the hilt of his bowie knife.

Of course there are some exceptions. Occasionally, in some western village, you will hear a voice ring out on the night air in words something like these: "Wild and woolly," "Hard to curry," "Raised a pet but gone wild," "Walked the Chisholm trail backwards," "Fought Indians and killed buffalo," "Hide out, little ones," and then you may expect to hear a few shots from a revolver. It is a cowboy out on a little spree, and likely will not hurt any one, as some friend, who is sober, generally comes to him, relieves him of his pistol and all is soon quiet again. As I took observations and noticed different individuals that night I could not help from contrasting the difference in the situations of the settlers, and our weary boys, who were either asleep or sat almost in silence around the camp fire. The settlers were at home; their wives, mothers, and sisters were near, and they were anxious to meet the savages and drive them from the land and save the settlements from the tomahawk and scalping-knife; they were impatient for morning to come and uneasy and anxious about the welfare and safety of their families; and well they might be, for one who was sleeping quietly that night twenty miles from the battle ground met his death next day at the hands of these same savages. On the other hand, our boys were four or five hundred miles from home, fighting to protect these people on this remote part of the Texas frontier from the raiding bands of savages who constantly harassed and made desolate their beautiful country.

None of our men were married; but they had parents, brothers, sisters and friends who were uneasy about their safety. The last thoughts on retiring at night and the first on arising in the morning were of the boys who were away off on the frontier exposed to all kinds of dangers, both day and night. That boy, lying in the house there, pale and bleeding, with his comrades around him, had a mother and sister in Gonzales county, four hundred and fifty miles away, who perhaps at this moment were taking their rest, little dreaming of the dangerous situation of the loved one. Suppose something could have whispered in the mother's ear the truth: "Billy was shot down this evening on the prairie, by the Indians, and now lies in a critical condition, with no chance for medical aid;" what a horrible night this would be for her! No more sleep; now she can only walk the yard and wring her hands in agony, and look towards the northwest where she knew her boy was, and wish she had the wings of a dove that she might fly to him, and, holding his drooping head in her lap, speak words of comfort and love.

But, then, it is best not to know. She remained in ignorance of this fact until the slow coaches of those days could convey the intelligence, and then it was not so hard to hear; the crisis had passed, and Billy was out of danger before she knew he was hurt,   His father also belonged to our company, and was with Garner, on a hunt, when we left the camp ; we intended to send a runner to notify him as soon as daylight came. I do not think Mrs. Jay slept any that night ; the scenes which were being enacted around her were new and strange. She informed us that they were just from Illinois, and were only stopping at the Keep ranch for a short time until her husband could buy land, he being then absent with his two sons for that purpose, not realizing the danger to which the family was exposed in their absence. They knew that they were on the frontier, and had been warned by the settlers to keep on the lookout for Indians, but thought it was more talk than anything else about so many Indians, and gave the subject but little thought.   They were delighted with the country, and were anxious to buy land and settle.   Cow hunters stopped nearly every day at the ranch to get water and rest themselves and horses, and she felt no uneasiness in the absence of her husband and sons, and now she was very uneasy about them, knowing their utter inexperience in an Indian country. She said she was looking for her husband back that day, and frequently walked out on the gallery and scanned the prairie to see if they were in sight ; and it was while so doing she saw the Indians crossing a swell in the rolling prairie, and thought they were cow hunters and was rather surprised to see so many together.   The idea never occurred to her that they were Indians.

In about half an hour she again walked out and saw our men crossing the same rising ground.   As we came along on the trail she thought it was another lot of cow hunters, and gave it no concern until Harvell dashed up and inquired for Dr. Jay and the boys. She told him they were not at home, and seeing that he had ridden hard asked him what was the matter.   He then informed her, in a few and hasty words, as he reined his horse around, that a large band of hostile Indians were back there and he was after men to help fight them ; that they were confronted by a small force of Texas rangers, but were not strong enough to do much good, and would likely all be killed if they fought them alone ; and so saying, he dashed off towards Clear creek, leaving her almost wild with terror.

She suddenly realized what it was to be on the frontier of Texas.   She then took a position where she could scan the prairie in the direction where she saw the Indians.   Both parties had disappeared from sight, behind the swells, and she was in hopes they had gone ; but suddenly she again saw the Indians come over a ridge not far from the place where she first saw them and halt in a long scattered line, looking back as if they were pursued.   The next instant she saw the rangers gallop up and get down from their horses, and puffs of smoke commenced darting out from the Indian line.   She knew, then, that the fight had commenced, but could not hear the report of the guns.

She then seized her children, who were around her, and rushed into the house, praying for help.   She threw herself on the bed and thought she would lay there until all was over, thinking herself and children would be the next victims when they finished the rangers.   But she could not stand it long, and again went out to look.   Our boys were holding their ground, and the Indians were scurrying around them, the mounted ones lying low on their horses and smoke puffing here and there.

The rangers were also firing rapidly, but remained on the ground by their horses.   Time and again she thought she would have to leave her post, she became so faint and weak at these strange and startling sights. She said she had often read little books about Indians and the rangers in Texas, but little thought she would ever witness one of these prairie fights. Only a short time ago she was in the densely populated State of Illinois, surrounded by her friends and relations; now she was on a Texas prairie witnessing a desperate struggle between a small band of rangers and a large war party of Kiowa and Comanche Indians, all alone, except her five helpless children. Their lives and hers were in the balance if the rangers were defeated. She expected nothing but a horrible fate for herself and little ones, and she hardly dared to hope that they would be victorious.

Mrs. Jay was a Christian lady, and fervently prayed to the Almighty to turn aside the darts of our enemies and shield and protect us in this our time of greatest need; and also prayed for herself and children that He would protect them; and "Oh," she said, "if the earnest prayers of a woman were of any avail I helped you out in that fight; and I prayed for protection for myself and children, and now look at the brave men encamped around my house and my children quietly sleeping. But, oh," she said, "I thought you were gone once, when you mounted and started off and the Indians ran among you. Part of the time you were hidden from my view behind the ridge, and my fears were increased, not knowing but that you were all killed. I could see some of the Indians nearly all the time, and I often fancied they started this way, and I would give up all hope and clasp my children in my arms. And oh, I was so glad when I saw you come in sight, advancing on the Indians, and the smoke puffing from your guns and part of the Indians giving way. I felt so elated I could scarce forbear to cheer. But when you moved around and got between the Indians and the house, and when I suppose they made their last close charge, I again lost hope. It seemed they had completely swallowed you up; the muzzles of the guns seemed close together, and everything was a confused mass of running horses and smoke. The Indians finally gave back, and I could only see a few rangers, and they seemed to be riding off until I lost sight of them altogether. I saw the Indians again charge and caught a glimpse of some of your men and most of the Indians again came back across the ridge, and as night was coming on I could not at that distance distinguish friend from foe. I was in great fear, for I knew not how it had terminated, and at dusk, when your men were near the house, I almost fainted, thinking they were the Indians, and was not entirely satisfied until I was accosted by one of the men, in English, which I knew was the voice of a friend. I am so glad," she continued, "that you all escaped so well, and I do hope and pray that this poor boy will recover. He looks so young to engage in such desperate combats as you have just passed through. I wish my husband was here; he is a good physician, and I am satisfied he could greatly relieve him if he was only here."

CHAPTER XII.

A BRAVE CHRISTIAN LADY—A RUNNER SENT TO THE CAMP—THE SABLE WARRIOR FROM BOLIVAR—PURSUIT OF THE INDIANS BY RANGERS AND SETTLERS THE DAY AFTER THE BATTLE.

WE tried to prevail on the good lady to take some rest, but she would not. I was proud of our boys that night as they stood around the camp fire answering the questions of the settlers, without boast or display, with the marks of bullets and arrows about their persons, seven out of eleven having been hit, either in their person or clothing.

Some time after midnight, as I was sitting by the bedside of my comrade, a negro came to the door and looked in, with his eyes about the size of Bland dollars. I asked him what he wanted.

"Is de young man what got shot by de Injuns in here?"

I told him he was.

"Yes, sah," said he. "I want to take a look at him."

"All right," said I. There he is on the bed. Come in."

The negro advanced to the bed carrying a large double-barreled shot-gun in his left hand, with a large shot-pouch and powder-horn on his right shoulder. After looking at the bloody sheet and Billy's pale-face a few moments, he exclaimed:

"Good gracious! Knows they have nearly killed dat boy shure nuff; but I guess us Bolivar boys will give 'em a round in de mornin'. I guess we can sling a few slugs into 'em dat dey can't pack through Wise county. Come in here, Joe, and look at dis'' (to another negro just outside the door who had come with him). ''What I been tellin' you 'bout Injuns; you don't know nothin' 'bout 'em. Come in here and see how dey will do you some day when you'se frolicking 'round over de country by yourself, and you jus' look out to-morrow when we go to charge and stick close to me.''

By this time Joe had got to the bedside, and seemed very much scared at the sight of blood.

Before daylight the men were mounted and ready for a start. Sergeant Cobb left myself and Gus. Hasroot with Billy. Taking me aside he said he did not think young Sorrells could live through the day, and if he died, that myself and Gus would have to bury him, as he knew not when himself or men would return, as he was going to use every exertion to overtake and fight the Indians again if there was any chance. He had now about thirty men under his command, and was anxious for another fight. Dan Edwards volunteered to go to our camp and notify old man Sorrell of his son's condition, and Larkin Cleveland to the camp on Big Sandy to notify Captain Baker of the fight.

Just as day began to dawn the men filed out at the gate, and were soon lost to view in the gloom of the early morning, and with a sad heart I returned to the bedside of my wounded companion. The minutes seemed like hours as I watched and waited. I was very sore from the long ride the day before, and my face was still swollen and painful. I was anxious for some messenger to return and bring the news, whether they fought again or not. I knew if they did it would be a desperate one, for the sergeant had determined, with the force

22

now under his command, to charge into their ranks, and if such were the case the Indians would fight desperately and men were bound to be killed, and all the boys of Company F were like brothers to me, and most of the brave settlers were men of families. and some of them would be left desolate.

About 10 o'clock I heard a footstep at the door, and on looking around saw the colored man from Bolivar with the big shot-gun. I was somewhat surprised to see him back so soon, and at first thought he might be a fugitive from the battle.

"Hello!" said I; "you got back quick. What news? Did you catch the Indians?"

"Yes, sah," said he; "dat is, dey had 'bout cotch 'em when I lef'. I would like to went on and help to give dem Injuns a rale good whippin', but business was 'tainin' me so down to Bolivar to-day I was obleeged to go back, and thought I would come by and see how de young man was. Yes, sah, we got to de pond whar de Injuns stopped and washed de blood off'n deyselves and hosses what dey got shot. I never seed de like; blood all roun' de pond and in de edge of de water, an' tracks —golly, thick as pigs' tracks. Yes, sah, I guess de boys has done give 'em a good maulin' by dis time," and with a flourish of his shot-gun he bade me good-day and joined his companion, Joe, at the gate; and these two sable warriors made tracks for Bolivar.

There were not many negroes on the frontier, and most of them had a mortal terror of Indians, but I saw one who was in the fight on Battle creek who stood at his post and fought when some of the white men ran in terror from the savages.

About noon Dr. Bobbitt arrived from Bolivar, and at once proceeded to examine Billy's wound, and pronounced it a very bad one, but could not find the ball; and after dressing it said he could do no more, but would remain with us through the night, and then he would be obliged to return.

The next morning our patient was still feverish and restless. The Doctor left some medicine for us to give him and then took his departure. We constantly scanned the prairie through the day, but no one came in sight until nearly sundown, when I saw three men bearing towards the ranch some distance off, and about dusk arrived on very tired horses. They were old man Sorrell, Dr. Gillespie and Larkin Cleveland. Edwards had carried the news to Mr. Sorrell, and he had hastened by the camp on Big Sandy and brought our physician with him. Cleveland, although nearly worn out, came back with them to pilot the way. I felt greatly relieved, you can imagine. Mr. Sorrell did not expect to find his son alive, and never spoke until he dismounted and took me by the hand and looked me straight in the face, and in a faltering voice said:

" Tell me the worst, Jack."

" Oh," said I, in a cheerful voice, " Billy is all right, and will be riding wild horses again in six weeks."

I never saw such a sudden change come in a man's face in my life. From a look of anguish and despair, his eyes fairly sparkled with joy, and with a firm, quick step entered the house. Billy greeted his father with a smile and expressed his joy at his arrival.

Dr. Gillespie made an examination of the wound, but said there was no chance to get the ball.

I was now greatly relieved. Billy had his father and the Doctor with him, and was doing as well as could be expected under the circumstances. I was also very anxious to hear from the gallant sergeant and his men.

Now, if I were writing an imaginary sketch, of course they would overtake them and entirely destroy the band, but such was not the case. The Indians succeeded in making good their escape, although the men trailed them forty miles before sundown. Some of the settlers came back by the ranch and gave us the particulars of the chase. They were delayed some time at the battle ground in trying to find the main trail, as the Indians had scattered off in various directions, carrying off the dead: but at the bloody pond, six miles from where we fought, they all came together.

CHAPTER XIII.

THE BLOODY POND—SETTLER ROPED AND DRAGGED TO
DEATH BY THE INDIANS—RETURN TO CAMP—A NOTED
INDIAN—MESSENGERS SENT TO FORT SILL—THE COR-
PORAL'S STRATAGEM.

FROM the pond the trail was plain, and they must
have left it about midnight, for they killed a man named
Hampton at sunrise next morning, twenty miles from the
battle ground. He was a short distance from the house,
chopping wood to get breakfast, when the Indians came
round a hill and cut him off from the house. As he
started to run they roped him and dragged him off across
the prairie in sight of his family. The Indians did not
stop to molest the family, as they knew they were pursued, or would be. Our men arrived at the ranch about
10 o'clock. Some cow hunters had found the body of
Hampton about two miles from the house, and brought
it in. His clothing was almost entirely gone, and he
was scalped and otherwise mutilated.

The wife of Hampton said the Indians had a dead
one with them, tied crosswise on a horse, and she knew
they had been fighting with the whites. This dead
Indian was the chief Sittanke. We afterwards learned
they buried him on the banks of Red river. The men
used every exertion to overtake the Indians, after they
left the ranch, but they had too much the start, and just
before sundown they came to the foot of the mountains,
and here the trail scattered and led off into dense thickets and deep cañons, and the pursuit had to be given up.

Here the sergeant was joined by Captain Baker, with the balance of the company. They had taken a near cut after hearing the news, guided by our trailer Marlett, who knew all the country, and told the captain he was satisfied the Indians would strike the rough country at this point. The Indians had stopped and killed some cattle near this place, the flesh of which was still warm. Bud Seglar secured some of the arrows which killed the cattle and tied them to his saddle. The boys were all glad to see one another, and regretted, those who came from camp, they were not with us in the fight. There were now about sixty men together, all well armed and mounted, and eager for a fight; but the enemy was beyond their reach. The men all camped together in the pass that night, and the next morning the rangers returned to camp and the settlers to their homes. They had one thing to console them: the Indians had been worsted on this trip, and driven beyond the settlements before they did much damage. The settlers, on their way back, closely examined the battle ground, and said there was more Indian sign on that prairie than they had ever seen there before. Bows, shields, quivers, blankets, lances, caps, robes, carbines, dead horses, etc., were scattered about.

The wounded mule was still on the ground, about two hundred yards from where he was shot. They also found several dead Indians, where they had been carried off and hid, that night after the fight; three of them were in a sink-hole, about half a mile from where they were killed. They accidentally came on another, lying full length on his back, in the tall grass, closely wrapped from head to foot in a fancy bed-spread. One of the men present recognized it as belonging to the Keenon family, who were massacred in December. He said he had often been at the Keenon ranch, and took notice of this bed-spread on account of its beautiful colors. Another one was found in a hollow, about a mile and a half west of the battle ground. A broken lance lay across his body. There was a dead horse also near him. This Indian was stripped, to secure some fancy rigging which he had on; and the old scars on his body denoted him to be a brave and daring warrior, and had been in some close places on the frontier. One of the old wounds was in the right breast, and seemed to have been made by a large rifle ball, which shattered two of the ribs near the breast bone, passed through the body and came out near the back bone. Another one was a deep cut in the left shoulder, which extended into the muscles of the arm. Oska Horseback, the Comanche chief, was also found. He had an ornament on his breast composed of white beads about an inch long, and fastened in rows to a piece of red cloth, which just covered the breast. The beads were made out of the finger bones of white men, which had been slain by him, or some of his people. Nearly all the settlers carried off some relic of the fight; some had scalps. Ferguson obtained three; he found the Indians in the sink-hole and scalped them.

Some of our boys came back with the citizens with orders from the captain for Mr. Sorrell and some of the boys to remain with Billy, and the balance to return to camp; and next morning two men, besides Mr. Sorrell, were left, and bidding them, and the good Mrs. Jay, farewell, we took our departure, and went by the way of the captain's camp, and from there to our own.

On the way back, one of our men, who had procured some Indian rigging and a sack of red paint, dressed himself like an Indian and painted his face. Late in the evening, as we were nearing Ball's ranch, the painted man and myself were riding ahead, through a small prairie, when we saw a man running his horse to a mott of timber ahead of us and a little to the left. He leaped from his horse behind a tree and covered us with his rifle. I saw his mistake at once, and shouted to him we were friends, at the same time riding towards him; but it was some time before he would lower his piece, and when we came up I discovered it was old man Ball. He recognized me, but told my companion he had better be careful how he rode in the neighborhood of Ball's ranch with that rig on.

Poor old man! He had been harassed so much by Indians, he was on the lookout, and ready to fight them at any time.

(It is surprising with what coolness one man will prepare to fight a band of Indians, single handed, on the border. On one occasion, when we were on a scout, we stopped to eat dinner and rest on Panther creek. We were sitting down in the tall grass, and hearing a noise near by, all sprang to their feet, and saw a man about one hundred yards from us with a wagon and yoke of oxen. His wagon was locked fast against a tree, and he was standing behind it with his gun. When we came to where he was, he told us he thought we were Indians, as he could not see us good, and was preparing to fight us. He intended to make a breastwork of his wagon, and that was why he ran it against the tree, so his team could not carry it off when the fight commenced.)

When the balance of our men came up, Mr. Ball invited us to spend the night at his ranch, which we did. He saw there had been an Indian fight and was anxious to learn the particulars.

We found the boys all well at camp, and they were

as glad to see us as if we had been gone a month, instead of four or five days.

In March, Captain Baker sent some papers to Sergeant Cobb with orders to forward them to the Indian agent, Tatum, at Fort Sill. Corporal William Murphy, Tom Garner and George McPhail were detailed to carry these dispatches. They arrived all right at the fort, and went to the agent's office. He gave them a kind welcome, but seemed greatly troubled and ill at ease, and said he feared trouble with the Indians. The soldiers had been ordered to Leavenworth, and the Comanches were insolent, and left the reservation whenever they were a mind to, and he was satisfied they were crossing the line into Texas, and joining bands of hostiles, who could not be brought to the reserve. He also informed the boys that a wounded Indian had come to the fort in February, and reported a fight in Texas, in which, he said, they had seven killed in the fight, including two chiefs, Sittanke and Young Horseback, and that they killed one of the white men.

This was the fight we had, and proves that some of the reserve Indians had joined the wild bands to raid on the Texas side. The agent also stated that the Comanches had laid a plot to kill him on a certain night, but was prevented from carrying out their plans by the Caddoes, who encamped around his house to protect him in the absence of the soldiers.

It was ration day when our boys were there, and the fort was full of Indians. A large crowd of them came into the agent's office and stood around our boys with a dangerous look in their black, snakish-looking eyes. They recognized them as rangers, and hated them with all their savage nature. They wanted to look at the carbines, but our boys would not allow them to put their hands on them. George McPhail had on a pair of revolvers, and before he could prevent it an Indian jerked one of them from the scabbard. George snatched out the other one, and presenting it at the Indian's breast, made him put it back. The Indians looked very angry, and, after muttering among themselves and giving the boys a black look, took their departure.

After the business for which they came had been attended to, the boys expressed their intention of setting out again that evening on their return, but the agent insisted on them remaining until morning, so that they could get some distance into Texas the next day before night, for he was satisfied if they started that evening and camped north of Red river, the Indians would follow and murder them if they could. Murphy said he would risk it, as he thought he could out-smart them; and so, after receiving a letter to be delivered to Captain Baker, set out on their return.

The boys noticed that the Indians watched them closely as they rode out of the fort. Murphy rode on until nearly dark, and then left the road and went into a small thicket near by, and dismounted, telling the boys not to remove their saddles, but hold their horses by the bridle, make no noise or strike a match. They remained here until about 10 o'clock, when a band of about fifteen Indians passed them, going towards the river. They expected to come upon the rangers in camp and massacre them, as the agent had feared, but they were completely foiled. In about two hours they came back, and passed on towards the fort. At a signal from Murphy the boys mounted and quietly returned to the road, and by daylight were many miles from their foes, and spent the next night in camp among their companions.

It was more quiet now on this part of the frontier than

it had been for some time. Our men scoured the country around, but could find no fresh trails of Indians. The people breathed more freely, and it was published in a Denton paper that Wise and Montague counties were now fully protected by the Texas rangers, and it has been said they never raided that part of the country where we fought them, again.

As soon as Billy Sorrell was sufficiently recovered from his wound, we were to have a ranger celebration at Decatur, Wise county. It was to be given by the citizens of said county, in honor of our recent fight. We had probably saved lives, besides considerable stock, for about 900 head of horses were under herd about six miles below the battle ground, on Hickory creek, and every one was satisfied the Indians were going after these horses, and would have driven them across Red river, if we had not overtaken and fought them.

CHAPTER XIV.

RANGER CELEBRATION AT DECATUR—A GOOD DINNER—
PRESENTED WITH A TEXAS FLAG—ACCIDENT IN THE
SQUARE — STARTING ON A LONG SCOUT—SUFFERING
FOR WATER—ARRIVE AT THE BRAZOS—A POETICAL
RANGER.

As soon as young Sorrell recovered, which was
nearly a month after the fight, he arrived at the captain's
camp. and our sergeant received orders to move his men
down there. We did so, and in a few days set out for
Decatur, and on arriving at that place were warmly
received by the citizens. Onr men went into camp near
the square, and had stables furnished in which to keep
our horses.

The people had collected from all parts of the county
and some from adjoining counties. The programme
was to have dinner at 1 o'clock, and then repair to the
court-house, where speeches would be delivered by
Colonel E. B. Pickett, Colonel Bowles, Sergeant Cobb,
and Miss Mary Pickett, who was to present our company with a flag. made by herself and other young ladies
of Wise county. At night there was to be a grand ball
at the court-house. Lieutenant Hill was going to present the boys who were in the fight with a fine revolver
apiece, with their names and date of the fight. which
was February 7th, 1871, engraved on the handles.
When dinner was announced, we repaired to the dining-
hall, where we found a long table, handsomely decorated and literally covered with everything which was

nice and wholesome, to eat. The rangers occupied the table first, and were waited on by a bevy of Wise county's most handsome daughters.

We did ample justice to the dinner; but I think some of the boys did not eat as much as they would have done had they been seated around a camp fire on the plains. There stood men who, a short time before, had shouted defiance to a picked band of Kiowa and Comanche warriors, outnumbering them four to one, surrounded, on the broad prairie, with no chance for succor; met charge after charge with a steady eye and unblanched cheek. Look at some of them now. when those beautiful girls approach and ask what they will be helped to; they cannot face them with steady nerves; they stand first on one foot and then on the other, mutter out something unintelligible, attempt to hand the plate, drop a knife, etc. For instance, look at that six-foot ranger here on my right. I saw him receive the fire of a Comanche Indian at the distance of thirty paces, without dodging, and now he is so confused and scared he has just told that black-eyed girl he did not use coffee, and I have seen him sit down around a camp fire and drink a level quart of it, strong and black, without sugar.

Everything passed off agreeably, and our boys acquitted themselves with credit. After dinner had been served to all, we then repaired to the court-house, which was soon closely packed. Colonel E. B. Pickett then spoke, followed by Colonel Bowles, who held an Indian scalp in his hand. Miss Mary Pickett then presented the flag to Sergeant Cobb, and delivered a nice address, which was replied to by the sergeant. It was a beautiful Texas flag—blue ground with lone star in the center, and beautifully embroidered. Miss Mattie Blythe then arose and called out the names of the men who were in the fight, and, as they answered, were told by our captain to take seats in front of the speakers' stand. She then presented the pistols furnished by the lieutenant. They were handsome weapons, and on each scabbard was a large Texas star. Three cheers were then given for the rangers, and the assembly broke up.

Late in the evening the rangers mounted their horses and rode around the square, Ed. Cobb in the lead, carrying the flag. In the wind-up, the boys gave a specimen of their horsemanship, charging furiously around the square, wheeling and turning at different points, and changing from one side to the other of their horses. Bill Archer's pistol was accidentally discharged, which killed his horse. By early candle light the ball commenced, which lasted until near midnight. All seemed to enjoy themselves, and we had a good time generally.

The next day our company left the pleasant little town of Decatur, to return to their duties as guardians of the frontier, carrying away many pleasant recollections of the celebration and the well wishes of the brave and generous people of Wise county.

We did not return to our old camp, as the grass was eaten up. Captain Baker, with the main part of the company, encamped in the hills northwest of Decatur, near the county line, and Ed. Cobb was sent further north, with sixteen men, and encamped on a little creek in Montague county.

In a short time Captain Baker sent out a scout for the purpose of taking a wider range than usual, and find out the state of affairs in different parts of the country. In the round, they were to take in Camp Colorado, Fort Griffin, and other places, some of them two hundred miles from our camp. The scout was ten men, and taken from both camps. From the captain's camp the following were selected: Charles Robinson, Cecil Robinson, Sam Cobb, Joel Payne, Dan Woodruff; and John Fitzgerald, Judson Wilhoit, A. J. Sowell, and Gustavus Hasroot, from Sergeant Cobb's camp; the whole to be under the command of Second Sergeant Joel R. Payne. One of our men, whose name I have forgotten, failed to go, which left the nine mentioned above.

We were provided with one pack mule to carry provision, mostly flour and coffee; we calculated to kill game for meat. The boys were well mounted and in high spirits when we started; but they little knew the hardships some of them were to undergo before they should again see Decatur. We were accompanied part of the way by some land buyers from down East. They were nice-looking men, but had never camped out or roughed it any. Mr. James, a citizen of Wise county, having business in the West, was also along. The two land buyers were well mounted, and had a pair of saddle-bags each and blanket, but I could discover no fire-arms about them, which somewhat surprised me, as I thought they would have been encumbered with such freight, traveling, as they were, on the extreme frontier of Texas. Some of our men asked them where their shooters were, and they merely said they were armed, which caused a smile among our men. They had asked permission to travel with us as far as Fort Griffin; the land which they wanted to look at was near Phantom Hill, further west.

In the afternoon, about 3 o'clock, I killed a large deer, which was very fat. We took such portions of it as we wanted, and went a short distance and camped, as we had been riding since morning without dinner.

Around the little pool of water near our camp the Indian tracks were thick and tolerably fresh. We called the strangers down there to look at their first moccasin tracks. We tried to start the trail from that point, but could not on account of the ground being so dry, the moccasins leaving no impression on the hard soil.

After fires were built and coffee put on to boil, the sergeant told all those who wanted meat, to cook and eat. One of the Eastern men cut a very thin piece, and, after putting it on a stick, held it about a foot from the fire. The other one did not attempt to cook any, and seemed perfectly lost. I broiled a side of ribs nice and brown, which looked very tempting to a hungry man, and our friend, who seemed to have no appetite, fished a small knife from his pocket, and said he would try some of that, if I had no objection. I told him to help himself to as much as he liked, and to bread and coffee, also. " But," said I, " if you use that kind of a Beldooke I will beat you ;" at the same time drawing my bowie and chipping off a bite about three inches square.

After a short rest, we went on further, and encamped for the night on a small creek. The grass was fine, and we saw several deer, but did not kill any. Sergeant Payne gave orders for no horses to be hoppled, but all be staked, as we knew Indians were about. Everything was quiet until about midnight, when Fitzgerald came on guard, and discovered that two of the horses were gone. He was about to notify Payne of this fact, when he heard a terrible plashing in the creek, as if horses were being driven hastily across. Thinking Indians were about, he gave the alarm, and the men were soon on their feet. John told them the Indians had crossed the creek with some of the horses. Payne grabbed his gun, and telling some of the men to follow him and others to stay at camp, started off in a run towards the creek, followed by some of the boys. Being somewhat behind, I heard Payne firing before I came up. This caused some excitement, and some of the men left the camp, thinking we were engaged in a fight; but it was a false alarm. Two of the horses had been hoppled, against orders, and they had strayed off, and they made the noise by jumping through the water, and when the sergeant arrived on the scene were close together, with something black between them, which he took for an Indian, and fired three shots before he was convinced of his mistake. It was a black stump about the height of a man. Next morning it was found to have been struck twice out of the three shots. On our return to camp, one of our land buyers was standing about half way between the camp and creek, with a small pistol in his hand; the other remained in camp near his horse.

From camp, next morning, we went in the direction of the Brazos river, aiming to strike it near Palo Pinto. During the day Sergeant Payne killed a large turkey, which we tied on our pack-mule Balaam, but had not proceeded far before it slipped down and popped Balaam in the flank, which caused this hitherto docile animal to kick up his heels and set off at a furious rate through the woods, getting rid of his pack as he went. Some of the men started in pursuit, while others followed to pick up our scattered utensils and provisions. The runaway was soon caught and the pack readjusted. We camped before sundown on a small running branch close to some mountains. Fitzgerald, being an inveterate hunter, soon set out towards the hills in search of game. Our camp was in a small grove of live oak saplings, near the creek bank. It is always the best policy to camp among trees in an Indian country, if possible, for in case of a sudden

23

attack at night they afford cover for the men, and very often saves a party from slaughter. The horses were all staked out and the mule was suffered to go loose, as he was never known to leave the horses.

About dusk. Fitz. came in and reported that he saw the tracks of two Indians between the mountains, where they had crossed a small sandy branch. We kept a good lookout on the horses, for fear the two Indians would try to mount themselves. About midnight the pack-mule, who had wandered off towards the foot of the mountain, suddenly snorted and dashed back to the camp. Every man was ordered up and kept in readiness, for we were satisfied the mule smelt Indians, and shortly afterwards some arrows struck among the small trees over our heads. The fire was put out, and every man strained his eyes to catch sight of an Indian; but we were not molested any more that night, and we supposed the arrows came from the two Indians whose sign Fitzgerald had seen that evening. We searched for them next day, but could not find them; and again set out on our journey towards the Brazos, the mountains of which we could see in the distance.

During the day, the men and horses suffered considerably for water. We struck a dry district and searched in vain for water to quench our thirst, after the supply in the canteens gave out. The day was very hot, being in June, and we were obliged to ride to the Brazos before we could get water.

Towards night we struck the river near the Hogback mountain. Our tired horses quickened their gait when they smelt the water, but we had to descend a steep, ragged bluff to get to it. The trail made by cattle and game on the north side of the river was very narrow, and wound like a serpent around the boulders down to the water's edge. We had to go down in single file, and in some places it was close rubbing for a man and horse to get through this narrow cut. Our mule always followed the crowd without being led, and as soon as he saw the water dashed ahead of us and started down first at a rapid gait, but soon lost his balance and got a fearful fall, rolling over several times before he could regain his feet; but we all succeeded in getting down without further accident, and man and beast soon quenched their thirst.

One of our men became very poetical, and made a song on our unfortunate little mule, who was now standing, very contentedly, up to his middle in the water, and seemed to be trying to take in enough to last him the balance of the scout. I will give you a few lines of the song as a sample of the poetical genius of a Texas ranger:

"Our pack-mule Balaam took a tare,
    And down the hill he run,
But struck his foot against a rock,
    And down poor Balaam come."

We camped near the river that night, and next day passed through the pleasant little village of Palo Pinto, and nooned it on Eagle creek, where there was plenty of good grass. From here we took our course for Camp Colorado, leaving Fort Griffin to the right, and the next day took leave of the land buyers, who could then make it to the Fort in a day's ride. We found game plenty, and had as much fresh meat as we wanted. The streams also were full of fish. On one occasion we saw about thirty deer in one bunch, and killed three.

CHAPTER XV.

TAKING LEAVE OF THE LAND BUYERS—PLENTY OF GAME—FOUL PLAY AT A RANCH—WILD TURKEYS— ARRIVE AT CAMP COLORADO.

ONE evening just before sundown we came out of a dense wood and struck a trail, which led down a small creek, and we were satisfied a stock ranch was not far off, and in a short time came in sight of it. The beeves, which were intended for market, were just being penned for the night; they were herded during the day. We saw some confusion among the hands when we first came in sight, but they soon discovered we were not Indians, and gave us a hearty welcome. Some of their hands had been run in a few days before by Indians, and they were on the lookout. We went down to the ranch and stopped long enough to cook a supply of bread, and listened to the tales and adventures of these hardy pioneers. They had plenty of everything in the way of provisions, and although there was no woman about the place, everything looked clean and nice.

One man interested me especially. He had a strange, wild look about him, and although an American, could not speak the English language good. He was captured by the Indians when he was three years of age and kept by them twelve years, and it was by accident he was discovered by his father, who traveled among the Indians trading. He had some mark about his person by which he was identified, and was induced by his father to return with him to Cheyenne city, and was at that place when it was taken by the Sioux, under Red Cloud, and the garrison massacred. His father was killed and himself wounded. He lay among the dead until after night, and then crawled off and made his escape. He was with the Indians at the battle of Round Mountain, when they were so badly whipped by the rangers under Van Dorn. He says they had been on a big raid in the Brazos valley, and knew they were pursued by a large force of rangers, and selected this place to make a stand and see if they could not defeat them. The mountain was flat on top and covered with bushes, rocks and briars. Their scouts kept them posted as to the movements of the whites, and they had time to select their battle ground. They got everything ready, and then waited one day before the rangers came in sight. The scouts came first, and after riding around some time became satisfied the Indians were on the mountain, and some of them went back to notify the commander, and about sundown the entire command came. The Indians were confident they could repel them, situated as they were, with nearly six hundred Comanche warriors ; but it made some of them quake to see two hundred Texas · rangers, splendidly mounted, riding around reconnoitering their position.

The rangers posted sentinels at various points, and then went into camp a short distance off. and soon their camp-fires lit up the wild scenery around. But few of the Indians slept that night, and at early dawn saw the rangers mounted and drawn up a short distance from the base of the mountain.

When the assault was made, most of the rangers came on foot. but some charged furiously up the side of the mountain on their horses, and twenty of them gained the summit and charged among the Indians. Those on foot soon came up, and the fight became general. Several of the rangers were killed on the mountain side as they went up, but the Indians were badly whipped, and soon scattered among the bushes and rocks, and succeeded in making their escape from the mountains in small squads. It being very rough, and cut up with deep gullies on one side, they left most of their dead and wounded on the mountain. This man said he himself was wounded. He was painted and dressed in the garb of an Indian, and thought himself that he was an Indian, as he could not remember anything before his capture. He said a ranger on a white horse shot him with a pistol. He fell and was carried off by a squaw. Twenty rangers were killed in this fight. The Indians lost about one hundred warriors. He then gave us specimens of his skill in throwing a knife, sticking it in a tree, a distance of ten steps, nearly every throw. He then gave several prolonged whoops, which were truly startling, and reminded me of the 7th of February.

We camped near this ranch on the creek and placed our guards for the night. Nothing occurred to disturb us until late in the night, when a horse suddenly dashed through camp, dragging a brush after him. Every man was on his feet in an instant, with gun in hand ; several of them had to jump behind trees to keep from being run over by the frightened horse, which kept turning and running back through the camp. Some of the men thought Indians had taken this means to make our horses break loose. Finally one of our men ·said he believed it was his horse, as he had tied him to a bush. It was so dark he could not distinguish the color, and shouldering his gun, went off in pursuit, and by the help of one of the guards, who was trying to find out what the clatter was about, caught him, and found out it was his own horse; and, fastening him securely, came back and reported, and was severely rebuked by Sergeant Payne for his carelessness, and the camp was soon quiet again.

We scouted some in this vicinity, but finding no fresh signs of Indians, continued our course towards Camp Colorado.

One day we stopped to noon near a stock ranch, and while there a man named Lawrence came to us and said a man had just been shot at the ranch. Sergeant Payne immediately set out with his men to investigate the affair, and make arrest, if necessary. We were met at the fence by a dozen rough-looking men, armed with carbines and revolvers, who demanded our business. Payne informed them we were rangers, and wanted to see the wounded man, and the one who shot him. They said the wounded man was in the house, but the man who had shot him was gone. We then dismounted, and six of us entered the house. We found the unfortunate man lying on his back on a low bedstead and a bullet hole in his breast. He seemed to be unable to speak, and the woman who sat crying in the house would answer none of our questions; and we were compelled to leave without finding out anything, but were satisfied there had been foul play at this place. The man Lawrence said he was a stranger in that part of the country, and that he lived up on the Savannah, and asked leave to travel with us that day, as he was afraid of the men at the ranch. To this Payne agreed, but did not like the man's actions much.

After we got some five or six miles from the ranch we met a crowd of armed men, who were on the hunt for Lawrence, and said he was a horse thief, and wanted to kill him, but were prevented from doing so by the rangers. Payne then had Lawrence disarmed, and we kept him prisoner until morning. By that time the lost horses, which the men thought he had stolen were found, and we returned him his arms and set him at liberty.

After leaving this place we rode hard all day and camped on Savannah creek, and the next night camped on the same creek, expecting every minute to fall in with a band of Indians, as several old trails led out through this country. Our camp was at the foot of some low hills, near the creek. About sundown the wild turkeys commenced flying from these hills and settling in the creek bottom. I am satisfied several hundred flew over our camp. This was a wild, but beautiful country. We were far out on the frontier, with no house, that we knew of, between us and Mexico. Early next morning some of the boys were out killing turkeys. They were large and fat, and we enjoyed them for breakfast. The men were all stout and in good health, and a Winchester carbine seemed like a toy in their hands. Our horses were also in good condition, the grass being good everywhere.

While we were saddling up to start, a difficulty occurred between Sergeant Payne and Charley Robinson. I do not now remember what it was about, but both men became very angry, and drew their pistols, and I sup-suppose would have commenced firing had not Sam Cobb, who was standing near, sprang between them. Others crowded around, and they agreed to drop it until some other time, and afterwards became good friends.

We arrived all right at Camp Colorado, and found Swisher's company still there, making regular scouts, but having no important fights with the Indians. After giving them all the information we could, got some supplies, and came out to Pecan bayou, where we camped and caught enough fish in a half hour's time to have fed fifty men. They were mostly blue catfish.

CHAPTER XVI.

START TO FORT GRIFFIN — HITSON'S RANCH — INDIANS ATTACK THE COWBOYS—INCIDENTS OF THE FIGHT—JOHN JACKSON CHASED BY INDIANS AND WOUNDED IN THE NECK.

AFTER leaving Pecan bayou, we shaped our course for Fort Griffin, and for some distance traveled over the same route we had come the winter before; but there was quite a change in the looks of the country. At that time it was midwinter, and everything looked bleak and desolate. The ground was frozen, and the tall grass was bent down with ice. Winter in the wilderness is a cheerless scene; but now it was springtime, and everything looked beautiful. The prairie was covered with green grass and flowers; birds were singing in the woods, and deer and antelope scampered off across the great prairies at our approach.

We deviated somewhat from our course and went by Hitson's ranch, on Battle creek. The hands were busy road-branding cattle for the trail. Hitson owned a large stock of cattle, and generally employed from fifty to seventy-five hands. The Indians seldom molested him on this account; they did not wish an encounter with Hitson's cowboys, for they had been worsted by them on several occasions. Once, when nearly all the hands were away, they ran one man in and came near killing him. His horse fell and threw him so violently to the ground that he lay stunned for a few moments, and while in this condition one Indian ran up, and, leaning over in his saddle, fired at him with a pistol, but missed his aim. By this time assistance arrived and the Indian fled.

We found Hitson to be a kind, clever man. He invited us in to take dinner with him. He had no family, and lived there a bachelor life with his hands. The dinner was served on a large goods box, turned down. It consisted of corn bread, fat beef, and very strong black coffee. As we had ridden since early dawn without stopping, and it was now past twelve, we did justice to the repast. Mr. Hitson seemed to be a man between forty-five and fifty years old; hale and hearty. He afterwards sold his ranch for four hundred and fifty thousand dollars, and removed to Colorado Territory.

After leaving the ranch, we traveled up the creek until we found plenty of mesquite grass, and camped. Before we left the ranch Mr. Hitson pointed to a mountain, several miles off, and informed us that a lot of hands were there gathering cattle for Jackson and Murphy; "but," said he, "most of them are new hands, who never saw an Indian or heard one yell, and some of these fine nights," said he (for the moon was full and the sky clear), "the Indians are going to burst them up completely."

Our camping place was under a large mesquite tree, which stood a short distance from the creek. As we were not hungry, we staked out our horses, spread our blankets, and all but one lay down to rest. When night came on a regular guard was placed, and one by one the boys dropped off to sleep, to dream, perhaps, of loved ones at home, far away towards the south, all unconscious of the dangers which lurked around, for we were apt to be aroused at any time by the war-whoop of the savage.

I lay and looked at the stars a short time, which so

thickly studded the sky, and being weary, with a long day's ride, soon fell into a dreamless sleep, and it seemed as if I had hardly closed my eyes when a hand was laid on my shoulder, and I instantly awoke and saw one of my comrades bending over me. " It is your time to go on guard, Jack," said he. " It is past midnight, and the moon is shining bright as day." " All right," said I. springing up; " turn in," and pulling on my coat, for the night had become chilly, I picked up my gun, and was soon keeping the lonely vigils of the night. I stood with my back to the tree and gazed out across the moonlit prairie. What a glorious night it was! I imagine it was such a night as this when the shepherds were watching their flocks on the plains of Bethlehem, when the heavenly host appeared and announced the birth of the Savior of mankind, and proclaimed peace on earth and good will to men ; but here, on this far-away frontier, the Angel of Death, instead of mercy and peace, was abroad. This was the night for roving bands of Indians to commit their depredations. I looked far out across the prairie, and could plainly see the dark mountain looming up, at the foot of which Hitson said Jackson's cowboys were herding cattle. Everything was quiet, still and beautiful, with the exception of the snoring of one of our boys, which grated so harshly on the senses that I was tempted to punch him with my gun.

I had been on guard, I suppose. about an hour, when I heard a shot in the direction of the mountain, and turning my head, heard another, and then another, and then a perfect fusilade at once. I knew too well what that meant on this far distant frontier. The Indians were making an attack on Jackson's camp. I instantly aroused the boys, telling them an Indian fight was on hand. Sergeant Payne sprang to his feet and ordered every man to his horse and saddle up quickly; we must go to their assistance. In a few seconds we were ready and about to mount, when we heard the clatter of numerous hoofs on the hard prairie soil coming in our direction. Payne ordered all the horses to be brought up to the tree, and if it were Indians to give them a volley as they came up. In the meantime we could still hear firing in the direction of the beefherd. We could plainly see two or three hundred head of horses coming towards us, and mounted men behind them. Indians running off horses, was our conjecture. "Be ready, boys; give them a salute as they come up," said the sergeant; but, while at full gallop, we saw a man dash around to the left and turn them, and they passed by, three hundred yards away. The moon was shining so brightly they could see our squad collected up on the prairie, and avoided us.

We learned afterwards that Hitson's hands were running their saddle horses in to corral them. They were grazing them on the open prairie, and when they heard the firing at Jackson's camp they knew Indians were there, and quickly rounding up the herd set out for the ranch. When the noise of running horses had died away, we listened again for firearms, but the fight was over, and not knowing in what force the Indians were, for sometimes they went in bands of two or three hundred, and as the fight was over, we were apt to encounter them on the open prairie, or be fired on by the now excited cowboys, for they were not aware there were any rangers in that vicinity. Taking all these things into consideration, Sergeant Payne decided to stay where we were the balance of the night, which we did, holding our saddled horses until morning.

At dawn we mounted and set out across the prairie

towards the camp. After some trouble and delay, we crossed a deep cañon, and were soon at the scene of the late battle. The first thing we noticed was a considerable number of dead horses. We got most of the particulars of the fight from a man named Crow, who was on guard when the attack was made. He said he was on guard near the horses, most of them being staked or hoppled. The beeves were in a strong pen, built of heavy logs. The men were sleeping near the beef pen, and near by stood a covered wagon. A short distance from the camp was a deep hollow. Crow was looking in the direction of this place when an Indian rode out of it and stopped in the open flat, and looked towards the horses. Crow, who was in a squatting position, instantly sprang to his feet and fired with a Spencer carbine, but missed his aim, and with a yell the Indian dashed towards the horses. Crow fired two more shots in quick succession, but was unable to bring him down. At the same time a large force of Indians charged the camp on the other side and commenced firing. By this time the hands were aroused. Some fought and some ran. Jackson and his veteran hands, who had been with him a long time, tried to save the horses, but could not. The Indians ran in among them and cut hopples and stake-ropes in quick succession, and ran them off. This accounts for so many horses being killed and crippled, as Jackson's men kept firing at the Indians while they were among the horses. The new hands, which Jackson had but recently brought from up the country, with but few exceptions, ran; five or six took refuge in the covered wagon, which was struck several times during the fight. The negro cook, who had been for years with Jackson on the frontier, snatched a pistol from the scabbard of one of the terror-stricken men and ran after a bunch of Indians, who were carrying off part of the horses, and fired among them so rapidly that some of them took to flight. One man ran off into the woods barefooted, with only his under clothing on, and did not return until the next day. His scant clothing was torn into shreds, and his feet badly lacerated by running through briars and over honeycomb rock. Some of the Indians kept up a furious yelling and firing, while others were carrying off the horses. One acted with great bravery, repeatedly dashing within twenty paces of the men who were firing. but so quick were his movements, and so dexterous was he in changing from one side of his saddle to the other, that he avoided several shots which were fired at him. Jackson, seeing this, ran around to that side and exclaimed: "Can't some of you fellows kill that d—d Indian." The Indian in question soon made another dash, and Jackson fired, killing his horse. but the Indian made his escape.

The fight was soon over, and all the horses, except those which were crippled, carried off. Daylight came, but they could not see a dead Indian ; several bows and and shields were picked up. An Indian is like a deer: he will sometimes go a long way after receiving a death shot. Jackson was as brave as a lion, and did all he could ; he had spent most of his life on the frontier, and was always cool in the hour of danger. On one occasion, while out in the woods near home, he came upon a band of Indians, and putting spurs to his horse, started for home with the red skins close at his heels. Seeing that some of them were as well mounted as he was, he drew his revolver and fired at the nearest ones until it was empty, and he then knew his safety depended on the speed of his horse, and he soon saw that he could outrun all of the Indians but one, and the race lay between the two.   The Indian soon came up with Jackson, and drew back his arrow to give him the fatal shot. Jackson, who was closely watching him, threw himself on the opposite side of his horse to avoid it, but the shaft struck him in the neck, almost cutting the jugular vein, and as they were now nearing the house the Indian left him.   Jackson was unable to recover himself in the saddle, and hung on to the pommel until he was nearly in a fainting condition from loss of blood.   On reaching the house the horse leaped the yard fence, and John Jackson fell off at his father's door.

CHAPTER XVII.

SERGEANT PAYNE — SCOUTS RUN BY INDIANS — DIS-
MOUNTED RANGERS—GENERAL SHERMAN ARRIVES AT
FORT GRIFFIN—CAPTURE OF THE·GOVERNMENT TRAIN
—INCIDENTS OF THE BATTLE.

WE did not tarry long at the cowboys' camp, but set
out on the trail of the Indians, which we followed until
noon, and had strong hopes of coming up with them,
but the country became so rough and uneven that we
finally lost the trail altogether.   It was then agreed that
two men should be sent out as scouts to look for the
trail or the Indians, and were to meet the sergeant and
party that night at Grier's ranch, on Hubbard's creek.
Dan Woodruff and myself were selected to hunt for the
lost trail.   After a fruitless search in the hills, Dan and
myself arrived at Greer's about sundown, and spent the
night there, but the rest of the boys failed to put in an
appearance; and not knowing what else to do, we, the
next morning, set out for Fort Griffin, distant abou thirty-six miles.   It seemed that it was impossible for our
scout to get into a fight with these Indians.   Had we all
remained together the frolic would have come off, for
when we least expected it Woodruff and myself came
upon them at Foil's creek, and only saved ourselves by
hard and desperate riding, and arrived safely at the fort,
where, on the next day, we were joined by Sergeant
Payne and his party, who had been lost in the brakes of
Hubbard's creek, which caused the delay.

It was now determined that we would start back to

our company without further delay, and report to the captain; and after getting some supplies went down and camped on the river, below the fort, ready for an early start on the following morning; but during the night a terrible storm came up, and four of our horses got loose and ran away, followed by the pack-mule. The men who found themselves afoot next morning, and a hundred and fifty miles from camp, were John Fitzgerald, Gus Hasroot, Cecil Robinson and A. J. Sowell. Search was made by the mounted men for the lost horses, but without success. We then employed two Tonkaway Indians to hunt. They found the trail, and followed it two days, but could not come up with them. Captain Sansom, of the rangers, had just arrived a short time before, and went into camp below us, on the river, but was now out, with the most of his men, scouting near Double mountain, the main hunting ground of the Comanches, and, as he was our senior captain, we decided to remain until his return and report to him, and accordingly went into camp on the river.

One evening, while here, we heard a cannon shot at the fort, and then several more in succession. Thinking likely that the place was being attacked by a large force of Indians, we hastily evacuated our camp carrying only our arms and ammunition, and set out for the fort, the loud boom of the cannon still echoing down the valley. As we were going through a little prairie, which skirted the hill upon which Fort Griffin was built, we saw the Tonkaway Indians swarming up the hill in the direction of the firing, and we hurried up the hill and soon came to the parade ground, where the battery was placed. The firing had ceased, and only the Tonks and a few soldiers were there.

I asked a soldier who passed near us what the firing

24

was about. "Firing a salute to General Sherman, sir, who has just arrived," was his dignified though polite answer, as he passed on. I saw the general that evening at the billiard-room of the officers. He had a stern expression on his face, somewhat resembling our esteemed Governor, John Ireland.

General Sherman was at this time making a tour of the Texas frontier, inspecting the posts. Every day we went up to the fort to see what was going on while we awaited the return of Captain Sansom. One evening, while there, a large government train, consisting of forty wagons, loaded with corn. passed through, en route to Fort Richardson. The teamsters were well armed, and it was thought could defend themselves against any Indian attack which would be made upon them. They saw no signs of an enemy until they arrived at Salt creek, some fifty miles from Fort Griffin, near what is now called the Monument Rock. Here they were suddenly surrounded by three hundred Kiowa and Comanche Indians. led by the four principal chiefs from the Fort Sill reservation—namely. Sittanke, Satanta, Big Tree and Kicking Bird. The teamsters hastily formed their wagons into a square, took refuge among them, and prepared to defend themselves as best they could against this largely superior force. The Indians charged them from all sides, and a desperate and bloody battle ensued. Numbers of the Indians were killed, but of no avail; one by one the beleaguered men were killed. At last the Indians closed in on them, the wagons were set on fire, and the bloody strife was over. Thirty-seven of the teamsters lay dead around the wagons, three made their escape, and one of them was badly wounded. He became so sore from his wounds that he was unable to walk, and had to crawl along, subsisting upon anything which came within his grasp—insects, lizards, berries, etc. Eleven days after the fight he arrived at Fort Richardson, reduced almost to a skeleton, but by careful treatment survived that terrible massacre.

In a short time after the massacre Gen. Sherman and escort arrived upon the scene. The wagons were still burning, and the bodies of the slain lying around. The Indians had carried off their dead, but the bloody ground around the wagons showed with what obstinacy the fight was carried on, and with what bravery and unerring aim these gallant soldiers had fought for their lives; but at last they had to fall and die between two forts garrisoned by eight hundred men.

CHAPTER XVIII.

PURSUIT OF THE INDIANS BY UNITED STATES SOLDIERS—
CAPTURE OF THE FOUR PRINCIPAL CHIEFS—COMANCHE
CHIEF KILLED BY SOLDIERS—SATANTA AND BIG TREE
SENT TO THE PENITENTIARY—AN ADVENTURE ON THE
CLEAR FORK.

GENERAL SHERMAN immediately dispatched a courier
to the commanding officer at Fort Griffin, ordering him
to send out force enough to overtake and punish the
Indians at all hazards, and recover the wagon mules,
which they had carried off. He was not yet aware of
the fact that the Indians who attacked the train were
from the Fort Sill reservation.

I and my comrades were in the fort when the messenger was discovered, on the north side of the river, running through the flat, and who never drew rein until he
dashed up on his panting steed to the headquarters of
the commanding officer, Colonel Wood. I remarked to
the boys that there was Indian news, and our supposition was that Sherman and escort had been attacked. In
a short time a bugle sounded, and about three hundred
cavalry assembled on the parade ground, and being
headed by an officer, started off at a quick pace towards
the scene of the disaster. They struck the trail at the
battle ground, we afterwards learned and followed
it until it divided, the smallest trail going in the direction
of Double mountain and the other towards Fort Sill.
A lieutenant with thirty men were sent after the smallest band, and the others kept the main trail, which led

directly to Fort Sill.   Most of the Indians who engaged
in the massacre had dispersed, but the four chiefs were
captured and sent down to Fort Richardson, to be tried
by the military; the mules could not be found.   On the
way down to the fort Kicking Bird said if they would
let him go he would bring back the mules.   This was
agreed to, so I understood; but the Indian, instead of
keeping his promise, gathered up some Comanches and,
taking the mules, left for parts unknown.   The other
three chiefs were carried in a light wagon, Sittanke being
on the seat with the driver and his hands tied; Big Tree
and Satanta were sitting together just in their rear, and
a file of soldiers rode on each side.   When they arrived
near the fort, Sittanke,* who had remained perfectly
quiet, with his blanket drawn closely around him, suddenly threw it off, with a glittering knife in his hand,
and, before any one could interfere, cut the driver's
throat, and sprang to the ground, carrying the driver's
carbine with him, and, taking shelter under the wagon,
commenced firing at the soldiers, wounding two of them
before he was dispatched.   The other chiefs remained
perfectly quiet while this was being enacted.   The body
of the dead chief was left on the prairie, and the other
two were safely landed in the guard-house at Fort
Richardson.

The lieutenant and his party overtook the band which
they were following near the Double mountains, where
they were engaged in shooting buffalo, and a running
fight ensued, in which two of the Indians were killed.

At the trial of the two chiefs they were sentenced to
imprisonment for life in the State penitentiary, but after
a short confinement were pardoned out by Governor

---

*This old chief was uncle to the Sittanke whom the rangers killed in the
fight near the Keep house in February.

Davis on a promise to remain quiet and peaceable and not leave the reservation. Big Tree, who was the war chief of the Kiowa tribe, never broke his parole, but the blood-thirsty and ever-restless Satanta disregarded his promises and commenced depredating again, but was recaptured and sent back to the penitentiary, where he soon after died. This old chief once captured the famous Buffalo Bill, but this noted scout outwitted him and made his escape.

I think if these murderers and highway robbers had been tried by the civil authorities they would have followed the spirit of Sittanke to the happy hunting ground in short order; but the suppression of these chiefs broke the power of the hostile Indians in the northwest.

In a few days we left the fort and went down to Captain Sansom's camp, and concluded to remain there until his return. Sansom's men reported plenty of antelope in this vicinity, and the next day I went out in search of some; but first kept up the river for some distance, hoping to kill a buffalo fish, as John Fitzgerald had killed a large one the evening before, but finding none I fired a shot at a large garfish, and concluded to quit the river and hunt antelope on the prairie. The bluff bank here was about twenty feet high, and I had to hunt for a place to go up. I soon found a narrow trail made by game and cattle coming to water. The bank being very steep, I took a running start, so as to get up easy, and coming out on the level prairie found myself face to face with an Indian. He was standing perfectly motionless, with a carbine on his left arm. He had heard my shot, and was looking for me. Now, an Indian was an Indian with me, and I could not tell a Tonkaway from a hostile, as he had nothing about him to indicate that he was friendly. My first impulse was to dodge back under the shelter of the bank, but thinking this might give him the advantage to get a shot first, if he was hostile, I presented my carbine at him, and he commenced holloaing: "Tonk! Tonk! Me Tonk!" I then advanced close to him, but was not satisfied as to his real character, for sometimes this is a ruse of the hostiles to throw a man off his guard and take the advantage, and I determined not to leave the ground first and turn my back on him. I then asked him what he was doing down there so far from the village, as I knew the Tonks seldom went far alone, as the Comanches, their most deadly enemy, were constantly on the lookout for them. He replied, in broken English, that he was hunting antelope. I then thought that the presence of the rangers on the other side of the river had induced some of them to hunt down here, as game was getting scarce near the fort; but still I wanted him to turn his back first, and, making a motion towards the prairie, told him to go on, then, and hunt his game, and without a word he turned square around and walked off across the prairie, without once looking back. He knew that I was a ranger, and that I mistrusted him, and seemed very willing he and I should part company; but if he had really been a Tonk I could have hunted and camped with him and been in no danger. They are one tribe who never fought the whites. I saw one at the village who said that he was one hundred and sixteen years old, and that he had killed deer along the Colorado river, where the capital of the State is now situated. After watching the Indian for some time, I turned off in another direction; but was unsuccessful as a hunter, and returned to camp empty-handed.

Sergeant Payne stayed at the fort most of the time, trying to devise some means of mounting us, so that we could start, as our time was already out for the scout, and he was anxious to report at camp. While here we received news of a fight between Captain Cox's company and the Indians. He had three of his men wounded and killed eight Indians. One evening a ranger galloped into camp bringing the intelligence that Captain Sansom had returned; that they had a fight, killing two Indians, and also brought orders from the captain to break up camp and move to the fort. This ranger had some rings in his pocket which he cut from the ears of a dead Indian. We all then set out and joined Sansom's men, who were encamped on the north side of the river, opposite the Tonkaway village. The captain was absent at the fort, but we received a hearty welcome from the boys, who said they had heard a good deal about Baker's men.

Some of the boys then gave an account of the chase in which they secured the scalps of two Comanches. After scouting some distance up Clear Fork and back towards Phantom Hill, they came upon what they supposed to be a large Indian trail, and followed it eagerly and rapidly, and in a short time came in sight of a large mott of timber, as they rode over the swell in the prairie, and could see many objects moving about among the trees, "There they are!" exclaimed several voices at once. The captain ordered a halt, and examined the timber a few moments, but could not make out whether they were Indians or not; but all agreed that they undoubtedly were, and one man even said he could see an Indian on a white horse. The captain then gave a few orders, and made a rapid charge on the timber, and soon traversed the distance, every man with his carbine in his right hand, ready to fire. As the objects had disappeared, the captain supposed the Indians had made a stand near the centre of the mott, or were escaping on the opposite side, and hastily gave orders for a portion of the company to charge through, and ·the balance of the men to divide into two squads and circle the timber to the right and left. These orders were carried out, when suddenly about two hundred Mustangs ran out and scampered off across the prairie. After examining the place they found a large spring near the center of the mott, and it was, no doubt, one of the watering places for these wild horses. After laughing over this grand charge and joking some of the men about seeing so many mounted Indians, they concluded, as it was nearly night, this would be a fine camping place, and when night spread its dark mantle over the lonely prairie the rangers were quietly sleeping on the spot where, a few hours before, they expected to fight a bloody battle with the scourge of the Texas frontier—the Comanches.

CHAPTER XIX.

CAPTAIN SANSOM SCOUTING — CHASING INDIANS AT DOUBLE MOUNTAIN—DEATH-SONG OF A BRAVE WARRIOR—SCALP-DANCE OF THE TONKAWAYS—PREPARING TO START FOR PEASE RIVER—DISBANDING THE RANGERS.

AFTER leaving this camp, they shaped their course towards the Double mountains, in the buffalo range, and one of the main hunting grounds of the Indians, and when not a great way from these noted peaks they began to see unmistakable signs of the proximity of the red hunters—moccasin tracks, the remains of slaughtered buffalo and other indices of their presence; and Tonkaway Bill, the scout, was kept ahead of the command with orders to report instantly if he sighted Indians, for Captain Sansom knew that if the Indians were not in force he would have to use every precaution to come upon them unawares. They were going through an open flat, with rising ground ahead, and could plainly see the scout going up this slight elevation, when the captain ordered a halt until he could reconnoiter the prairie beyond. The scout went slowly when nearing the crest of the ridge, and when his eyes came on a level with the open ground beyond, he was seen to suddenly stop and lower his head, and, turning his pony around, bent low in the saddle and came rapidly back to where the company had halted, and riding up to the captain, commenced in his broken English: "Captain, me see two Comanches; me no know how many more; maybe so plenty; me see two." The captain then ordered the pack-mules to be driven into a ravine near by and left in charge of Tonkaway Bill's squaw. While this was being done, the old chief, Casteel, who had accompanied the expedition, dismounted, and pulling out a broad strip of red flannel, tied it to the tail of his horse, and then remounting, pointed to it, and thus addressed the rangers: "When we fight Comanches, and heap run and heap shoot, you see this, you no shoot me; you know me Casteel." The old chief well knew that in a mixed-up fight on the prairie the rangers could not tell one Indian's back from another, and had taken this precaution to prevent mistakes during the confusion of the fight, like the Lipan chief, Flacco, in the fight on the Nueces, who, when the firing commenced, tied a red handkerchief around his head and remained near Captain Hays during the combat.

In a few moments everything was ready, and the captain gave the order to advance at a lively gait to the crest of the ridge, and when they arrived at this point saw the two Indians sitting on their horses, about three hundred yards off, but no others were in sight. The Comanches fled at sight of the whites, and a lively chase commenced across the prairie, the timber being about two miles off. Every few moments some one fired, and the Indians urged their horses to the utmost speed, and being well mounted the rangers did not gain much on them; but, finally, one of them, in jumping his horse across a ditch, his girth broke and the saddle and Indian came to the ground. The other one, who was some yards in advance, seeing the unfortunate condition of his companion, half turned his horse, as if he would come to his assistance, but seeing a whole company of rangers coming at full speed, saw it was useless, and renewed his exertions to save himself. The dismounted Indian ran a short distance on foot, as his horse had run off when he fell, and then came back towards his enemies, throwing down his weapons and holding up his hands; but, as the rangers kept firing as they came up, he soon fell, pierced by several balls. This delayed them some, and the other Indian had gained on them considerably. Five or six of the best mounted men now undertook to run him down before he gained the timber; it all depended on who rode the best horse, for he was out of the range of carbines. But after running a mile further they saw the Indian's horse was beginning to fail; but he was also nearing the timber. Captain Sansom, seeing this, urged his horse forward, shouting to the foremost man to shoot the horse. By this time they were in range again, and after a few shots the horse fell dead in his tracks, shot through with a Winchester ball. The Indian hastily disengaged himself from his fallen steed, and pulling two revolvers, took one in each hand and came back to meet his foes, uttering loud whoops of defiance, and firing at those who were near him, and it took considerable skill in dodging and wheeling their horses to avoid his rapid shots. Some of the men dismounted and fired, hitting him several times; but this brave warrior continued the unequal combat until his pistols were empty and himself completely riddled with bullets. He then dropped his weapons and stood erect, with his arms folded across his breast. There was such a look of proud defiance in his features, and something so noble in the attitude in which he placed himself, that the rangers ceased to fire. He was bleeding from a dozen wounds, most of them fatal shots, but still he stood erect and gazed far off across the prairie, not deigning to look at his enemies, who had now silently

gathered around him. By this time the captain, the
Chief Casteel, and about half the men had ridden up,
and sat gazing with astonishment at this curious finale
of the chase. Presently the Indian began to sing, still
looking far off, not even turning his eyes, when the other
men came up and crowded around him. It was, indeed,
a touching scene, and one which is seldom witnessed on
the frontier. This lone Indian, standing on the prairie
with his arms crossed majestically on his breast, with a
far-off look in his eyes, singing his death song, with about
thirty Texas rangers in a circle round him on their panting steeds.

When his song was finished, he stood a few moments
and then commenced swaying to and fro, and finally
sank to the earth, dead. Captain Sansom asked Casteel
if he knew what he was singing. He said "Yes;" he
understood all he said, for he was acquainted with their
language, and that he was recounting all the brave
deeds he had done, the scalps he had taken, what a good
warrior his father was, etc. The party then turned and
rode slowly back to the place where the mules had been
left, leaving the body of this brave red man where it
had fallen. These two Indians were evidently part of
the band which had been scattered by the soldiers, and
if so, participated in the capture of the government train
and the massacre of the teamsters, and deserved to be
killed. The scalp of the Indian was taken off by the
Tonks.

When the party returned to where the first Indian was
killed, they found the squaw, in whose charge the pack-
mules were left; but when the firing commenced had
deserted them and followed the rangers, brandishing a
revolver in her hand, and when she came to where the
dead Indian lay, reined up, and, leaning over, shot him

in the crown of the head, then dismounted and scalped him. When the Tonkaways returned to their village they had the scalp dance.

Upon the return of Captain Sansom from the fort, he was informed that some of Baker's men were in camp, and he expressed a desire to see us. When presented to him, we acquainted him with our situation, and he said he was just preparing to go on a long scout; that his Tonkaway spies had just got in, and reported a large camp of hostile Indians on Pease river, numbering some four hundred warriors, and that he was going to start for that point on the following morning, and would furnish us horses to go with him, as he was going to send an order for Cox and Baker to join him on the route. This worked exactly into our hands, and we felt greatly relieved. Thirty Tonkaway warriors and fifteen buffalo hunters were also going with the expedition, which would make the force nearly two hundred of rangers, Indians and hunters. The Tonkaway Indians came across the river from their village about sundown, and camped to themselves near by. They looked terrible in their war garb and paint, and would make a man shudder to think of being surrounded by such fierce-looking demons.

Our expectations of speedily joining our company and probably participating in a terrible Indian battle were doomed to disappointment. Captain Sansom returned to the fort that night, when the stage arrived, and received a letter from Governor Davis, ordering him to immediately repair to Austin, with all the rangers under his command; so instead of starting to Pease river on the following morning, Captain Sansom set out for the capital, and we went back to our old camp, on the river below the fort. Sergeant Payne went to the fort to buy provisions. Captain Sansom had offered us transportation to Austin; but we were satisfied that our captain would not move until his scouts got in. Payne would not insist on us going with Sansom's men, though he thought it would be best, but said if we wanted to join our own company, we would set out without delay, and he would keep the mounted men with us, as the country was entirely unsettled, with the exception of a few stock ranches, from forty to a hundred miles apart, and we were almost certain to come in contact with Indians before we got through.

We disposed of our saddles, bridles, blankets, etc., to a squatter, getting about one-fourth their value. We retained only our carbines, pistols, ammunition, and a tin cup apiece, and canteens; I also kept half of a blanket to lay upon at night. I do not remember the day of the month, but it was in June, when we bade farewell to Fort Griffin, and set out on our toilsome march. We concluded it would be best to keep down the river some distance and then take a northeast course for Decatur, which led across a rugged chain of mountains, deep cañons and rapid streams. We calculated to live on game killed by the way. The distance was about one hundred and fifty miles. Some salt was about all we were hampered with in the way of provisions, except a loaf or two of bread purchased at the fort.

CHAPTER XX.

DISMOUNTED SCOUTS STARTING BACK TO CAMP, DISTANT
ONE HUNDRED AND FIFTY MILES—CAMPING ON THE
CLEAR FORK OF THE BRAZOS—A PERILOUS SWIM AND
A NARROW ESCAPE FROM DROWNING.

At noon on the first day we stopped on a little creek
about nine miles from the fort. The day was warm,
and we rested in the shade of some large elm trees. To
the east of us was a range of low hills. After remaining an hour or so, we were about to resume our journey
when we were startled by a shot in the direction of the
woods. "Be easy, boys, and keep silent until we see
what it means," remarked Sergeant Payne; and then
several more shots were fired, and, looking through the
bushes, saw about thirty Indians coming over the ridge
towards the spot where we were, and as usual, we could
not tell whether they were Tonks or hostiles, and made
a general scattering through the brush, hiding like par-
tridges, where we could watch them without being seen.
We saw now that the Indians seemed to be firing at
some trees as they slowly rode down the hill into the
little valley, but our fears were soon relieved when we
saw a white man, with a captain's uniform, ride over
the hill behind the Indians, accompanied by several soldiers. Every man then came from his hiding place into
the open ground, and were then discovered by the
Tonks, who instantly halted, not knowing what kind of
a lay-out we were, as some of our men wore long hair
and buckskin, and might be taken for a Comanche seen

through the brush. The captain, seeing the halt, galloped to the front, and when the Tonks came up and recognized us as rangers, were glad to see us. The captain said he had been scouting, but could see no fresh sign since the massacre at Salt creek, and wishing us good luck moved on with his dusky scouts, and we continued our journey down the river and camped near its banks.

The evening had been excessively warm, and towards night black, angry clouds banked up in the northwest, and the low-muttered thunder at intervals threatened a storm, and shortly after night it commenced raining, and such a rain! It was no use trying to keep dry. It seemed as if the clouds had burst and poured out a perfect deluge of water at once. We stood it as best we could under the circumstances, and got but little sleep. The whole country was flooded with water, and it seemed as if day would never come; but it did at length, and what a sight for travelers, especially pedestrians! Water everywhere! The Clear Fork of the Brazos was out of its banks, and running at a fearful rate, and when morning came belied its name, for its waters were almost as red as blood. This was caused from the red soil of Paint creek washing into it some distance above us. The rain was over, and the rolling thunder, which .resembled the discharges of artillery during the night, was dying away in the distance. The next thing now was something to eat. We had a little bread; not more than enough for one man, and no meat at all, and on looking around we saw that we could not continue our journey, as a deep creek, which was now overflowed, was directly across our path, and emptied into the river just below where we had stopped for the night, and concluded to remain where we were for the

25

present; and some of the boys set off up the creek in search of game, while Sergeant Payne drew a hook and line from his pocket and said he would try for some fish. We had no doubt but what we could get plenty to eat; but our amazement was great as, one by one, the hunters returned empty-handed, not even finding a quail or rabbit. Well, here we were: no breakfast, no dinner, the sun sinking in the west with but little prospect for supper. But after awhile the gallant sergeant returned with a catfish weighing at least a pound and a half, to be divided among seven men—hungry men at that. The fish was cleaned, however, and laid on the coals, and when it was done, those seven men devoured it.

That night we got some sleep, and next morning arose feeling sore and hungry. The creek and river had fallen somewhat, but was still too high to ford, and seeing we would have to remain another day, the hunters again scattered out in hopes of finding game, and it was a wonder to us that it was so scarce this far from the fort, but we all anticipated better luck this time. The horses fared well, for the grass was fine. Those remaining in camp began to get restless when noon came and nothing had been brought in. One man, who went out horseback came in and said he could see no sign of game, but as he had to keep mostly in the open ground, we thought the footmen would be more successful. But, as the day before, one at a time, they came in with no better fortune, and in vain the sergeant whipped the stream with his line, until he gave it up in disgust. A fish the size of the one he caught the day before would now be called a monster. Well, have the hunters all got in? Count up. No; John Fitzgerald, the mighty Nimrod of the company, was still out.

They all had faith in John. Some said they knew

John would bring in something: but the day wore on, and the sun had nearly run its course; the men were actually suffering for something to eat. Only a small piece of fish and a bite of bread in thirty-six hours, and in vain we looked towards the hills for the appearance of the absent hunter; and now, for the first time, the idea occurred to us that John might be lost, and why not! This was a strange country to him. "Fire some guns, boys," said Payne, "and if he he is in hearing it will guide him to camp." Two shots were fired in quick succession, and were answered by a loud report from a carbine close by. Every eye was turned in that direction, and there was John, slowly approaching the camp, almost fagged out with fatigue and want of food; but he had game. Yes, John had killed a turkey, a small one, it is true—a hen—but its proportions looked awful in comparison with the sergeant's catfish.

The tired hunter sat down to rest while his companions hastily prepared the banquet. It was soon ready, and the boys gathered around. At last they had met the enemy, and were anxious for the fray to commence. Knives were drawn and the combat opened. It was short but decisive. There was nothing left of that turkey but the slick bones and feathers. The boys all expressed themselves as feeling better. Pipes were lighted, and some might have raised their voices in song, but the shades of night were drawing around, and it was time to put out fires and place guards; fires and songs might attract the attention of a band of gay and festive Comanches. It was not likely, however, that any hostiles were in this vicinity at present, for the Tonk scouts had just passed through here, and the trail of a Comanche never escapes their eyes.

Next morning we were all hungry again, and nothing

to eat, and it seemed almost useless to hunt. One of the men, on the previous day, while crossing a high ridge, discovered a settlement across the river south of our camp. We had heard of the Lee settlement down this way, and this, we thought, must be it. We then examined the river to see if a horseman could ford it. One party followed the course of the river to the mouth of the creek, but there was no chance of crossing that way, for the bluffs were high on one side or the other of the river, all the way. If we could find a crossing the sergeant said he would send a man to the settlement for provisions enough to last until we could continue our journey.

It was not our intention to follow the river much further, for our course was more north, and we were going nearly east. The sergeant and party returned from up the river, and reported no chance for a horseman to cross. There was one place which seemed to be a crossing when the river was down, but it was still deep and running very swift, and the going-out place on the other side was so narrow that if a horse went down below it, it would not be able to land at all. The idea, therefore, of crossing on horseback was given up for that day at least.

The only chance was for some one to swim the river, procure some provisions from the settlers, and then swim back across the river with it—a feat not easily accomplished. There were only certain places where even a man could ascend the bank; some places the bluff being twenty feet high and perpendicular. It was finally agreed that two men had better swim the river and bring enough bread to last until the next day, when we calculated the whole party could cross, go by the Lee settlement, and get bread enough to last a couple of days, and also some salt, for after we left this settlement we knew we would have to subsist for days on fresh meat, without bread, and salt was extremely necessary. Volunteers were called for, and John Fitzgerald and Cecil Robinson were the first to step out.

I will here give the names of our party, who were assembled this afternoon on the high bluff of the Clear Fork of the Brazos, devising ways and means to procure something to subsist upon while we were hemmed in by the turbid waters. It was now about the 1st of July, 1871. The names of the party are as follows: Sergeant Joel R. Payne, John Fitzgerald, Sam Cobb, A. J. Sowell, Gustavus Hasroot, the two Robinson brothers, Charley and Cecil. Two of our scouts had returned some time ago with Mr. James.

Charley at first objected to his brother undertaking to swim the river, for he was young—only seventeen years of age—and not very stout, and was fearful that he would not be able to stem the current; but Cecil was determined to go, and the two began to strip for the trial. They selected for their starting-place a point further up the river, where they could have the advantage of the current, which they knew would carry them some distance down the river before they would be able to cross it and make their landing good at a certain point below the high bluff on the other side. They fastened their clothing to the crown of their heads, and, sliding in, struck out boldly for the other side.

John, being short and strong in the arms and chest, soon crossed the main current, and made the landing place all right; but as soon as Cecil struck it, he went down in spite of all he could do. The balance of us kept down the river where we could watch him and render such assistance as lay in our power. Charley shouted to him to come back to the side on which we were, but he still continued to battle with the current in his endeavors to reach the other side. Fitzgerald had landed, and was running down the bank in order to help him if he could; but Cecil finally crossed the current and swam to the other side, but the bank was so steep that he could not get up, and had to still keep down the river, although nearly exhausted, but finally came to a cypress limb which dipped the water, and went out on that and down the body of the tree. A loud shout went up from the boys on our side, which was answered from the other side, and they soon disappeared through the bushes, and we returned to camp to pass off the time as best we could until their return.

We were getting very restless, and anxious to be on the move. We were tired of our camp; tired of watching the bloody-looking water glide by. The rangers were being disbanded all over the State, and probably at this time our company was breaking up, and we here on the bank of this swollen river, one hundred and fifty miles from our command, and four of us afoot, with an unknown country (to us) to traverse, unsettled, and constantly crossed to and fro by hostile Indians.

The sun was nearly down when we heard a faint whoop up the river, and saw the boys preparing to cross. By the time we arrived opposite, they were ready for the plunge. They took particular pains in adjusting their bread and clothing, and then launched out. John went down about one hundred yards and then crossed; but young Robinson was again unsuccessful, and went down rapidly with the current, and what made it worse we saw that in his efforts to land he had displaced his wallet of bread, which now hung around his neck, tied so securely that he could not remove it. He made several efforts to pull it off, but could not. His strength was fast giving way, and finally he went under. His brother uttered a cry, and commenced throwing off his clothes, and could hardly be prevented from leaping off the bluff. Fitzgerald again plunged into the river, and came, with swift strokes, to Cecil's assistance, who, meanwhile, had arisen some distance below the point where he went under, and made some feeble attempts to swim. Payne shouted to him to cease his efforts and drift with the current, if he could, until Fitz. got to him. By this time we were nearly back to camp, but here there was an eddy and a perfect whirl of water against the bank. Fortunately the drowning boy was caught in this whirl and brought to the bank, and before he could drift out again a long pole was reached him, to which he clung, and was carried down the river to a low place in the bank, where we landed him like a big catfish. He lay some time on the bank before he was sufficiently recovered to walk. He had thirty biscuits hung about his neck, and when they became saturated with water were very heavy, and soon exhausted his strength. But he was soon all right, with the exception of the loss of his hat, which was by this time probably several miles down the river. That night we feasted, like sailors, on soaked biscuits.

CHAPTER XXI.

LEAVING CAMP—CROSSING THE MOUNTAINS—SEPARA-
TION OF THE SCOUTS—LIVING ON GAME—SORE FEET
—KILLING A TURKEY—THE STONE HOUSE IN THE
WILDERNESS—A LARGE TRAIL OF INDIANS—WHY WE
WERE HERE.

EARLY the next morning we again examined the river,
but did not think it advisable to make an attempt to
cross until evening, as we had to be very careful with
our arms and ammunition. We had plenty of bread to
last us through the day. About 3 o'clock we repaired
to the place where there seemed to be a ford, and one
of the mounted men put his horse in and made it across
without having to swim far. He then returned, and the
three horsemen carried our guns, pistols, belts of cartridges, etc., and we all soon made it across; and, bidding farewell to the old camp, set out for the Lee settlement, guided by Fitzgerald and Robinson, the latter
having a handkerchief on his head in lieu of a hat.

Arriving at the house of old man Lee, we informed
him that we would like to procure some more provisions,
and also spend the night there, and set out early next
morning on our journey. The old man received us
kindly, telling us we were perfectly welcome, and anything that we needed which was on the ranch was at our
disposal. The horses of the mounted men were put up
and fed, and all invited into the house, where he
informed his wife and daughters who we were. They
received us politely, and set about preparing supper,

which was in due time announced; and for the first time since the celebration in March we ate from a table.

We had not forgotten how to conduct ourselves in the presence of pretty girls; and they being communicative and intelligent, and in nowise put out by our half-savage garb, for they were used to seeing men dressed in buckskin and loaded with pistols and knives on this far-away western frontier. The time passed off pleasantly. The old man remarked as we were about to break up for the night not to be surprised if an Indian alarm was sounded before day in the settlement. His neighbors, about a dozen in number, were from a quarter to two miles off. Telling the old man that if a row was kicked up before day that we would be on hand, we were soon resting quietly, after the toils and hardships through which we had passed; but no hostile foe awoke the hardy pioneers of this little settlement that night, and we arose next morning greatly refreshed.

We had a good breakfast, and our small wallets were filled with nice biscuit and other refreshments, and one of the girls hunted up a second-hand hat and gave it to young Robinson; and after bidding them farewell, and thanking them for their kindness, for they would receive no pay, we again turned our faces towards the wilderness. But could we have seen but a short distance into the future we would have turned back and stood guard around this old man and his family; for, shortly after we left, this settlement was attacked by the Indians, who burned the houses and killed or carried into captivity the inmates. Old man Lee was killed in the horse lot, his house set on fire, and his lovely daughters carried into a captivity worse than death. But such was life at that time on the frontier of Texas.

So sudden was the attack, the old man was cut off

from the house, and, being unarmed, fell an easy prey to his blood-thirsty and cruel foes.

When we again struck the river, we crossed without much trouble, and took a northeast course through the hills. We calculated when we set out from the fort to remain together, but saw, after traveling some distance through this rough country, that we would gain time to separate, for we were continually coming in contact with deep ravines and cañons, also rough and rocky mountains, where the mounted men could not proceed, and would consequently have to make a detour to the right or left to avoid these obstacles, and which, if we remained together, would cause the footmen to make tedious circuits, as we could go through many places the horses could not. It was some time before Payne would agree to this plan, but finally, seeing the necessity of it, consented.

We told the sergeant that we would keep as near on our course as we could, as we had all agreed that in this direction lay Decatur. In the meantime Payne and his party could travel rapidly where the country permitted, and soon reach camp, and inform Captain Baker of our situation, and if we did not arrive on time to send out a party to search for us. After coming to this conclusion, we divided what bread we had, and after many farewells and some misgivings we separated.

After our companions left us, and we could see them no more. a sense of loneliness crept over us. Here were four of us, with more than a hundred miles to traverse, across mountains, cañons, honey-comb rock, etc., and with some beautiful prairie country. After resting ourselves and holding a consultation as to our future actions, now that we were alone and without a commander, we slowly journeyed on. The boys now asked me to take

the lead and travel such a course as I thought best across
this pathless country. I told the boys that I was not
competent to undertake the task which they were about
to impose on me, but if such was their wish I would do
the best I could, and this was my plan. In the first
place, we would keep a northeast course, and shoot no
game, except for our subsistence, and to cook and eat
before sundown, and light no fires at night, and to travel
some distance after night and then lay down in the tall

(The Lost Scouts.)

grass, and it would take a keen-sighted Indian to find
us. We were also to avoid prairies as much as possible
for fear of encountering a mounted band of Indians, for
then our chances would be slim of saving our scalps;
but in the rocks and cañons, brush or timber, with two
hundred rounds of ammunition, we felt that we could
hold our own against great odds. The boys all agreed
that this was the safest plan, and observed it all the way
through. We had to pass within twelve or fifteen miles

of the spot where, a few days before, three hundred painted savages had yelled around the doomed men in charge of the train, and we were apt to come in contact with a roving band of hostiles at any time, and it behooved us to be ever watchful and on our guard.

The first night after the boys left us we were on a high mountain when night closed in around us, and it soon became so dark we could not see our way, and we lay down and slept good until morning. It was well that we stopped when we did, for the mountain had gradually narrowed to a point, and was steep and rugged, with deep chasms on each side, and we had to retrace our steps for some distance before we could descend into the valley.

That morning we ate our last biscuit, and began to look out for some kind of game, as we now had to subsist on that without bread; but game was plenty, and we soon killed a turkey, which we cooked, and after eating a protion of it, carried the balance with us, and no more killed until that was gone, for the report of a gun might draw an enemy to the spot, and we would only shoot when necessity demanded it.

After three days' traveling, climbing mountains and walking over rough, rocky country, our feet began to blister, and we suffered at every step. We wore heavy boots, and not being used to traveling on foot, we made but slow progress. Ascending a mountain on the fourth day, and looking back, we could still see the brakes of Clear Fork, from whence we started, but still we slowly toiled on, with skinned heels and blistered soles.

We found plenty of game and pure water, and would have fared well if we could have traveled without so much pain and misery at every step. We often stopped in cool, shady places, beside running streams, and bathed and rested our tired and blistered feet, and were loth to depart and wend our way across hot prairies or up rugged hills. One morning, about the 6th of July, we started early, before the dew had dried from the grass, and had traveled but a short distance when we came upon a large Indian trail, which had been made but a few hours before, probably just before daylight, as the dew was fresh knocked from the grass. They were going in a west direction, and we crossed the trail going northeast, and therefore had no fear of encountering them. If we had lighted fires at our camp that night the Indians would have discovered us, as we had slept in the valley, and the Indians passed over a high divide, which overlooked our camp; but we were lying asleep in the tall grass, all unconscious of the danger which was so near. We got away from the trail as soon as possible, as some of them might return for something, and discover us, for our Indian hunt was over, and we were now strictly on the dodge. From the looks of the trail there might have been thirty or forty of them.

After getting clear of the trail, we traveled on for some distance over a tolerably open but broken country, and then entered a thick forest in a level country, but occasionally cut through by a deep gully. We were about to stop and rest, for it was about noon, when we saw the walls of a rock building through the trees just ahead of us. We were surprised at this, for we did not expect to find a habitation yet for days, but, on nearing it, we saw that it was unfinished and unoccupied. The walls were very thick, and the rock well joined together. It was partitioned off into several rooms, with numerous doors and windows. The floor, also, was smoothly laid with large stones, but there was nothing by which we could tell how long it had been there, or why it was left in this unfinished condition, for it was roofless, and the grass was nearly waist high around its weather-stained walls, and a pile of rotten boards lay under a large tree near the south door. It was a pleasant, cool place to rest in, and we staid there some time.

After leaving this place, we soon came out of the woods into an open, beautiful country, and a broad valley bordering a swift-running creek. Game was in abundance, and the soil looked rich and mellow; but the red man still kept this beautiful country a howling wilderness, while thousands of human beings were homeless, struggling to maintain large families on old worn-out farms in other States. That was what we were here for, on this clear, bright evening, almost dragging our weary limbs along and limping at every step with blistered and swollen feet, that this paradise of northwest Texas might be opened up for settlers. When near the creek a deer was killed, part of it cooked and eaten, and what we could carry of it stowed away in our wallets, and again moved on, and as usual lay down after dark.

CHAPTER XXII.

AGAIN ON THE MOVE — BLISTERED FEET — A RANGER
SINKS IN HIS TRACKS, AND IMPLORES HIS COMRADES
TO LEAVE HIM—MAKING A PAIR OF MOCCASINS—THE
BIG TRACK—HONEYCOMB ROCK —NOTHING TO EAT—
PLENTY AGAIN—ARRIVE AT CAMP—DISBANDED.

NEXT morning it was almost impossible for us to
travel. Our feet were so swollen it was with great pain
and difficulty that we succeeded in getting our boots on,
and after going a short distance were compelled to stop
and pull them off. After resting for some time we again
set out, but were compelled to abandon our boots and
walk in our sock feet, which relieved us for awhile, but
the sharp stones soon wore our socks away, and we were
left barefoot, but we still continued to slowly advance,
and spent the night in some low hills, among rough and
jagged boulders. Next morning Hasroot said he was
unable to travel, but finally made the attempt, and by
frequent halts got several miles by 3 o'clock in the evening. It was distressing to see him trying to get along.
The soles of his feet were puffed out and almost in one
solid blister, and it was painful to even walk on the prairie grass. The others were suffering great pain, but he
was the worst used up, and what made it more difficult
was the weight each man had to carry. In addition to
our venison, we had a carbine, sixty cartridges and a
heavy army revolver each. Finally, about three hours
by sun, Gus sank down and said he was unable to proceed any further, and begged us to go on and leave him,

and he would make it to some settlement when he got able to travel, or he would remain there until a party could be sent back from camp after him.

Of course we would not agree to this, as we knew not how far it was to camp, or what might happen after we separated to prevent us from carrying out this plan. We therefore prepared to spend the night where we were with our unfortunate comrade, and probably by morning we could move on a short distance further. I still had part of a light blanket, which I was carrying along to sleep on at night, and the idea occurred to me that I might convert this into a pair of moccasins for Gus, and having some buckskin strings, set about the work, and completed them before I lay down for the night. I put four layers of the blanket for the soles, which made them very soft and durable. When the work was done, I turned to my companion to inform him what a nice present I had for him, but he was fast asleep and his troubles forgotten.

Had we thought of this sooner, and used our buck-hide the same way, we might have made it better.

The following morning, when Gus awoke and discovered the huge moccasins I had manufactured for him, and I told him to try them on, as they were for his benefit, he said: " Where did you come across them fellows? Have you killed old Big Foot, a giant, or the Old Man of the Mountains? They are not seven-league boots, are they, that I can jump in and step over to camp before night and tell the boys your situation?" I explained to Gus that they were neither of the articles mentioned, but a nice pair of moccasins I had manufactured myself out of the last remnant of my blanket while he slept. Gus then changed his humor, and looked quite serious as he proceeded to put them on. The

Big Foot whom he mentioned was not the famous Big Foot Wallace, the great scout and Indian fighter of Western Texas, but an Indian the rangers and settlers had often trailed, but could never catch, and who had one uncommonly large foot and one small one.

After eating a light breakfast of venison, we prepared to move on, telling Gus to lead out and see how he could navigate in his blanket moccasins. He did so, and was surprised at himself to see how much better he could get along, and we could hardly keep apace with him, as we were suffering great pain at every step; but we were cheerful, as we saw that Gus was good for the day.

We took it slowly, often halting to cool our feverish feet in the cool mountain streams, which we often crossed, and in this way traveled eight or ten miles before we again lay down for the night. If Indians had been on our trail this day I think they would have abandoned the pursuit as soon as they caught sight of the track which Gus made, for if he had been proportioned in stature to the track he made he would have been about twelve feet high.

When morning dawned we arose greatly refreshed, but our feet were still sore and tender; but we had avoided the honeycomb rock as much as possible, for it was the worst obstacle we had to encounter in the way of traveling. As there are people who do not know what honeycomb rock is, I will try to describe it to the best of my ability. It is generally found in the low foot hills, and sometimes extends out into the prairies. It is not in large boulders, but in small fragments, scattered over the surface, sometimes for miles around, and is thickly perforated with small holes, resembling the cells of a honeycomb, with sharp, jagged points sticking up.

26

In some places it seems like a solid rock-bed beneath the surface. With these sharp points sticking out, it is almost impossible to travel over it, and as many of them are hidden by the grass, it is not possible to travel over them unshod without being wounded at almost every step.

This morning we had nothing to eat, as our supply of meat had given out, and we had sighted no game since that we could get a shot at; and it always seems the case. If men are out, this way, and run short of provisions and begin to suffer for something to eat, game seems shy and hard to get. I recollect hearing my father tell of a circumstance of this kind when he was a ranger at an early day in Texas. They were on a scout near the head of the Guadalupe river, and their provisions gave out, but it created no anxiety, for game had been seen in abundance, and they calculated to kill some next chance; but night came, and they camped without supper, and the next day the same, and the next and the men began to suffer terrible pangs of hunger. Every eye was constantly roaming in search of game, but none came in sight, and they spent the third night in this condition. There was not much sleeping done, and by daylight they were again in the saddle. The men began to have a strange, wild look about them, and talked but little. About 8 o'clock they crossed a creek, and just as they got up the opposite bank there stood a large bear, not more than forty steps away. Calvin Turner, who was in advance, instantly checked his horse, and raised his rifle. The men all checked up, and remained perfectly motionless, with bated breath, watching the effect of the shot. At this moment the bear reared up on its hind feet, as if to get a better look at them, thus presenting the fairest mark a hunter could wish. Turner was a man of steady nerves, and drawing a careful bead, touched the trigger, and the cap popped without discharging the piece. The bear sprang off into the woods, as if he had been shot from a catapult, and before another rifle could be raised was out of sight. A perfect yell of chagrin and astonishment arose from the men as they dashed off in hopes of coming up with him again, but the search was vain; the bear made good his escape. Turner was uncontrollably wild with rage, and drawing his bowie knife, hacked the stock of his faithful old rifle, which had never gone back on him before, and wound up by shedding tears over his failure, when fifty hungry and starving men were at his back with loaded rifles, depending on his steady nerves and sure aim to fetch the meat. But fate was not entirely against them, for that evening a deer was killed and evenly divided among the men, a fire was lighted, and the feast began. One man ate up his share while searching for a good stick to broil it on.

After leaving our camp we traveled on until noon without finding any game, and stopped in some dry hills without water. The day, too, was excessively hot, and together with our painful mode of locomotion, aggravated our thirst. Fitz. thought he heard the yelp of a turkey, and took a short stroll in the hills, but could find nothing. After resting some hours, we again set out, with a long stretch of prairie ahead, which looked dry and hot, and made our feet ache to think of the steps we would have to make in order to cross it; but there was no other chance, for the prairie stretched for miles to the right and left.

We were now suffering with thirst, and the sooner we started the better, for we had to cross that prairie before we could get a drink, and bracing up as best we could under the circumstances, we set out. The distance was much greater than we anticipated, and the heat of the sun was almost unbearable, it being now about the middle of July. Besides, the prairie in places was thickly strewn with honeycomb rock. The sun was sinking low in the west when we began to near the confines of the prairie, and we steered our course for a small hill covered with large elm trees, whose shade looked cool and inviting after the long, hot tramp across the prairie without water. We could also see the serpentine course of a creek, which meandered towards the southeast from this point of timber, and we judged its fountain head must be there, and the thoughts of a cold spring buoyed us up and hastened our lagging footsteps. When nearing the grove a small bunch of wild cattle ran out from behind the hill, and made off across the prairie in a northwest direction, and this also confirmed our belief that a spring was there, and gave us great joy, for it indicated that we were nearing the settlements. In this almost unlimited cattle range they often strayed from the ranches, and became almost as wild as the deer and antelope. As we drew near, we noticed a cottonwood tree growing at the foot of the hill on the north side. I remarked to the boys that I would bet a coonskin against Gus Hasroot's moccasins that we would find a spring at the root of that tree, and even before we arrived at the spot we heard the gurgling sound of running water. We forgot our blistered feet and ran to it, and such a spring! It was delightful to look at. A stream of water came out from under the roots of the cottonwood almost as large as a man's arm, and nearly ice cold. There was a rattling of tin cups, and our thirst was soon quenched. We then ascended the hill and sat down in the dense shade of the elms to rest. The next thing now to be thought of was something to eat, and in looking around discovered a thicket of wild plums. Numbers of them had ripened and fallen to the ground, perfuming the air with their delicious odor. They were the Chickasaw plum, and as sweet as any cultivated variety. After eating as many as we wanted, one of the boys set out after the cattle, in hopes of getting a shot, as by this time we were very hungry. We had no scruples about doing this; we knew the rangers were welcome to kill cattle to subsist on, when placed in a situation like this. Cattle were not as valuable then as now, and the Indians were constantly depredating upon them. Stock men were more than willing to furnish beef to men who were trying to rid the country of these dreaded and subtile foes; and how quick the change has come! Only twelve years have rolled away since we traversed these lonely wilds afoot, and now the country is thickly dotted with farm houses and stock ranches; peace and plenty on every hand, and no one to make them afraid. The savages have been driven across the border, and no longer molest the Texas settlers. They have forever left the hunting grounds of their fathers, no more to return and dispute it with the white man. They have vanished like a vision of the night, and a hawk's eye could not discover an Indian's track.

Our hunter, by taking advantage of a thicket, arrived in gunshot of the cattle, and brought down a fat calf. One of the boys went to his assistance, and they soon brought it in. A fire was raised, and we were soon feasting on fat broiled ribs, well salted, with occasional draughts of cold water. By the time the repast was finished night was at hand, and putting out our fire, we drew back into the dense shadow of the trees and lay down to sleep, which soon came after the toils of the day.

We arose early next morning, so as to make good time while it was cool, and when day dawned were ready to start. We followed the course of the little creek a short distance, and saw great numbers of small trout and perch in the clear water; but as the course of the creek did not correspond with ours, we soon left it and began to cross the Keechi mountains.

Some of the country now began to look familiar to us, as we had scouted near this range in June, soon after starting on this trip. We knew now that if we could hold out that in a few days we could make it to camp. We could still walk, and Hasroot's feet were getting well; but the soles of his moccasins were fast wearing out and would soon be gone.

After getting through the low foot hills, we deviated somewhat from our course, and ascended a high peak, so as to get a good view of the country. Here we rested for a time, feasting our eyes on the grand and beautiful scene before us.

The broad valley of the Keechi river lay at our feet, the stream stretching away to the south, till the timber, which lined its banks looked dim and smoky in the distance. The view to the north was shut in by a range of mountains. The valley was as green as a wheat field in spring, with a thick coat of mesquite grass. This valley was once the home of the Keechi tribe of Indians, and it was here in these mountains that Miss Hunter was held a captive forty-six days, but was restored to her people by them paying a heavy ransom.

After gazing on this enchanting scene for some time, we descended the mountain and entered the valley, and after walking about a mile over the soft mesquite grass, came to the river. We soon found a shallow place and crossed over, keeping up the stream until time to rest and eat dinner. After remaining about two hours, we left the river and struck out across the open country. It was not so warm to-day as it had been, and the country was level and clear of stones for some distance, and we made pretty good time, and that night slept in the hills, with the Keechi some distance behind us.

The next day we saw more cattle, and crossed an old road running east and west. These were cheering signs, and we expected every minute to come upon a ranch; and about 3 o'clock that evening, as we emerged from the hills into the valley, we saw a house about half a mile off, directly in our course. This hastened our movements, and we soon arrived at the place, but everything betokened it a deserted ranch. The gate to the yard fence was broken down, and high weeds had grown up around the house. There was a gallery fronting to the south, with open hall between two log cabins, all under one roof. There were chairs, tables, bedding, clothing and various other things scattered about in the passage-way and rooms. It seemed that no one had occupied this place for a year or more. and we conjectured that they had been run off by Indians. On the south side of the house there was a small field, and plum and peach orchard close by. We refreshed ourselves with delicious ripe plums, which were in abundance, almost to the door. The peaches were not yet ripe. There was also a spring and milk-house near by, and altogether it was a beautiful situation, commanding a fine view of the surrounding country; but the place itself looked lonely and desolate, and we soon took our departure. The sun was getting low, and we wanted to travel while it was cool. We afterwards learned that this place had been settled by a family from one of the northern states, who lived here several years. They had a small stock of cattle, and were doing well; but during a raid by the Indians through this part of the country the entire family were killed. Some of the children were found dead and scalped at the milk-house, as if they had sought refuge there when the savages made the attack on the house. As these people had no relations in this country, everything remained as it was the day of the massacre, except that the bodies had been removed.

After leaving this place our journey was soon completed. On the second day we struck Big Sandy creek, which was familiar to all of us. We took a bath in the creek, and then ascended a hill to see what we could see.

"Decatur!" we all simultaneously exclaimed, as we gained the summit and cast our eyes to the east. Yes, there it was, about three miles off, and to the right. We had only missed our course this far in coming one hundred and fifty miles, and about 3 o'clock this forlorn-looking remnant of the scout walked into the square, with bare and blistered feet, long hair and greasy jackets. Rangers and citizens crowded around us. The news soon spread through the town that the lost rangers had got in, and we stood in our tracks the next five or ten minutes and shook hands.

Payne, Dave Smith, Bud Seglar, Jim Seglar, Dawson Hodges, and others were just preparing to start in search of us, with guides who knew the country. Most of our scouting had been done further to the north and northwest, and our men were not familiar with the country we had just come through. We had been out just forty-four days, the last and longest scout that we made. While standing here, answering questions and shaking hands, one of my old messmates, Charley Figurs, came through the crowd, and taking me by the arm, told me to follow him; and leading the way to Brown's store, made me a present of a pair of fine boots, and, although painful, I pulled them on. If this ever meets the eye of Charley, he may rest assured that I shall always hold him in grateful remembrance.

The boys had a brush with the Indians in our absence, and captured thirty-six head of horses. They ambushed them in a pass at night, as they were going out through the mountains with their stolen property.

We reported to the captain, who was glad to see us, and had been very uneasy at our long absence.

In a few days we set out for the capital, and were disbanded.

Occasionally we see some of the boys, and hear from others. Some have passed away. Gus Hasroot and Charley Robinson died in Gonzales county; Gregg was killed in a fight with horse thieves in northern Texas; Bill Archer was drowned while crossing Red river; and Bill Taylor died in Santa Fé.

I will here insert a letter which I received from Joel R. Payne five or six years after we were disbanded:

COLUMBIA, TENN., July 12th, 1876.

A. J. Sowell, Esq., Seguin, Texas:

Dear Jack—Time, with his furrowed brow, has brought about many changes for your old friend and comrade, and not the least among them is the reduction of his once robust frame to almost nothing but skin and bones. Sickness of the severest and most fatal type—consumption—has told very severely upon me in the last twelve months, and at last I have been compelled, from loss of strength, to quit work and retire—not on five thousand a year, but without a dime—penniless.

And yet, my dear boy, I am surrounded by very kind friends, who do not let me want for anything it is in their power to furnish me I neither suffer for love or attention. My kind wife is my constant companion, ever ready to cheer me with kind and loving words, and never once faltering in her duty to her husband. Under all these circumstances, is it a wonder that I should still cherish a hope of getting well? If I should express one wish that I would like to have granted more than any other, it would be that our heavenly Father would grant me a few more years of life, that I might make some provision for my wife before I am called upon to "shuffle off this mortal coil" and bid the world an everlasting good-night.

I feel that a great many years of my life have been foolishly wasted. Had I acted properly—had I done right when I became of age, I might to-day have been independent, so far as the goods of this world are concerned. But I did *not* do right. I went heedlessly into reckless dissipation, and though my career was short, it was bright while it lasted. I finally saw the errors of my ways—when it was too late, however, and after two years of reckless dissipation I found myself stripped of all my little fortune and broken down in mind and bodily health. Since then I have been struggling along, working for a salary. I have a little property left, which will probably net me four or five hundred dollars. With this amount I want to go to Texas in the fall and see if I cannot rebuild my sunken fortunes. The only danger I apprehend now is from hemorrhage from the lungs. I have already had four, but my physician says there is no particular danger if I will be quiet for a time and abstain from work and an over amount of bodily or mental exertion. My idea is to resume work the 1st of August, and continue until the 1st of September or October, when I want to go back to Texas. I think I will either go to Wise or Montague counties, or go somewhere west of Austin or San Antonio.

I presume you are still at work on your book. If you are, and I can be of any assistance, either in the way of furnishing items or helping you in getting it published, let me know, and I am at your command. You must be sure and tell me all about Dr. Gillespie, and all my other old friends. I suppose you have a family by this time, and have lost all desire to go back to the frontier. I've been thinking perhaps that you and I might get a commission and raise a company. I would be in my glory if I could get back.

I will wait until I hear from you before telling you all the news. Do you ever hear from Figurs? I haven't seen or heard from him in four years. Has George McPhail ever got back? My kind regards to your family. Write on receipt of this.

Faithfully your friend,

JOEL R. PAYNE.

I will state that I never heard from Payne again, although I answered his letter.

THE END.

LaVergne, TN USA
04 December 2010
207349LV00003B/33/P

9 781149 522196